Latin to GCSE
Part 2

Name ...Stell..............

Form ....

St Paul's Girls' School   W6 7BS

Latin to GCSE:
Part 2

By
Henry Cullen
John Taylor

Bloomsbury Academic
An imprint of Bloomsbury Publishing Plc

B L O O M S B U R Y
LONDON · OXFORD · NEW YORK · NEW DELHI · SYDNEY

Bloomsbury Academic
An imprint of Bloomsbury Publishing Plc

50 Bedford Square	1385 Broadway
London	New York
WC1B 3DP	NY 10018
UK	USA

www.bloomsbury.com

BLOOMSBURY and the Diana logo are trademarks of Bloomsbury Publishing Plc

First published 2016
Reprinted 2016 (twice), 2017 (twice)

© Henry Cullen and John Taylor, 2016

Henry Cullen and John Taylor have asserted
their rights under the Copyright, Designs and Patents Act, 1988, to be
identified as Authors of this work.

British Library Cataloguing-in-Publication Data
A catalogue record for this book is available from the British Library.

ISBN: PB: 978-1-78093-441-9
ePub: 978-1-47428-565-0
ePDF: 978-1-47428-564-3

Library of Congress Cataloging-in-Publication Data
A catalog record for this book is available from the Library of Congress.

Typeset by RefineCatch Limited, Bungay, Suffolk
Printed and bound in India

CONTENTS

ILLUSTRATIONS

GLOSSING

The chapter vocabularies for Part 1 and Part 2 cover the GCSE Defined Vocabulary List. GCSE words are underlined and glossed in blue when they first occur. The underlining is repeated for words that recur in the same passage: they should then be learned. They can be checked in the chapter vocabularies, or in the Latin to English vocabulary in the back of the book.

Non-GCSE words are underlined and glossed, again with the underlining repeated. Proper names are normally underlined and glossed at their first occurrence in a passage, but the underlining is not repeated.

The practice papers in Chapter Twelve follow the conventions of GCSE papers.

NOTE ON ENGLISH TO LATIN MATERIAL

As in Part 1, English to Latin sentences are included throughout the book. By this point all have the Stretch and Challenge (S&C) sign because they use a wider range of grammar and vocabulary than will be tested by the optional English to Latin sentences at GCSE. They remain a useful way of consolidating the language and it is hoped that students will not be deterred from attempting at least some of them.

GCSE-style English to Latin sentences are provided in Chapter Twelve in the five practice papers and in ten additional exercises, along with an explanation of the restricted grammar and vocabulary required for them.

ABBREVIATIONS

abl	ablative
acc	accusative
adj	adjective
adv	adverb
comp	comparative
conj	conjunction
dat	dative
dep	deponent
f	feminine
fut	future
gen	genitive
ind	indirect
indecl	indeclinable (does not change its endings)
inf	infinitive
irreg	irregular
lit	literally
loc	locative
m	masculine
n	neuter

nom   nominative

num   numeral

pl   plural

prep   preposition

pron   pronoun

qu   question

refl   reflexive

s-dep   semi-deponent

sg   singular

subj   subjunctive

sup   superlative

usu   usually

voc   vocative

1, 2, 3   first, second, third person; first, second, third *etc* declension
1st, 2nd, 3rd   first, second, third *etc* conjugation

Note also two abbreviations of Latin expressions that are common in English, and frequently used in the explanations of grammar in this book:

e.g.   *exempli gratia*   for (the sake of) example
i.e.   *id est*   that is (*introducing further explanation*)

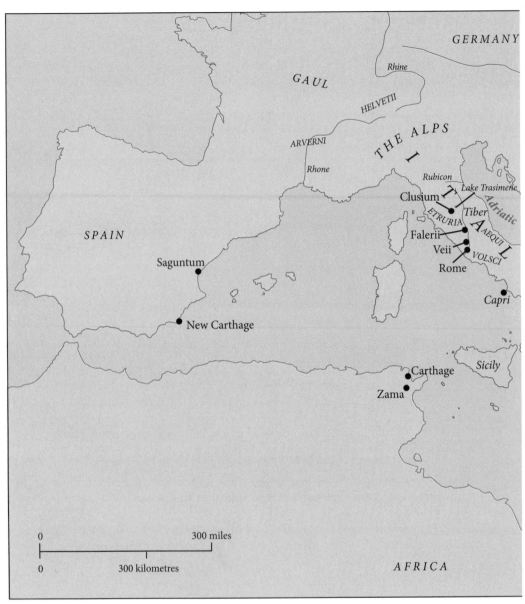

The Ancient World

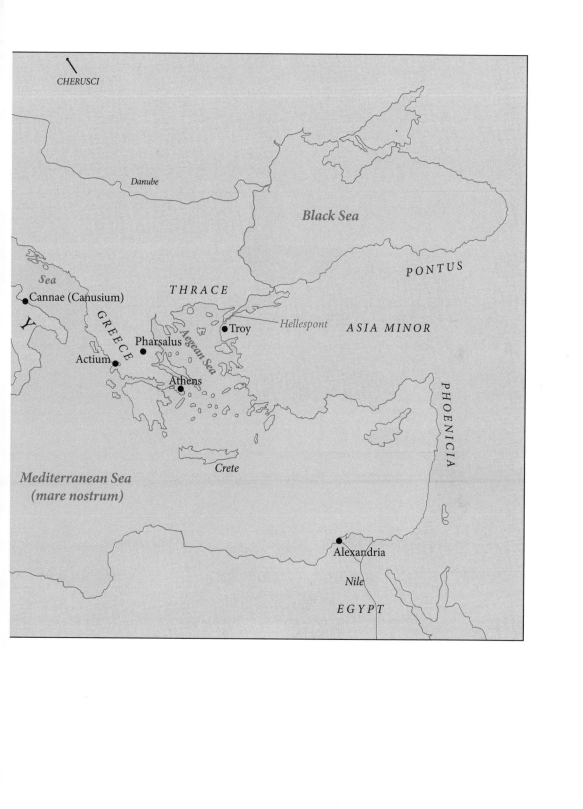

CHERUSCI

Danube

Black Sea

PONTUS

THRACE

Sea

Cannae (Canusium)

GREECE

Pharsalus

Aegean Sea

Troy

Hellespont

ASIA MINOR

Actium

Athens

PHOENICIA

Crete

Mediterranean Sea
(mare nostrum)

Alexandria

Nile

EGYPT

Chapter Seven

THIS AND THAT: *hic* and *ille*

The words *hic* (this) and *ille* (that) are called *demonstratives* because they point out or demonstrate the person or thing you are talking about: *hic* for what is near at hand, *ille* for things further away. They are very common in Latin, just as in English.

this, *pl* these

		m	*f*	*n*
sg	nom	hic	haec	hoc
	acc	hunc	hanc	hoc
	gen	huius	huius	huius
	dat	huic	huic	huic
	abl	hoc	hac	hoc
pl	nom	hi	hae	haec
	acc	hos	has	haec
	gen	horum	harum	horum
	dat	his	his	his
	abl	his	his	his

- Note the distinctive genitive and dative singular endings (underlined) across all three genders. For the genitive, compare *eius* and *cuius* (met in Chapters Five and Six). The dative here adds -*c* to the -*i* that most pronouns have: compare *ei* and *cui*.

- The masculine and neuter ablative singulars have a long o (i.e. adding -*c* to the equivalent second declension ending).

- The plural is regular 2-1-2 in declension apart from the neuter nominative and accusative (and even this resembles regular 2-1-2 by being the same as the feminine nominative singular).

Though classed as a pronoun, *hic* is commonly used like an adjective with a noun. It agrees with the noun (in number, gender and case), and normally comes in front of it:

hic vir heri aderat.   (hic *used like an adjective*)
This man was here yesterday.

But the same meaning could be expressed by *hic* alone:

hic heri aderat.   (hic *used as a pronoun*)

When part of *hic* is used on its own, a word such as *man, woman, thing, people* is supplied in English according to the gender and number of the pronoun. This is particularly common in the neuter:

nuntius haec nobis dixit.
The messenger told us these things (*or* this*).

* Though *haec* is plural in Latin, the singular is more natural here in English.

Often *he/she/it/they* (like the equivalent part of *is, ea, id*) is the appropriate translation:

milites nostri vicerunt. hos heri vidi.
Our soldiers were victorious. I saw them yesterday.

Exercise 7.1

Translate into English:

1. hic nauta fortis est.

2. cur haec dicis, amice?

3. pater huius pueri senator erat.

4. quis hos libros <u>movit</u>?

5. donum huic feminae dare constitui.

6. ubi emisti hunc cibum?

7. dux horum militum periit.

8. puer his verbis matri tandem persuasit.

9. hoc vinum malum est.

10. servus <u>crudelis</u> hoc gladio dominum necavit.

moveo -ere movi   I move (something)
crudelis -e   cruel

Exercise 7.2

S&C

Translate into Latin:

1. This girl writes well.
2. I greeted this old man.
3. When did you hear these things, boys?
4. We were carrying the food into this house.
5. The master punished these slave-girls.

---

that, *pl* those

		m	*f*	*n*
sg	*nom*	ille	illa	illud
	acc	illum	illam	illud
	gen	illius	illius	illius
	dat	illi	illi	illi
	abl	illo	illa	illo
pl	*nom*	illi	illae	illa
	acc	illos	illas	illa
	gen	illorum	illarum	illorum
	dat	illis	illis	illis
	abl	illis	illis	illis

(regular 2-1-2 plural)

- Again note the distinctive genitive and dative singular endings (underlined) across all three genders, like those of other pronouns.

Like *hic, ille* can be used either with a noun or on its own:

illi pueri semper clamant.
Those boys are always shouting.

illam in foro hodie vidi.
I saw that woman in the forum today.

As with *hic,* just *he/she/they* is often the appropriate translation. So the last sentence above could also be translated:

I saw her in the forum today.

Often a nominative part of *ille* is used as the subject of a sentence, referring to someone who was mentioned in the previous sentence but was not its subject, i.e. it marks a change of subject:

dominus servum diu petebat. ille tandem rediit.
The master was looking for the slave for a long time. He (*i.e.* the slave) finally returned.

As we saw in Part 1, the subject can be contained in a Latin verb, so pronouns are used less often than in English. A series of verbs in a passage can have the same subject, but a change of subject between sentences is usually signalled by a noun or pronoun.

- Note that the third person pronoun *is, ea, id* (met in Chapter Five as *he, she, it*) can also be used like an adjective meaning *that* (i.e. the same as the equivalent part of *ille*):

    legistine omnes eos libros?
    Have you read all those books?

Exercise 7.3

Translate into English:

1. illae naves celeres erant.
2. illa bene dicit.
3. cibum illi seni da!
4. illi iuvenes stulti sunt.
5. <u>captivum</u> conspeximus. ille tamen effugit.
6. multos clamores ea nocte audivimus.
7. vidistine illas feminas?
8. dominus illius servi crudelis erat.
9. quid in eo templo invenisti?
10. illud non faciemus.

captivus -i *m*   captive, prisoner

Exercise 7.4

Translate into Latin:

1. I was reading that letter.
2. Those soldiers were brave.
3. What is the name of that ship?
4. I shall give money to those boys.
5. The girl fears that horse.

Background: the early days of the Roman Republic

Figure 7.1 *Horatius defends the Tiber bridge against Lars Porsenna.* Engraving. (Photo by Rischgitz/Getty Images)

After the rape of Lucretia, the expulsion of the last king Tarquinius Superbus, and the establishment of the Republic with Brutus as the first consul, the Romans were determined never again to be ruled by kings. But Tarquinius was unwilling to go without a fight. After leaving Rome he took refuge with Lars Porsenna, the Etruscan king of Clusium, a powerful city north of Rome (Tarquinius himself had come from an Etruscan family). Tarquinius persuaded the Etruscans to besiege Rome and reinstall him as a puppet ruler under their control. The Etruscans captured the Janiculum Hill on the north-west bank of the Tiber. The historian Livy (writing about 500 years later, in the time of the Emperor Augustus) recounts these events in a series of stories about noble deeds, designed to inspire his own contemporaries with a vision of Rome's glorious past. Many stories of early Rome show enemies admiring Roman qualities: courage and determination, but also decency in the conduct of war. Enemy leaders are portrayed as having a similar sense of honour: they are impressed by the Roman example, as Livy's readers are intended to be. The accuracy of the stories is hard to determine, though they probably contain a kernel of historical fact. The stories of Horatius, Mucius Scaevola and Cloelia are set in about 508 BC. There was then only one bridge across the Tiber.

Exercise 7.5

Horatius

Horatius holds the bridge against the invading Etruscans (508 BC).

hostes urbi <u>iam</u> appropinquabant. Romani qui in agris habitabant trans <u>pontem</u> in urbem fugerunt. magnum erat periculum, magna tamen <u>virtus</u> unius viri <u>clari</u>, cuius nomen erat <u>Horatius</u>. 'cives mei,' inquit 'nonne periculum intellegitis? hostes mox trans hunc <u>pontem</u> venient, et in foro Romano eos videbitis. verba mea audite! vos
5 <u>pontem</u> delere iubeo. ego hostibus <u>resistam</u>, et hoc <u>modo</u> urbem servabo.'

<u>primo</u> duo <u>comites</u> cum Horatio in <u>ponte</u> erant. hi tres viri fortiter pugnabant; post eos Romani <u>pontem</u> delebant. ubi parva <u>pars pontis</u> manebat, Horatius <u>comites</u> in locum <u>tutum</u> discedere iussit. Horatius nunc in <u>ponte</u> <u>solus</u> contra multos <u>stabat</u>. duces hostium ferociter spectavit. illi timebant quod Horatius
10 multos in hoc bello <u>iam</u> necaverat. sed tandem magno cum clamore <u>tela</u> in unum Romanum iecerunt.

Horatius magna <u>virtute</u> se <u>defendebat</u>. subito tamen, ubi Romani <u>pontem</u> deleverunt, clamorem eorum audivit. tum Horatius deum <u>fluminis</u> vocavit. '<u>Tiberine</u> pater' inquit 'accipe haec arma et hunc militem in aquam tuam.' deinde
15 in <u>flumen</u> <u>desiluit</u> et, quamquam hostes multa <u>tela</u> in eum iaciebant, ad <u>alteram</u> <u>ripam</u> <u>tutus</u> <u>tranavit</u>. <u>sic</u> unus vir urbem servavit.

	iam	now, already
	pons pontis *m*	bridge
	virtus -utis *f*	courage
	clarus -a -um	famous
3	Horatius -i *m*	Horatius
	resisto -ere	I resist (+ *dat*)
	modus -i *m*	way, manner
	primo	at first
	comes -itis *m/f*	companion, comrade
7	pars partis *f*	part
	tutus -a -um	safe
	solus -a -um	alone, only
	sto stare	I stand
	telum -i *n*	missile, javelin
12	defendo -ere	I defend
	flumen -inis *n*	river
	Tiberinus -i *m*	Tiberinus (*god of the river Tiber*)
	desilio -ire -ui	I jump down
	alter -era -erum	the other
16	ripa -ae *f*	bank (of river)
	trano -are -avi	I swim across
	sic	in this way

- Note in this passage the common word order *magno cum clamore* (with a great shout). Common adjectives denoting size or quantity usually come in front of the noun. When a preposition (which also needs to come in front of the noun) is used as well, the order is usually *adjective–preposition–noun*. Another frequent example is *magno in periculo* (in great danger).

COMPARATIVE ADJECTIVES

A *comparative* adjective is used to compare two people or things, to express the fact that one has a particular quality to a greater extent than another. In English a comparative is usually formed by adding *-er* to a short word (*long* becomes *longer*), or putting *more* in front of a longer word (*difficult* becomes *more difficult*).

happier

		m/f	*n*
sg	*nom*	laetior	laetius
	acc	laetior-em	laetius
	gen	laetior-is	laetior-is
	dat	laetior-i	laetior-i
	abl	laetior-e	laetior-e
pl	*nom*	laetior-es	laetior-a
	acc	laetior-es	laetior-a
	gen	laetior-um	laetior-um
	dat	laetior-ibus	laetior-ibus
	abl	laetior-ibus	laetior-ibus

- The comparative is 3-3, i.e. third declension, with one set of forms for the masculine and feminine and another for the neuter.

- The syllable *-ior* is added to the gentive singular stem of the adjective. This applies whether the ordinary adjective is 2-1-2 (like *laetus*) or third declension (like *fortis* or *ingens*, with comparatives *fortior* and *ingentior*). Note that the ablative singular here is *-e*, like the third declension nouns (not *-i*, like ordinary third declension adjectives), and the neuter nominative and accusative plural is *-a* (not *-ia*).

- Note the distinctive neuter nominative and accusative singular (without *-ior-*), which might be mistaken for a second declension masculine form like *filius*.

Exercise 7.6

Put the following into the comparative, keeping the same gender, number and case:

1. longus
2. miserum (*m acc sg*)
3. laetas
4. fortes (*m nom pl*)
5. ingentia (*n nom pl*)

There are two ways of expressing a comparison:

1. A comparative adjective is very often followed by *quam* (= than). The two people or things being compared are in the <u>same case</u>. In a simple comparison this is often nominative:

> dominus stultior est quam servus.
> The master is more stupid than the slave (is).

But the items either side of *quam* can be in any case, according to their job in the sentence:

> senex librum longiorem mihi quam fratri dedit.
> The old man gave a longer book to me than (he gave) to my brother.

2. A simple comparison (where the items compared would be nominative or accusative) can alternatively be expressed by missing out *quam* and putting the second noun in the ablative (*ablative of comparison*):

> dominus stultior est servo.

lit The master is more stupid, by (the side of *or* the standard of) the slave.
i.e. The master is more stupid than the slave.

- Note that *quam* also has other meanings. When it is not in a comparison, it usually means *how*, either as a question (*quam fortis es?* = how brave are you?) or an exclamation (*quam fortis es!* = how brave you are!).

- Remember that the feminine accusative singular of *qui, quae, quod* is also *quam* (*puella quam vidi . . .* = the girl whom I saw . . .), but that is only a *homonym* (i.e. an unrelated word coincidentally spelled in the same way).

- The adverb *multo* (= [by] much) is often used with a comparative to stress the amount of difference:

> dominus multo stultior est quam servus.
> The master is much more stupid than the slave.

Exercise 7.7

Translate into English:

1. ego stultior sum quam frater.

2. quis fortior erat quam dux noster?

3. servi crudeliores sunt domino.

4. puella quam heri conspexi multo pulchrior erat quam comites.

5. consilium facilius petimus.

6. nonne haec verba difficiliora sunt quam illa?

7. quam gravis hic gladius est! multo gravior est quam ille.

8. quam irata erat mater tua? num iratior quam mea?

9. nonne equus meus iam celerior est tuo?

10. hostes multo ferociores sunt militibus nostris.

Exercise 7.8

S&C

Translate into Latin:

1. The old man was braver than his son.

2. Are the gods more miserable than we are?

3. I have never read an easier book.

4. Who is more savage than our master?

5. I have never written a more difficult letter.

REVISION CHECKPOINT

Make sure you know:

- the demonstrative pronouns *hic* (this) and *ille* (that), used alone or with nouns

- comparative adjectives, formed by adding *-ior* to the genitive stem

- the use of *quam* (than), and the ablative of comparison

SUPERLATIVE ADJECTIVES

A *superlative* adjective tells us that a person or thing has a quality to a very great extent, or to the greatest extent of any in a group. In English the first meaning is expressed by using *very*, the second usually by adding *-est* to a short word (*long* becomes *longest*), or putting *most* in front of a long word (*difficult* becomes *most difficult*).

very happy, happiest

		m	f	n
sg	nom	laetissim-us	laetissim-a	laetissim-um
	acc	laetissim-um	laetissim-am	laetissim-um
		etc	etc	etc

- The syllables *-issim-* are added to the genitive singular stem, and the superlative is regular 2-1-2 in form. This applies whether the ordinary adjective is 2-1-2 (like *laetus* is) or third declension (e.g. *fortis* or *ingens*, superlatives *fortissimus* and *ingentissimus*).

- The context usually enables you to tell whether *very* or *-est/most* is the better translation.

  quod epistulam tuam acceperat, puella laetissima erat.
  Because she had received your letter, the girl was very happy.

  hic servus stultissimus omnium est.
  This slave is the most stupid of all (the slaves).

The presence of a genitive plural after a superlative, as in the second example, is a reliable indication that *the most . . .* is needed in English.

Exercise 7.9

Put the following into the superlative, keeping the same gender, number and case:

1. longos
2. forti (*m dat sg*)
3. stultam
4. tristis (*f nom sg*)
5. crudelem (*m acc sg*)

Exercise 7.10

Translate into English:

1. navem gravissimam ad mare trahebamus.
2. cur illum librum longissimum legere cupis?
3. hic captivus semper <u>audacissimus</u> est.
4. quis fuit fortissimus militum?
5. nova ancilla semper laetissima est.
6. ego stultus sum; tu stultior; ille stultissimus.
7. ille nuntius verba tristissima dixit.
8. hic erat crudelissimus dominorum quod servos suos saepe puniebat.
9. viri ferocissimi in hac insula olim habitabant.
10. templum quod in media urbe vidimus ingentissimum erat.

audax -acis   bold, daring

Exercise 7.11

S&C

Translate into Latin:

1. I built the longest wall.
2. These boys are very stupid.
3. Our mistress was always very brave.
4. I was carrying the heaviest of the gifts.
5. That woman and her husband are very happy.

IRREGULAR COMPARATIVE AND SUPERLATIVE ADJECTIVES

An adjective is often given with its comparative and superlative forms:

ordinary form		*comparative*	*superlative*
laetus	*happy*	laetior	laetissimus

This is particularly useful if they are irregular. A number of adjectives have slightly irregular superlatives, which are still very easy to recognise.

- Adjectives with masculine nominative singular ending -*er* have the superlative ending -*errimus*:

miser	*miserable*	miserior	miserrimus
pulcher	*beautiful*	pulchrior	pulcherrimus
celer	*swift*	celerior	celerrimus

Note how *pulchrior* loses the *e* in the comparative, as the adjective itself does after the masculine nominative singular.

- A few third declension adjectives with masculine/feminine nominative singular ending -*ilis* have the superlative ending -*illimus*:

facilis	*easy*	facilior	facillimus
difficilis	*difficult*	difficilior	difficillimus

More care is needed with the very irregular forms. Note that these are often irregular in English too. In language generally, the most common words are typically the most irregular, because they have got bashed around with use. They quickly become familiar because they are met so often.

bonus	*good*	melior	*better*	optimus	*best, very good*
malus	*bad*	peior	*worse*	pessimus	*worst, very bad*
magnus	*big*	maior	*bigger*	maximus	*biggest, very big*
parvus	*small*	minor	*smaller*	minimus	*smallest, very small*
multus	*much*	plus	*more (of)*	plurimus	*most (of), very much (of)*
multi	*many*	plures	*more*	plurimi	*most, very many*

- Note that *plus* in the singular behaves like a neuter noun meaning *a greater amount*, e.g. *plus cibi* (more food). This is parallel to the use of *multum*, e.g. *multum cibi* (much food), which we saw in Chapter Three.

Exercise 7.12

Give an English derivative of:

1. optimus
2. minimus
3. maior
4. pessimus
5. plures

Exercise 7.13

Translate into English:

1. villa senatoris maior templo erat.
2. nova ancilla cenam pessimam paravit.
3. plurimi cives in foro aderant.
4. peiorem cibum numquam consumpsi.
5. pater plus pecuniae filio dedit.
6. melius vinum numquam bibam.
7. haec navis celerrima omnium est.
8. urbem maximam <u>ibi</u> invenimus.
9. murus eius minor erat meo.
10. puellam pulcherrimam in foro conspexi.

ibi   there

Exercise 7.14

S&C

Translate into Latin:

1. I have never read a worse book.
2. That horse is very small.
3. We have never had a better king.
4. This is the best of the slave-girls.
5. All these words are very easy.

COMPARATIVE AND SUPERLATIVE ADVERBS

The comparative of an adverb formed from an adjective is the *neuter singular* of the comparative adjective (nominative/accusative): the distinctive but misleading ending *-ius*. Hence for example:

    comparative   laetius   more happily

Because a superlative adjective is 2-1-2 in declension, the superlative adverb is predictably formed in the same way as the adverb of a normal 2-1-2 adjective: remove *-us* from the masculine nominative singular and add *-e*. So for example:

superlative   laetissime   very happily, most happily

These patterns apply to irregular comparatives and superlatives as well as regular ones.

A comparative adverb is often followed by *quam* (than), just as a comparative adjective is:

senator civibus facilius persuasit quam ego.
The senator persuaded the citizens more easily than I (did).

- Note a special meaning of *quam* when it is put in front of a superlative adverb: *as . . . as possible*. So for example:

  quam celerrime   as quickly as possible

- The superlative adverb *minime* (= very little, least) can also mean *No* in answer to a question:

  'dormisne?' 'minime'
  'Are you asleep?' 'No.'

- Failure to distinguish between adjectives and adverbs is a common mistake at GCSE.

Exercise 7.15

Translate into English:

1. milites portam fortissime custodiebant.

2. puer peius scribit quam puella.

3. haec puella senatori audacissime respondit.

4. hostes quam celerrime fugerunt.

5. servus iratius dixit quam dominus.

6. iuvenis stultissime villam <u>incendit</u>.

7. 'viamne facillime invenisti, serve?' ille 'minime' respondit.

8. filia senatoris semper optime dicit.

9. milites nostri audacius pugnabant quam hostes.

10. omnes laetissime discesserunt.

incendo -ere -i   I set (something) on fire

Exercise 7.16

Translate into Latin:

1. This boy runs more quickly than his brother.
2. The old man slept very well.
3. The slave was working more happily than his master.
4. I shall send a letter as quickly as possible.
5. The citizens were defending the city very bravely.

REVISION CHECKPOINT

Make sure you know:

- superlative adjectives, formed by adding *-issimus* to the genitive stem
- irregular comparatives and superlatives
- comparative adverbs (ending *-ius*) and superlative adverbs (mostly ending *-issime*)

Exercise 7.17

Mucius Scaevola

Mucius fails in his attempt to assassinate Porsenna, but impresses the king with his bravery (508 BC).

Etrusci, quorum rex Porsenna erat, Romam oppugnabant. cives perterriti magno in periculo erant. in urbe tamen erat iuvenis fortis, Gaius Mucius nomine. Mucius consilium audacissimum cepit: castra enim hostium intrare constituit. senatoribus igitur 'patres,' inquit 'consilium optimum habeo quod
5 nos liberabit Romamque servabit. cupio enim castra Etruscorum intrare. ibi auxilio deorum Porsennam necabo. post mortem regis, Etrusci ab urbe nostra discedent.' senatores et consilium et virtutem eius maxime laudaverunt.

Etrusci -orum *m pl*		Etruscans
Porsenna -ae *m*		Porsenna
Gaius -i Mucius -i *m*		Gaius Mucius (*also called just* Mucius)
castra -orum *n pl*		camp*
7	et . . . et	both . . . and
	laudo -are -avi	I praise

* Note that *castra* (= camp) is plural in form but singular in meaning.

Figure 7.2 *Renaissance engraving of Mucius Scaevola burning his hand*. Between 1584 and 1610, Andreani, Andrea, c.1560–1623. (Photo by: Universal History Archive/UIG via Getty Images)

Mucius igitur gladium in <u>vestibus</u> <u>celavit</u> et nocte Roma abiit. ubi ad <u>castra</u>
hostium advenit, magnam turbam circum regem invenit. Mucius hominem
10 conspexit qui pecuniam militibus dabat. 'Porsennam habeo' sibi dixit, et statim
hunc gladio necavit. non tamen regem sed <u>scribam</u> eius necaverat. milites
Mucium ad Porsennam traxerunt. rex eum rogavit 'quis es? unde venisti?' tum
ille 'civis Romanus sum' respondit. 'me Gaium Mucium vocant. ego, qui mortem
tibi paravi, mortem mihi non timeo. me necare potes; sunt tamen Romae
15 multi iuvenes qui post me venient et te necabunt.'

rex <u>et</u> iratus <u>et</u> perterritus erat. primo nihil dixit. tandem 'milites' inquit 'te
punire iubebo.' Mucius tamen ad <u>aram</u> ambulavit et <u>dextram</u> in <u>igne</u> diu tenebat.
'<u>dolorem</u>' inquit 'non timeo.' Porsenna 'virtutem tuam' inquit '<u>et</u> timeo <u>et</u> laudo.'
deinde Mucium liberare constituit. illum, postquam Romam rediit, cives
20 'Scaevolam' vocaverunt.

	vestes -ium *f pl*	clothes
	celo -are -avi	I hide (something)
	scriba -ae *m*	secretary
	ara -ae *f*	altar
17	dextra -ae *f*	right hand
	ignis -is *m*	fire
	dolor -oris *m*	pain
	Scaevola -ae *m*	'Lefty' (*lit* left-handed)

ACTIVE AND PASSIVE

With an active verb the grammatical subject is the person or thing doing the action:

The boy *kicks* the ball.

With a passive verb the grammatical subject is on the receiving end of the action:

The ball *is kicked* by the boy.

Passive verbs in Latin are easy to recognise. Most present, imperfect and future active forms can be converted to their passive equivalents by a simple formula: remove the active person ending, and add the passive one instead. Here are the basic person endings for each:

		active	*passive*
sg	1	-o *or* -m	-r (*added to* -o, *or in place of* -m)
	2	-s	-ris
	3	-t	-tur
pl	1	-mus	-mur
	2	-tis	-mini
	3	-nt	-ntur

- The vowel(s) in front of these passive person endings are usually the same as in the active.

PRESENT PASSIVE

conjugation		1st	2nd	3rd	4th	mixed 3rd/4th
		I am carried	I am warned	I am dragged	I am heard	I am taken
sg	1	portor	moneor	trahor	audior	capior
	2	portaris	moneris	traheris*	audiris	caperis*
	3	portatur	monetur	trahitur	auditur	capitur
pl	1	portamur	monemur	trahimur	audimur	capimur
	2	portamini	monemini	trahimini	audimini	capimini
	3	portantur	monentur	trahuntur	audiuntur	capiuntur

* Note here the ending *-eris* (instead of the expected *-iris*).

- The present passive can be translated (e.g.) *I am being carried*, implying *at this moment*, as well as *I am carried*.

Exercise 7.18

Translate into English:

1. laudamur
2. traditur
3. custodiuntur
4. teneris
5. salutamini

Exercise 7.19

Convert from active to passive, keeping the same person and number, then translate:

1. punit
2. amamus
3. duco
4. iubetis
5. mittunt

AGENT AND INSTRUMENT

Consider the following simple sentence (consisting of subject, object and active verb):

servus dominum necat.
The slave kills the master.

When this is made passive, the original object becomes the subject, and the original subject becomes the *agent* (the *person by whom* the action is done), expressed by *a* (or *ab* if the next word starts with a vowel or *h-*) and the ablative:

dominus a servo necatur.
The master is killed by the slave.

If we are told the *thing with which* the action of a passive verb is done, this is called the *instrument* and is also put in the ablative, but <u>without</u> *a/ab*:

dominus gladio necatur.
The master is killed with a sword.

Both agent and instrument can be expressed in the same sentence (*a/ab* showing which is the agent):

dominus a servo gladio necatur.
The master is killed by the slave with a sword.

- Only verbs that are *transitive* (i.e. ones that in the active have an accusative direct object) can be made passive in this way.

- In Part 1 we met *a/ab* meaning *from* or *away from*, also with the ablative. But there is not much risk of confusion: *a/ab* meaning *from* is usually followed by a noun referring to a place, whereas *a/ab* meaning *by* is followed by a noun referring to a person, and then a passive verb. In both situations, the preposition focuses a meaning the case has already (*from/by*).

Exercise 7.20

Translate into English:

1. nova villa iam aedificatur.
2. nos Romani numquam ab hostibus vincimur.
3. clamores puerorum saepe in via audiuntur.
4. a domino vocaris, serve.
5. illa verba Romae numquam dicuntur.
6. rex ab uxore gladio necatur.
7. verba deorum non semper intelleguntur.
8. vinum in hac taberna venditur.
9. porta nunc fortiter a militibus custoditur.
10. num a patre punimini, pueri?

Exercise 7.21

S&C

Translate into Latin:

1. We are greeted in the street.
2. The food is being eaten by these boys.
3. The letter is at last being written.
4. You are being watched by the senator, citizens.
5. The door is being attacked with a sword.

IMPERFECT PASSIVE

conjugation		1st	2nd	3rd	4th	mixed 3rd/4th
		I was being carried	I was being warned	I was being dragged	I was being heard	I was being taken
sg	1	portabar	monebar	trahebar	audiebar	capiebar
	2	portabaris	monebaris	trahebaris	audiebaris	capiebaris
	3	portabatur	*etc*	*etc*	*etc*	*etc*
pl	1	portabamur				
	2	portabamini				
	3	portabantur				

- Note how the formula for converting active person endings to passive works again here, and how all these have *-ba-* in the ending like the equivalent active forms, making the imperfect passive very easy to recognise.

The imperfect passive is usually translated e.g. *I was being carried*, implying something that was in the middle of happening or went on for a long time. Another possible translation in some contexts is *I used to be carried*.

Exercise 7.22

Translate into English:

1. puniebar
2. salutabatur
3. defendebamini
4. spectabantur
5. movebamur

Exercise 7.23

Convert from active to passive, keeping the same person and number, then translate:

1. videbas
2. ducebamus
3. vocabat
4. custodiebatis
5. mittebam

Exercise 7.24

Translate into English:

1. urbs decem annos oppugnabatur.
2. aqua a puellis bibebatur.
3. pecunia in templo custodiebatur.
4. ego a sene de periculo fluminis monebar.
5. liber diu scribebatur.
6. nonne in periculum ducebamini, milites?
7. urbs a civibus armis defendebatur.
8. cena mea diu parabatur.
9. a turba spectabamur.
10. ille liber saepe legebatur.

Exercise 7.25

Translate into Latin:

1. Many words were being written.
2. The wall was being destroyed by the boys.
3. We were being praised for a long time.
4. Shouts were often heard in the forum.
5. Why were you being attacked with a sword, master?

FUTURE PASSIVE

conjugation		1st I shall be carried	2nd I shall be warned	3rd I shall be dragged	4th I shall be heard	mixed 3rd/4th I shall be taken
sg	1	portabor	monebor	trahar	audiar	capiar
	2	portaberis*	moneberis*	traheris	audieris	capieris
	3	portabitur	monebitur	trahetur	audietur	capietur
pl	1	portabimur	monebimur	trahemur	audiemur	capiemur
	2	portabimini	monebimini	trahemini	audiemini	capiemini
	3	portabuntur	monebuntur	trahentur	audientur	capientur

* Note the ending *-beris* instead of the expected *-biris*.

- As with the future active, note the distinction between two sets of endings: a passive version of *-bo*, *-bis*, *-bit* for first and second conjugations, and a passive version of *-am*, *-es*, *-et* for third and fourth.
- Note that *traheris* is spelled in the same way as the equivalent part of the present passive (but the future is pronounced with a long *e*). You need to use the context to tell the tenses apart.

Exercise 7.26

Translate into English:

1. salutabor
2. custodientur
3. defendemur
4. iubeberis
5. accipiemini

Exercise 7.27

Convert from active to passive, keeping the same person and number, then translate:

1. vocabo
2. laudabimus
3. inveniet
4. spectabis
5. mittetis

Exercise 7.28

Translate into English:

1. cibus noster mox parabitur.
2. omnes laudabimini, puellae.
3. nonne portae a militibus custodientur?
4. haec villa mox vendetur.
5. ego in silva numquam inveniar.
6. haec templa novo modo aedificabuntur.
7. num a domino audiemur?
8. rex hoc gladio necabitur.
9. quando liberaberis, serve?
10. vinum cras bibetur.

Exercise 7.29

S&C

Translate into Latin:

1. All the food will soon be eaten.
2. The horse will be led into the garden by the slave.
3. That boy will be punished tomorrow.
4. Surely we shall not be captured by the enemy?
5. These words will soon be understood.

REVISION CHECKPOINT

Make sure you know:

- the distinction between active and passive
- present passive endings (*-r, -ris, -tur, -mur, -mini, -ntur*)
- agent (*a/ab* and the ablative) and instrument (ablative alone)
- imperfect passive (e.g. *portabar*)
- future passive (e.g. *portabor* or *trahar*)

Exercise 7.30

Cloelia

Fearing further attempts on his life, Porsenna makes a treaty to withdraw the siege, but the Romans have to hand over young men and women as hostages (508 BC).

erat inter <u>obsides</u> quos <u>Porsenna</u> ceperat puella Romana, <u>Cloelia</u> nomine. haec puella fortisima erat. 'virtus <u>Mucii</u>' sibi inquit 'ab omnibus nunc laudatur; virtus mea mox ab omnibus laudabitur.' castra <u>Etruscorum</u> prope <u>Tiberim</u> erant; Cloelia, postquam effugere constituit, <u>paucas</u> comites secum duxit. <u>custodes</u>
5 primo nihil audiverunt, quod puellae tacebant. deinde tamen Etrusci eas prope flumen conspexerunt. puellae tamen, quamquam multa <u>tela</u> ab hostibus iaciebantur, Tiberim <u>tranaverunt</u> et Romam <u>tutae</u> advenerunt.

Porsenna, ubi de <u>fuga</u> earum audivit, iratus erat. nuntios igitur Romam statim misit qui Cloeliam <u>poposcerunt</u>. Romani, quod <u>foedus</u> de <u>obsidibus</u> fecerant,
10 eam ad regem remiserunt. Porsenna et virtutem puellae et <u>fiduciam</u> Romanorum laudavit. 'Cloelia' inquit 'et <u>dimidia pars</u> obsidum liberabuntur et Romam remittentur.' Cloelia, quae hos <u>obsides</u> legere poterat, nunc pueros secum duxit: 'illi' inquit 'mox pugnare poterunt.' ubi omnes Romam redierunt, Cloelia diu a senatoribus civibusque laudabatur. tandem Porsenna suos e terra Romanorum
15 duxit.

	obses -idis *m/f*	hostage
	Porsenna -ae *m*	Porsenna
	Cloelia -ae *f*	Cloelia
	Mucius -i *m*	Mucius
3	Etrusci -orum *m pl*	Etruscans
	Tiberis -is (*acc* -im) *m*	the river Tiber
	pauci -ae -a	a few
	custos -odis *m/f*	guard

	telum -i *n*	javelin, missile
7	trano -are -avi	I swim across
	tutus -a -um	safe
	fuga -ae *f*	escape
	posco -ere poposci	I demand
	foedus -eris *n*	treaty
10	fiducia -ae *f*	good faith
	dimidia pars *f*	half

PRESENT ACTIVE PARTICIPLE

A *participle* is an adjective formed from a verb. It has characteristics of both; it has endings showing number, gender and case like an adjective, and has a tense (and may have an object) like a verb. Most Latin verbs have three participles: present active, perfect passive and future active.

The present active participle is translated *-ing* in English, e.g. *carrying* (but note this is an adjective meaning *while carrying*, not a noun meaning *the act of carrying*).

carrying

		m/f	*n*
sg	*nom*	portans	portans
	acc	portant-em	portans
	gen	portant-is	portant-is
	dat	portant-i	portant-i
	abl	portant-e*	portant-e*
pl	*nom*	portant-es	portant-ia
	acc	portant-es	portant-ia
	gen	portant-ium	portant-ium
	dat	portant-ibus	portant-ibus
	abl	portant-ibus	portant-ibus

* If the participle is used purely as an adjective the ablative singular ending is *-i*, but more often (as we shall see in Chapter Eight) it is *-e*.

- The model for this is a third declension (3-3) adjective like *ingens*, using in the first part of the ending the characteristic vowel(s) for the conjugation. Because that vowel is *e* for second and third conjugation, their present participles decline just like *ingens* (except for the variant ablative singular noted above). The first conjugation has *-a-* in the first part of the ending as shown above, and the fourth has *-ie-*. These exactly match the vowel(s) used before the *-bam*, *-bas*, *-bat* endings in the imperfect tense. Thus:

conjugation	2nd	3rd	4th	mixed 3rd/4th
	warning	dragging	hearing	taking
	m/f	m/f	m/f	m/f
sg nom	monens	trahens	audiens	capiens
acc	monentem	trahentem	audientem	capientem
	etc	etc	etc	etc

- Note carefully the unusual present participle of the irregular verb *eo* (I go): nominative *iens* (as you might expect), but then stem *eunt-*, so accusative singular *euntem*.

Exercise 7.31

Give the following forms:

1. running (*m/f/n nom sg*)
2. shouting (*m/f nom pl*)
3. waiting (*m/f/n abl pl*)
4. guarding (*m/f acc sg*)
5. going (*m/f/n gen sg*)

The tense of any participle tells us when the action happens *in relation to the main verb of the sentence*. A present participle therefore describes an action taking place <u>at the same time as</u> the main verb. So a present participle with a past main verb describes two things happening simultaneously in the past.

The literal translation of the present active participle is *(while) X-ing*:

exiit ridens.
He went out laughing.

puerum cenam consumentem vidimus.
We saw the boy eating his dinner.

In these examples the translation *-ing* sounds fine in English, but often the participle is better expanded into a clause introduced by *when* or *while*. If the main verb is past (as it usually is in a passage) the present participle comes out like an <u>imperfect</u> tense (whose person also comes from the main verb):

     per viam ambulantes, clamorem audivimus.
lit   Walking along the road, we heard a shout.
i.e. <u>While we were walking</u> along the road, we heard a shout.

Note also here that extra information about the action of the participle (here *per viam*) usually comes in front of it. If the participle is used with a noun, the extra information is sandwiched:

puellas ad forum festinantes vidimus.
We saw the girls (while they were) hurrying to the forum.

This example illustrates another point: it is important to work out who or what the participle agrees with. Sometimes this can be ambiguous, as here (because the nominative and accusative plural are the same): *festinantes* could alternatively be nominative, agreeing with *we* (the subject supplied from the verb ending):

We saw the girls while (we were) hurrying to the forum.

In this situation, only the context (and sometimes word order) enable you to decide between the alternatives.

Any participle, like any adjective, can be used on its own as a noun (supplying from the grammar and context a word such as *man, people, things*). The present participle is often used like this in the genitive plural, and can be difficult to recognise:

turba audientium adest.
lit A crowd of listening ones is here.
i.e. A crowd of listeners (*or* people listening) is here.

Exercise 7.32

Translate into English:

1. servos fugientes vidi.
2. puer ridens villam intravit.
3. in silva ambulans pecuniam inveni quam olim celaveram.
4. quid de milite fugienti audivisti?
5. senes in taberna sedentes conspeximus.
6. cibum ancillae laboranti dabo.
7. clamor pugnantium diu audiebatur.
8. puellam epistulam scribentem videre poteram.
9. servi fugientes punientur.
10. num custodes dormientes invenistis, cives?

Exercise 7.33

S&C

Translate into Latin (using present participles; no separate words needed for 'while' or 'who'):

1. We saw the woman sitting in the garden.
2. While eating dinner I heard a shout.
3. Laughing, the friends departed from the forum.
4. The woman gave money to the girl who was crying.
5. The running horses were being watched by the crowd.

Background: social conflict in Rome (1)

As the Roman Republic developed, there was increasing conflict between the patricians (wealthy aristocrats who held political power) and the plebeians (ordinary people, some of them poor) who formed the bulk of the population. The poor, especially those serving in the army, were constantly in debt. Feeling that the Senate was not doing enough to help with their problems, they went on strike and withdrew to the Sacred Mountain, about three miles outside the city. There was alarm in Rome, as the plebeian soldiers were vital to the defence of the city. The Senate sent Menenius Agrippa to negotiate. The parable he told had the desired effect, and afterwards two 'tribunes of the plebs' were created to look after their interests, as well as a plebeian assembly. Problems nevertheless continued.

Exercise 7.34

A military strike

Soldiers go on strike in protest at their poor conditions; they are told a parable, which persuades them that the patrician class serves a purpose (494 BC).

olim erat inter Romanos magna <u>discordia</u>. milites enim, quos <u>consules</u> in bellum ducebant, cum hostibus saepe pugnaverant sed minimam pecuniam acceperant. in forum igitur convenerunt. duces suos irati <u>culpabant</u>. unus miles 'ego' inquit 'patriam defendens laete pugnavi. hostes Romanorum saepe vicimus. agri tamen
5 nostri ab hostibus delentur; cibum igitur non habemus. <u>patricii</u> nobis pecuniam <u>commodant</u>, sed nos <u>plebeii</u> ab eis punimur quod <u>rependere</u> non possumus. mox servi erimus.' haec verba ab omnibus laudabantur. milites igitur ab urbe discesserunt in montem qui prope urbem erat. Romani, quod milites muros defendentes <u>non iam</u> habebant, magno in periculo mox erant.
10 tandem cives perterriti <u>Menenium Agrippam</u>, virum bonum, ad milites mittere constituerunt. ille, ubi in montem venit, <u>fabulam</u> militibus <u>narravit</u>.

'olim erat in <u>corpore</u> magna <u>discordia</u>. partes enim corporis <u>ventrem</u> ma̠
clamore <u>culpabant</u>. "venter" inquiunt "cibum semper consumit quem nos ei
15 damus. sed in medio corpore sedens, <u>nihil</u> facit." <u>dextra</u> igitur "cibum" inquit
"ad <u>os</u> non portabo." <u>os</u> "cibum" inquit "non accipiam." <u>dentes</u> "cibum"
inquiunt "non <u>manducabimus</u>." <u>venter</u>, quod cibum non habebat, magno in
periculo mox erat. non tamen <u>ventrem</u> vicerunt partes <u>corporis</u>, sed in periculum
mortis venerunt. <u>sanguinem</u> enim, quem <u>venter</u> <u>corpori</u> <u>praebet</u>, <u>sine</u> auxilio eius
20 non habuerunt.' Agrippa his verbis militibus persuasit; mox in urbem redierunt.

	discordia -ae *f*		disagreement
	consul -ulis *m*		consul
	culpo -are		I blame
	patricii -orum *m pl*		patricians, nobles
6	commodo -are		I lend
	plebeii -orum *m pl*		plebeians, common people
	rependo -ere		I pay back
	non iam		no longer
	Menenius -i Agrippa -ae *m*		Menenius Agrippa (*also called just*
10			Agrippa)
	fabula -ae *f*		story
	narro -are -avi		I tell
	corpus -oris *n*		body
	venter -tris *m*		stomach
15	nihil		nothing
	dextra -ae *f*		right hand
	os oris *n*		mouth
	dens dentis *m*		tooth
	manduco -are		I chew
19	sanguis -inis *m*		blood
	praebeo -ere		I provide
	sine		without (+ *abl*)

PERFECT PASSIVE PARTICIPLE

This is the most common participle, and one of the most important building-blocks
in Latin grammar. It literally means *having been X-ed*.

(having been) carried

		m	*f*	*n*
sg	*nom*	portat-us	portat-a	portat-um
	acc	portat-um	portat-am	portat-um
		etc	*etc*	*etc*
		(regular 2-1-2)		

The perfect passive participle may be regular or irregular in formation, according to conjugation, with the following endings added to the present stem:

first	-atus *as above*
second	*often* -itus *(like fourth), some irregular*
third	*irregular, but follow various patterns*
fourth	-itus

conjugation:

1st	2nd	3rd	4th	*mixed 3rd/4th*
(having been)	(having been)	(having been)	(having been)	(having been)
carried	warned	dragged	heard	taken

portatus -a -um   monitus -a -um   tractus -a -um   auditus -a -um   captus -a -um

---

Exercise 7.35

Give the following forms:

1. having been warned (*f nom pl*)
2. having been taken (*m/n gen pl*)
3. having been dragged (*n nom/acc pl*)
4. having been greeted (*m nom sg*)
5. having been guarded (*m acc pl*)

A list of important perfect passive participles is given in the next section.

Again the tense of the participle is in relation to the main verb, i.e. the action described by the perfect passive participle <u>precedes</u> that of the main verb. The literal sense *having been X-ed* usually sounds awkward in English and is better avoided. Just *X-ed* is often fine:

hostes victi discesserunt.
lit   The having been defeated enemy left.
i.e.   The defeated enemy left.

- This use of *defeated* must of course be distinguished in English from its use as a simple past tense (e.g. *we defeated them*).

Because this participle is passive, it can have an agent and/or instrument like any passive verb:

epistulam a senatore missam numquam accepi.
I never received the letter sent by the senator.

As we saw with the present participle, other information (here the agent, *a senatore*) is sandwiched between the noun and the participle.

The perfect passive participle is often better replaced in English by a clause beginning *who/which* (like a relative clause), *after/when* (like a time clause), or *since/because* (like a causal clause). The reason for this range of possibilities is that English prefers a more exact statement of the how the actions described by the participle and the main clause are related, whereas in Latin the participle just expresses a loose connection of time (one thing happened before the other), and beyond that leaves it up to the reader to work out the link.

> villam a patre aedificatam vidi.
> I saw the villa <u>which had been built</u> by my father.
> (*perfect passive participle translated as a relative clause*)

- Translation as active (*which my father had built*) is also possible here: this is discussed in Chapter Eight.

> nuntius a rege auditus discessit.
> The messenger left <u>after he had been heard</u> by the king.
> (*perfect passive participle translated as a time clause*)

> hostes superati fugere cupiebant.
> The enemy wanted to run away <u>because they had been overpowered</u>.
> (*perfect passive participle translated as a causal clause*)

Often there is more than one possibility:

> milites nostri urbem ab hostibus oppugnatam intraverunt.
> Our soldiers entered the city <u>which had been</u> attacked by the enemy.
> Our soldiers entered the city <u>after it had been</u> attacked by the enemy.
> Our soldiers entered the city <u>because it had been</u> attacked by the enemy.

Because the perfect passive participle refers to something that had already been done when the action described by the main verb happened, it comes out as a <u>pluperfect</u> (*had been*) if the main verb is in a past tense, as it usually is. (Compare how a present participle comes out as an imperfect.) With a present or future main verb, it stays as a perfect (*has/have been*).

- If the perfect passive participle is translated as a time clause, *after* is the safe choice to show that one action preceded the other (whereas *when* could also be used with an imperfect in English to translate a present participle).

Exercise 7.36

Translate into English:

1. nuntius diu exspectatus tandem advenit.
2. cenam ab ancilla paratam consumpsimus.
3. uxor militis necati miserrima erat.
4. de verbis ibi auditis nihil dicere constitui.
5. regem gladio necatum vidimus.
6. pecuniam olim a fratre celatam inveni.
7. servus paucas horas custoditus effugit.
8. puellae vocatae cibum dedi.
9. servi liberati laetissimi erant.
10. templa a Romanis aedificata semper manebunt.

Exercise 7.37

S&C

Translate into Latin (using perfect passive participles; no separate words needed for 'which', 'because' or 'after'):

1. The ship which had been carried into the sea was heavy.
2. Because they had been warned by the old man, the citizens stayed in the forum.
3. After they had been punished, the slaves decided to run away.
4. We found the book which had been hidden in the temple.
5. The gate once attacked by the enemy was being guarded well.

COMMON PERFECT PASSIVE PARTICIPLES

Here are twenty common perfect passive participles of verbs you have met so far, which should be learned. Most of them are irreglar, but they often have English derivatives that help you to recognise them. Others can be checked in the Latin to English vocabulary, and a fuller list of irregular Principal Parts can be found in the Reference Grammar.

present tense	perfect passive participle	meaning
		having been . . .
accipio	acceptus -a -um*	received
capio	captus	taken, captured
conspicio	conspectus	noticed, caught sight of
deleo	deletus	destroyed
dico	dictus	said, spoken
do	datus	given
duco	ductus	led
facio	factus	made, done
iacio	iactus	thrown
interficio	interfectus	killed
invenio	inventus	found
iubeo	iussus	ordered
lego	lectus	read, chosen
mitto	missus	sent
moveo	motus	moved
pono	positus	placed, put
relinquo	relictus	left
scribo	scriptus	written
video	visus	seen
vinco	victus	conquered

* all are regular 2-1-2 in declension

Exercise 7.38

Translate into English:

1. pecuniam in via inventam habeo.
2. cives fugere iussi iter sine periculo fecerunt.
3. cibum in horto relictum consumpsimus.
4. hostes urbem captam incenderunt.
5. equum heri visum emere constitui.
6. cuius erat liber in aquam iactus?
7. uxor epistulam a sene scriptam legere non poterat.
8. templum deletum miseri vidimus.
9. amicum conspectum salutavi.
10. gladium a te motum invenire non potui.

Exercise 7.39

Translate into Latin (using perfect passive participles; no separate words needed for 'which', 'after' or 'because'):

1. I was looking for the letter which had been sent by my brother.
2. The city conquered by the enemy will be destroyed.
3. I received the money after it had been found in the forum.
4. Because he had been seen in the street, the slave was terrified.
5. The horse which had been led into the forum frightened the children.

REVISION CHECKPOINT

Make sure you know:

- present active participle (e.g. *portans*, gen *portantis*)
- perfect passive participle (e.g. *portatus -a -um*)
- common/irregular perfect passive participles

Background: social conflict in Rome (2)

The aristocrat and military hero Coriolanus (who had gained his name for an almost single-handed attack on the enemy town of Corioli) was strongly opposed to the increased power the plebs had recently acquired. In a time of famine he opposed a plan to keep the price of imported grain down to an affordable level. The tribunes put him up for trial, but before the case came to court Coriolanus, disenchanted with his own people and seeking vengeance, joined Rome's enemy the Volsci whom he had previously fought. Coriolanus later provided Shakespeare with the name and subject of a famous play.

Exercise 7.40

Coriolanus

Coriolanus suffers for his treachery (about 488 BC).

Coriolanus qui dux Romanorum fuerat ab urbe fugit ad Volscos qui bellum cum
Romanis tum gerebant. illi eum laete acceperunt. mox Coriolanus, imperator
Volscorum factus, bellum contra patriam suam gessit. agros Romanorum delevit,
multa oppida cepit, castra prope Romam posuit. nuntios a senatoribus missos
5 non accepit.

feminae igitur Romanae ad matrem uxoremque eius venerunt, auxilium petentes.
'venite nobiscum' inquiunt 'ad castra hostium. nos feminae urbem armis
defendere non possumus, sed precibus lacrimisque eam servabimus.' ubi ad
castra advenerunt, comes Coriolani, qui magnam turbam feminarum
10 conspexerat, ei 'mater tua' inquit 'uxorque adsunt, cum duobus parvis filiis.'
Coriolanus igitur ad matrem festinavit et feminas salutavit. mater tamen irata
rogavit 'cur me salutas? hostisne es an filius? captivane sum in castris tuis an
mater?' haec verba animum Coriolani moverunt. matri tamen 'Romam verbis
tuis servavisti' inquit 'sed filium tuum posthac numquam videbis.' deinde milites
15 ab urbe abduxit. quod tamen hoc fecerat, Volsci Coriolanum necaverunt.
Romani tamen, a periculo sic liberati, unum animum nunc habebant.

	Coriolanus -i *m*	Coriolanus
	Volsci -orum *m pl*	Volscians (*Italian tribe living south of Rome*)
	gero -ere gessi	I wage (war)
2	imperator -oris *m*	general, leader
	oppidum -i *n*	town
	preces -ium *f pl*	prayers
	lacrima -ae *f*	tear
	an	or
12	captiva -ae *f*	(female) captive, prisoner
	animus -i *m*	mind, spirit
	posthac	after this
	abduco -ere abduxi	I lead away

SUMMARY OF CHAPTER SEVEN GRAMMAR

This and *that*:
The pronouns *hic* (this) and *ille* (that), also used like adjectives with nouns.

Comparative adjectives:
Used to compare two people or things, translated *-er* or *more* . . . Endings in *-ior*, neuter *-ius* (3-3). Comparison by using *quam* (than) with the two nouns in the same case, or omitting *quam* and having the second noun in the ablative.

Superlative adjectives:
Used to say a person or thing has a quality to a very great extent, or to the greatest extent of a group, translated *very* . . . or *-est*. Endings in *-issimus -a -um* (2-1-2).

Irregular comparative and superlative adjectives:
Variant superlatives (*-errimus -a -um; -illimus -a -um*), and very irregular comparatives and superlatives of common adjectives, e.g. *bonus, melior, optimus* (good, better, best).

Comparative and superlative adverbs:
The comparative adverb is the neuter singular of the comparative adjective, e.g. *laetius* (more happily); the superlative adverb changes the *-us* of the superlative adjective to *-e*, e.g. *laetissime* (very/most happily).

Active and passive:
With an active verb the grammatical subject does the action; with a passive verb the grammatical subject is on the receiving end.

Present passive:
Changes active endings to *-r, -ris, -tur, -mur, -mini, -ntur*, e.g. *portor* (I am carried).

Agent and instrument:
Agent is the person by whom the action of a passive verb is done, expressed by *a/ab* with the ablative; instrument is the thing with which it is done, expressed by the ablative alone.

Imperfect passive:
Changes *-bam* of the imperfect active to *-bar*, e.g. *portabar* (I was being carried).

Future passive:
Changes *-bo* of first and second declension to *-bor*, e.g. *portabor* (I shall be carried), and *-am* of third and fourth to *-ar*, e.g. *trahar* (I shall be dragged).

Present active participle:
A participle is an adjective formed from a verb. The present active participle declines like *ingens*, with vowels appropriate to the conjugation, e.g. *portans*, gen *portantis* (carrying).

Perfect passive participle:
Formed like a 2-1-2 adjective, e.g. *portatus -a -um* (having been carried); various ways to translate this in a sentence (*after, when, because, who/which*); list of common perfect passive participles to be learned.

CHAPTER SEVEN VOCABULARY

a/ab (+ *abl*) — by (*agent with passive verb*)
animus -i   *m* — mind, spirit, soul
audax -acis — bold, daring
captivus -i   *m* — captive, prisoner
castra -orum   *n pl* — camp
celo -are -avi -atus — I hide (something)
clarus -a -um — famous, clear
comes -itis   *m/f* — companion, comrade
consul -ulis   *m* — consul
corpus -oris   *n* — body
crudelis -e — cruel
custos -odis   *m/f* — guard
et . . . et — both . . . and
flumen -inis   *n* — river
gero -ere gessi gestus — I wage (war)
hic haec hoc — this, *pl* these; he, she, it
iam — now, already
ibi — there
ille illa illud — that, *pl* those; he, she, it
imperator -oris   *m* — general, leader; emperor
incendo -ere -i incensus — I set on fire, I burn (something)
laudo -are -avi -atus — I praise
maior -us — bigger, greater
maxime — very greatly
maximus -a -um — biggest, greatest, very big/great
melior -us — better
minime — no; least, very little
minimus -a -um — very little, smallest
minor -us — smaller, less
modus -i   *m* — manner, way, kind
moveo -ere movi motus — I move (something)
multo — much, by much (*with comparative*)
narro -are -avi -atus — I tell, I relate
nihil   *n* — nothing
optimus -a -um — best, excellent, very good
pars partis   *f* — part
pauci -ae -a — few, a few
peior -us — worse
pessimus -a -um — worst, very bad
plurimus -a -um — very much, *pl* very many, most
plus *gen* pluris — more of (+ *gen*); *pl* more
primo — at first
quam — than (*in comparison*);
how . . .!/? (*exclamation or question*)

quam celerrime (*or other sup adv*)	as (quickly) as possible
resisto -ere restiti	I resist (+ *dat*)
sanguis -inis *m*	blood
sic	thus, in this way
sine	without (+ *abl*)
solus -a -um	alone, on one's own, lonely, only
sto stare steti	I stand
virtus -utis *f*	courage, virtue

50 new words

Chapter Eight

PRINCIPAL PARTS (3)

As we saw in Part 1, this is a system for giving important parts of a verb, from which other information about it can be worked out. For most verbs there are four, and we have now met all of them:

present tense (first person singular)
infinitive
perfect tense (first person singular)
perfect passive participle* (masculine nominative singular)

* In older and in more advanced books, the fourth principal part is given in a form called the *supine*, which ends *-um* like the *neuter* of the perfect passive participle.

Verbs are commonly quoted with their principal parts in the form:

porto, portare, portavi, portatus   I carry

From this you can tell that the meanings of the other parts are *to carry, I (have) carried, having been carried*. With regular forms, the principal parts are often abbreviated:

porto, -are, -avi, -atus

As usual with Latin words abbreviated with a hyphen, you remove the last syllable of the first form quoted, then add the alternative endings.

Some verbs do not have the fourth principal part because they cannot be made passive.

Principal parts are a way of plotting information. As we saw in Part 1, if just the first person singular of the present tense was quoted, you could not tell a first conjugation verb from a third conjugation one (since both end in -o). If just the infinitive was quoted, you could not tell a second conjugation verb from a third conjugation one, since both end in -*ere* (though pronounced differently: the first *e* is long in second conjugation verbs, short in third). By seeing all four parts together you can work out all you need to know.

- From this point onwards, new GCSE verbs glossed in passages and sentences will be given with full principal parts for learning (even if not all are required in the immediate context).

PERFECT PASSIVE

Like the equivalent active tense, the perfect passive is used to describe something that *was done* once in the past, or *has been done* (recently and/or with continuing effects). It must be carefully distinguished from the imperfect passive, which describes something that *was being done*.

conjugation		1st	2nd	3rd	4th
		I was/have been carried	I was/have been warned	I was/have been dragged	I was/have been heard
sg	1	portatus* sum	monitus sum	tractus sum	auditus sum
	2	portatus es	monitus es	tractus es	auditus es
	3	portatus est	*etc*	*etc*	*etc*
pl	1	portati sumus			
	2	portati estis			
	3	portati sunt			

similarly for mixed 3rd/4th conjugation:
I was/have been taken   captus sum, captus es *etc*

*Note that the participle is always nominative, but changes its ending according to the number and gender of the subject (so it can be singular or plural, and masculine, feminine or neuter: e.g. *portatus, portata, portatum* in the singular, and *portati, portatae, portata* in the plural).

The perfect passive is made up of the *perfect passive participle* with the *present* tense of the verb *to be* used as an auxiliary verb (i.e. acting as part of another verb). The present is used because the participle is perfect tense already. The perfect passive literally means *I am in a state of having been carried*, i.e. *I have been carried* or simply *I was carried*.

- Beware of the danger of translating the perfect passive as *I am carried* (which would be a present passive): this is a very common mistake at GCSE.

Exercise 8.1

Translate into English:

1. laudata est
2. iussi estis
3. relictus sum
4. visi sunt
5. superati sumus

Exercise 8.2

Translate into Latin (use either m or f where the gender is unclear):

1. They have been conquered.
2. She was greeted.
3. I was led.
4. You (*sg*) have been guarded.
5. He was killed.

Exercise 8.3

Translate into English:

1. servus in hortum missus est.
2. hae puellae in via a pueris conspectae sunt.
3. celeriter fugere iussi estis, cives.
4. gladius e flumine tractus est.
5. multi clamores illa nocte auditi sunt.
6. de periculo mortis monitus sum.
7. omnes ab hostibus capti sumus.
8. cena optima tibi parata est, amice.
9. cur in forum ductus es?
10. consilium militis a duce acceptum est.

Exercise 8.4

S&C

Translate into Latin:

1. The city has finally been set free.
2. We were seen in the forum by the consul.
3. The dinner was prepared by the slave-girls.
4. You have been led into danger, soldiers.
5. When were the gifts given to you, master?

Exercise 8.5

Cincinnatus

Cincinnatus, an impoverished aristocrat who would later be seen as a model of the best Roman values, is called from the plough to high command but scrupulously lays aside power when the crisis is over (458 BC).

<u>Minucius</u> dux Romanus et milites eius in montibus cum <u>Aequis</u> pugnabant. ab hostibus nunc <u>premebantur</u>. ubi haec Romae nuntiata sunt, cives timentes <u>Cincinnatum</u> <u>dictatorem</u> facere cupiverunt. ille optimus miles erat, sed <u>pauper</u>: in parvo <u>fundo</u> trans <u>Tiberim</u> habitabat. nuntii a senatoribus missi eum agrum <u>arantem</u>
5 invenerunt. Cincinnatus, ubi nuntios appropinquantes vidit, uxorem <u>togam</u> parare iussit. nuntii ubi advenerunt 'milites nostri' inquiunt 'ab hostibus <u>premuntur</u> et cives perterriti sunt. periculum grave est. hostes ad portas urbis mox venient. auxilium tuum rogamus.' tum Cincinnatum <u>togam</u> <u>gerentem</u> <u>dictatorem</u> salutaverunt. ille igitur multos milites ducens quam celerrime ad
10 castra Minucii festinavit. postquam Minucium servavit, hostes vicit et <u>sub iugum</u> misit. ubi Romam intravit, duces hostium in <u>triumpho</u> ducti sunt, et capta arma <u>ostenta sunt</u>. deinde tamen Cincinnatus, postquam <u>imperium</u> suum <u>deposuit</u>, ad agros rediit.

Figure 8.1 *Engraving showing Cincinnatus called from the plough to be dictator of Rome.* Engraving by N. Thomas, after S.D. Mirys, 1785. (Photo by Hulton Archive/Getty Images)

		Minucius -i *m*	Minucius
		Aequi -orum *m pl*	the Aequi (*a hill tribe north-east of Rome*)
		premo -ere	I overwhelm, I crush
		Cincinnatus -i *m*	Cincinnatus
3		dictator -oris *m*	dictator (*granted sole power to deal with an emergency; not a negative term*)
		pauper -eris *m*	poor man
		fundus -i *m*	farm
		Tiber -eris (*acc* -im) *m*	the Tiber
4		aro -are	I plough
		toga -ae *f*	toga (*robe worn by Roman men on formal occasions*)
		gero -ere*	(*here*) I wear
		sub (+ *acc*)	under (*implying motion*)
11		iugum -i *n*	yoke (*made of crossed spears; defeated enemies had to walk under it as a symbol of humiliation*)
		triumphus -i *m*	triumphal procession
		ostendo -ere -i ostentus	I show
		imperium -i *n*	power
13		depono -ere deposui	I put down, I lay aside

*Note that *gero* (met in Chapter Seven) can mean *I wear* (clothes), as well as *I wage* (war).

PLUPERFECT PASSIVE

The pluperfect passive is used to describe an action that already *had been done* by some point in the past.

conjugation		1st I had been carried	2nd I had been warned	3rd I had been dragged	4th I had been heard
sg	1	portatus* eram	monitus eram	tractus eram	auditus eram
	2	portatus eras	monitus eras	tractus eras	auditus eras
	3	portatus erat	*etc*	*etc*	*etc*
pl	1	portati eramus			
	2	portati eratis			
	3	portati erant			

similarly for mixed 3rd/4th conjugation:
I had been taken   captus eram, captus eras *etc*

*As with the perfect passive, the participle is always nominative, but changes its ending according to the number and gender of the subject.

The pluperfect passive is formed in a comparable way to the perfect. Here the auxiliary verb is the *imperfect* tense of the verb *to be*: added to the participle, which is perfect tense already, it creates the pluperfect, which is two stages back. The pluperfect passive literally means *I was* (already, at some time in the past) *in a state of having been carried*, i.e. *I had been carried*.

- Note that the pluperfect active (e.g. *portaveram*) uses *-eram, -eras, -erat* as a set of endings attached to the perfect stem, but the pluperfect passive uses *eram, eras, erat* as a separate auxiliary verb.

- Beware of the danger of translating the pluperfect passive as *I was carried* (which would be a perfect passive): just like translating the perfect passive as *I am carried* instead of *I was/have been carried*, this too is a very common mistake at GCSE.

Exercise 8.6

Translate into English:

1. liberati eramus
2. acceptus eras
3. rogata eram
4. servati erant
5. custoditae eratis

Exercise 8.7

S&C

Translate into Latin (use either m or f if the gender is unclear):

1. They had been sent.
2. It had been built.
3. You (*pl*) had been found.
4. She had been praised.
5. I had been ordered.

Exercise 8.8

Translate into English:

1. captus eram; deinde effugi.
2. epistulam inveni quae tibi missa erat.
3. illa verba numquam audita erant.
4. cur cepisti pecuniam quae deis data erat?
5. nuntius qui in foro conspectus erat subito discessit.
6. muri multas horas custoditi erant.
7. turba e foro mota erat.
8. cur Romam missi eratis, milites?
9. multum cibi a pueris consumptum erat.
10. templum quod a rege aedificatum erat in bello deletum est.

Exercise 8.9

S&C

Translate into Latin:

1. The words of the messenger had been heard by everyone.
2. That book had been written by the old man.
3. You had been sent to the shop, girls.
4. The weapons had been dragged from the forum.
5. Five horses had been found near the road.

REVISION CHECKPOINT

Make sure you know:

- principal parts (present tense first person singular, infinitive, perfect tense first person singular, perfect passive participle), e.g. *porto, portare, portavi, portatus* (I carry, to carry, I [have] carried, having been carried), and the information that can be deduced from them

- perfect passive (perfect passive participle with *sum* as auxiliary verb), e.g. *portatus sum* (I was/have been carried)

- pluperfect passive (perfect passive participle with *eram* as auxiliary verb), e.g. *portatus eram* (I had been carried)

Exercise 8.10

Verginia

In a story of the arrogant behaviour of an aristocrat (echoing the earlier treatment of Lucretia), Verginia's father drastically defends her honour (about 449 BC).

Appius Claudius decemvir erat. puella pulchra, Verginia nomine, in via ab eo conspecta erat. Appius tum amore incensus est. Verginia plebeia erat. Appius multum pecuniae et magnum imperium habebat. Verginia tamen, quae sponsum habebat, Appium respuit. Appius igitur, quod puellam capere cupiebat, consilium
5 crudele cepit. amicus eius, ab Appio iussus, ubi Verginiam in foro vidit, 'haec puella' falso inquit 'est ancilla mea. filia servi est, non civis Romani.' Verginia perterrita in ius vocata est. ibi erat magna turba, et Appius iudex in medio sedens.

Appius verba amici sui audiebat. tum pater puellae, Verginius nomine, intravit. 'ego' inquit 'civis Romanus sum et pater Verginiae. filiam meam custodire cupio.' haec
10 verba a turba laudata sunt. Appius tamen 'lictor,' inquit 'turbam move! da viam amico meo! ancillam enim suam capere cupit.' tum pater Verginiae, quod nullum auxilium vidit, cultrum a taberna lanii rapuit. 'hoc uno modo, filia,' inquit 'te liberare possum.' et puellam cultro statim necavit. omnes qui aderant ingentem clamorem fecerunt. Appius lictorem Verginium capere iussit. ille tamen, cultrum
15 adhuc tenens, viam sibi ad portam fecit; deinde Roma discessit. comites eius civibus ostenderunt et corpus puellae et scelus quod ab Appio factum erat.

	Appius -i Claudius -i *m*	Appius Claudius (*also called just* Appius)
	decemvir -viri *m*	Decemvir (*one of a board of ten magistrates*)
1	Verginia -ae *f*	Verginia
	plebeius -a -um	plebeian, of the common people
	sponsus -i *m*	fiancé
	respuo -ere -i	I reject
	falso	falsely
7	ius iuris *n*	law-court
	iudex -icis *m*	judge
	Verginius -i *m*	Verginius
	lictor -oris *m*	lictor (*attendant and bodyguard of magistrate*)
11	nullus -a -um	no, not any
	culter -tri *m*	knife
	lanius -i *m*	butcher
	rapio -ere rapui raptus	I seize, I grab
	adhuc	still
16	scelus -eris *n*	crime

IF CLAUSES (CONDITIONALS)

A clause containing *si* (if) is known as a *conditional*, because it sets a condition: if one thing is true, something else follows. Simple conditionals with present or past tense verbs translate naturally into English ('tense by sense'):

> si tu ades, ego laetus sum.
> If you are here, I am happy.

> si nihil audivisti, dormiebas.
> If you heard nothing, you were asleep.

It is possible to mix tenses:

> si puer hoc dixit, stultus est.
> If the boy said this, he is stupid.

A future conditional has a *hidden* future verb (a future tense in Latin but translated into natural English as a present):

> > si hunc librum leges, omnia intelleges.
> *lit*   If you will read this book, you will understand everything.
> *i.e.*   If you read this book, you will understand everything.

- This is the same rule we saw in Chapter Six for a time clause (with *ubi*) referring to the future.

The *if* clause can come anywhere in the sentence:

> servus fortis erat si illud fecit.
> The slave was brave if he did that.

The other part of the sentence is usually a statement, but can be a command or a question:

> si librum habes, lege.
> If you have a book, read it!

> si librum habes, cur non legis?
> If you have a book, why are you not reading it?

A negative conditional uses *nisi*, which can be translated either *if not* or *unless*:

> > nisi tu ades, miser sum.
> > If you are not here, I am miserable.
> *or*   Unless you are here, I am miserable.

Exercise 8.11

Translate into English:

1. si illam puellam laudas, stultus es.
2. si puer senem servavit, fortissimus erat.
3. laetissimus sum si amicos pecuniamque habeo.
4. nisi viam mihi ostendes, numquam redire potero.
5. si me audire potestis, statim respondite!
6. omnes te salutabimus si Romam venies.
7. si librum meum nunc habes, ubi invenisti?
8. ancilla tristis est nisi ab omnibus amatur.
9. si bellum gerimus, semper vincimus.
10. pueros punire debemus si hoc fecerunt.

Exercise 8.12

S&C

Translate into Latin:

1. If the boys are quiet, they are working well.
2. I do not trust the senator if he said these things.
3. If we overcome the enemy, we shall be happy.
4. Unless I can sleep, I am miserable.
5. If the citizens are afraid, they must guard the gates

Background: Roman power expands in Italy

The gradual extension of Roman power and influence into the surrounding part of Italy led to a series of conflicts, although these were often just minor border raids. Veii, the richest member of a league of Etruscan cities, proved more difficult. The Romans captured it only after a ten-year siege (like the Greeks in the Trojan War of old), and through the ingenuity of the talented general Camillus. This was not the last time he would intervene decisively to help his city, yet after the capture he showed signs of excessive pride, which the Romans always considered dangerous. Camillus fell into and out of favour with his fellow citizens. But the story of his encounter with the treacherous teacher at Falerii is intended once more to show the superiority of honourable to self-interested behaviour, though it makes the further point that doing the right thing is often also advantageous.

Exercise 8.13

Camillus at Veii

The Romans under Camillus capture the Etruscan city of Veii after a long siege (396 BC).

Romani <u>Veios</u>, urbem <u>Etruriae</u>, decem annos <u>obsidebant</u>, <u>sicut</u> <u>Graeci</u> <u>Troiam</u>
olim <u>obsederant</u>. milites, quod diu ibi manere debebant, miserrimi erant. <u>vineas</u>
magno <u>labore</u> fecerunt, sed hostes eas statim incenderunt. multi milites interfecti
sunt, sed Romani urbem capere non poterant. tandem <u>signum</u> a deis missum
5 acceperunt. erat <u>enim</u> prope Veios <u>lacus</u>: aqua <u>sine</u> <u>causa</u> <u>surgebat</u>. <u>haruspex</u> 'ubi
aqua cadet' inquit 'urbs <u>quoque</u> cadet.' Romani <u>canalem</u> fecerunt; aqua cecidit.

deinde <u>Camillus</u> imperator factus est. bellum novo consilio <u>conficere</u> constituit.
dona deis et <u>praemia</u> militibus <u>promisit</u>. milites, qui nunc laeti erant, <u>cuniculum</u> <u>sub</u>
muris Veiorum fecerunt, per noctem laborantes. tum <u>alii</u> Romani portas urbis
10 oppugnaverunt, <u>alii</u> per <u>cuniculum</u> cucurrerunt et in templum <u>Iunonis</u> exierunt.
hi milites, postquam hostes a <u>tergo</u> oppugnaverunt, portas <u>aperuerunt</u>. <u>ceteri</u>
Romani intraverunt et urbem tandem ceperunt.

	Veii -orum *m pl*	Veii (*city about ten miles north of Rome*)
	Etruria -ae *f*	Etruria (*region of central Italy*)
	obsideo -ere obsedi	I besiege
1	sicut	just as
	Graeci -orum *m pl*	the Greeks
	Troia -ae *f*	Troy
	vinea -ae *f*	siege-shed (*wooden cover for troops attacking*)
3	labor -oris *m*	work, toil
	signum -i *n*	sign
	enim	for (*comes second word*)
	lacus *m*	lake
	sine (+ *abl*)	without
5	causa -ae *f*	cause, reason
	surgo -ere surrexi	I rise
	haruspex -icis *m*	soothsayer
	quoque	also
	canalis -is *m*	channel
7	Camillus -i *m*	Camillus
	conficio -ere	I finish
	praemium -i *n*	prize, reward
	promitto -ere promisi promissus	I promise
	cuniculus -i *m*	tunnel
8	sub (+ *abl*)	under
	alii . . . alii	some . . . others
	Iuno -onis *f*	Juno (*queen of the gods*)
	tergum -i *n*	back
	aperio -ire -ui	I open
11	ceteri -ae – a	the rest (of)

- The proper name *Camillus* will not be glossed again in this chapter.

- Note that we have now met the preposition *sub* (under) both with the accusative (for motion under) and the ablative (for position under). Compare the use of *in* with the accusative (into) and with the ablative (in).

SELF AND *SAME*: *ipse* and *idem*

Two important pronouns, also used as adjectives with nouns, are *ipse* (-self) and *idem* (the same).

-self, *pl* -selves

		m	*f*	*n*
sg	*nom*	ipse	ipsa	ipsum
	acc	ipsum	ipsam	ipsum
	gen	ipsius	ipsius	ipsius
	dat	ipsi	ipsi	ipsi
	abl	ipso	ipsa	ipso
pl	*nom*	ipsi	ipsae	ipsa
	acc	ipsos	ipsas	ipsa
	gen	ipsorum	ipsarum	ipsorum
	dat	ipsis	ipsis	ipsis
	abl	ipsis	ipsis	ipsis

(regular 2-1-2 plural)

- Again note the distinctive genitive and dative singular endings.

Latin uses *ipse* to give emphasis. It implies *in person* (not through someone else). Its use corresponds to English examples such as I made it <u>myself</u> or I wrote to the king <u>himself</u>.
As the hyphen in translation (*-self*) shows, *ipse* usually belongs closely with another word (but is not in Latin actually attached to it). Though classed as a pronoun, it is very often used like an adjective with a noun or another pronoun:

reginam ipsam vidi.
I saw the queen herself.

illi ipsi omnia audiverunt.
Those men themselves heard everything.

The nominative of *ipse* can be used regardless of person, agreeing with the subject of the verb:

ipsi nihil audivimus.
We ourselves heard nothing.

- Note carefully the distinction between *ipse* and *se* (which is always a third person pronoun, always reflexive, and never nominative):

miles ipse servum necavit.
The soldier himself killed the slave.

miles se necavit.
The soldier killed himself.

Nevertheless *ipse* is sometimes added to a reflexive pronoun for extra emphasis (but it cannot here be translated separately in English):

miles se ipsum semper laudat.
The soldier always praises himself.

Exercise 8.14

Translate into English:

1. libros a rege ipso emptos habeo.
2. multos senatores et consules ipsos in via conspeximus.
3. quid ipse in bello fecisti, pater?
4. miles stultus se ipsum semper laudabat.
5. ancilla cenam sibi et reginae ipsi paravit.
6. consilium imperatoris ipsius optimum est.
7. quis custodiet ipsos custodes?
8. hostes auxilio deorum ipsorum vincere poteramus.
9. milites per urbem et per forum ipsum ambulabant.
10. nuntius adest; dux ipse mox adveniet.

Exercise 8.15

Translate into Latin:

1. The general himself was in the camp.
2. I did not see the goddess herself.
3. What did you yourself hear, slave?
4. I gave the letter to the consuls themselves.
5. This boy is the son of the king himself.

the same

		m	f	n
sg	nom	idem	eadem	idem
	acc	eundem	eandem	idem
	gen	eiusdem	eiusdem	eiusdem
	dat	eidem	eidem	eidem
	abl	eodem	eadem	eodem
pl	nom	eidem	eaedem	eadem
	acc	eosdem	easdem	eadem
	gen	eorundem	earundem	eorundem
	dat	eisdem	eisdem	eisdem
	abl	eisdem	eisdem	eisdem

- This is the pronoun *is, ea, id* with *-dem* stuck on the end, and minor adjustments of spelling. The *-s* of the masculine nominative singular has disappeared, so *idem* not *isdem*. The neuter ending in *-d* already does not double it (so neuter nominative and accusative singular, like masculine nominative, are *idem*). Any part of the original pronoun ending *-m* changes it to *-n* before *-dem* is added, to ease pronunciation (so e.g. masculine accusative singular *eundem*, not *eumdem*). Again note the distinctive genitive and dative singular endings (this time with *-dem* added).

Like other pronouns, parts of *idem* can be used alone (supplying a suitable noun in English from gender, number and context), or like an adjective with a noun:

hic senex eadem semper dicit.
This old man always says the same things.

eundem librum saepe legebam.
I often used to read the same book.

Exercise 8.16

Translate into English:

1.　ille equus eadem semper facit.

2.　tres pueri idem nomen habebant.

3.　filiaene eiusdem patris estis?

4.　duo consules eodem anno interfecti sunt.

5.　in eadem urbe omnes habitamus.

6.　bellum cum eisdem hostibus saepe gessimus.

7.　eandem feminam in foro hodie conspexi.

8.　idem vinum in eadem taberna semper bibo.

9.　et dominus et servi eundem cibum consumebant.

10.　omnes dona eidem deae dederunt.

Exercise 8.17

Translate into Latin:

1. The messenger spoke the same words again.
2. Did you see the same girl yesterday, master?
3. The man and the woman were killed with the same sword.
4. I found many parts of the same body.
5. We seek the help of the same gods.

Exercise 8.18

The spoils of Veii

The Romans take spoils from the captured city of Veii, including a statue of Juno. Camillus on his return to Rome becomes dangerously proud.

Camillus milites <u>praemia</u> de urbe capta rapere iussit. ubi dona deis dare parabat, in terram subito cecidit: malum <u>signum</u> esse <u>videbatur</u>, quod Roma ipsa <u>postea</u> ab hostibus capta est. nunc tamen Romani laeti erant. multa pecunia <u>Veiis</u> Romam missa est; multi cives venditi et servi facti sunt. milites <u>statuam</u> <u>Iunonis</u> capere iussi
5 sunt. iram tamen deae timebant. unus miles <u>statuam</u> rogavit: 'o dea, cupisne iter Romam facere?' <u>statua</u> capite <u>nutare</u> <u>visa est</u>: ceteri milites spectabant. dea igitur Romam portata in novo templo a Camillo aedificato posita est. Camillus ipse, ubi Romam rediit, urbem in <u>triumpho</u> intravit. equi <u>albi</u> <u>quadrigam</u> trahebant. alii eum imperatorem optimum vocabant, alii deum.

	praemium -i *n*	prize, reward
	signum -i *n*	sign, omen
	videor -eri visus sum*	I seem, I appear
	postea	afterwards, later
3	Veii -orum *m pl*	Veii
	statua -ae *f*	statue
	Iuno -onis *f*	Juno
	nuto -are	I nod
	triumphus -i *m*	triumphal procession
8	albus -a -um	white
	quadriga -ae *f*	chariot

*Note that *videor* (the passive of *video*, literally *I am seen*) when followed by an infinitive usually means *I seem* or *I appear*. The underlying thought is the same: X *was seen* to happen (even if it was surprising or unexplained), so it *seemed* or *appeared* to happen. It is given here with its infinitive and perfect tense, both passive in form. (We shall see in Chapter Nine that its principal parts are like those of a deponent verb, which is passive in form but active in meaning.)

> ### REVISION CHECKPOINT
>
> Make sure you know:
>
> - conditional clauses with *si* (if) or *nisi* (if not/unless), tense by sense, but 'hidden future' – future in Latin, present in English – if reference is to the future
> - the use of *ipse* (-self) and *idem* (the same), with or without a noun

FUTURE ACTIVE PARTICIPLE

1st conjugation   about to carry

		m	*f*	*n*
sg	*nom*	portat-ur-us	portat-ur-a	portat-ur-um
	acc	portat-ur-um	portat-ur-am	portat-ur-um
		etc	*etc*	*etc*
		(regular 2-1-2)		

- This is *formed from* the perfect passive participle, inserting the syllable *-ur-* before the ending, but is *active* in meaning. Similarly for the other conjugations:

1st	*2nd*	*3rd*	*4th*	*mixed 3rd/4th*
about to carry	about to warn	about to drag	about to hear	about to take
portaturus	moniturus	tracturus	auditurus	capturus
-a -um	-a -um	-a -um	-a -um	-a -um

There is a whole range of possible translations for the future active participle: *about to . . ., going to . . ., intending to.* There is sometimes a suggestion of purpose (*aiming to . . .*). Like other participles, the future active one is often better translated as a clause (e.g. *when . . .*). Like other participles too, its tense is in relation to that of the main verb, so with a passage set in the past a future participle may come out as e.g. *when they were about to do X.*

	pueri discessuri clamorem audiverunt.
lit	The boys, about to leave, heard a shout.
i.e.	When the boys were about to leave, they heard a shout.

The future active participle is similarly used with the imperfect tense of the auxiliary verb *to be* to form a 'made up' tense expressing *future in the past*.

senex pecuniam celaturus erat.
The old man was going to hide the money.

- Note the following future participles of irregular verbs:

sum (I am)   futurus -a -um   about to be
eo (I go)   iturus -a -um   about to go

iter difficile futurum timeo.
I fear the journey, which is going to be difficult.

Romam iturus semper laetus sum.
I am always happy when I am about to go to Rome.

Exercise 8.19

Translate into English:

1. puellae donum empturae ad tabernam ambulant.
2. iter facturus cibum parabam.
3. bellum longum futurum erat.
4. imperator miltes pugnaturos fortes esse iussit.
5. nonne montem ascensuri periculum timetis?
6. nuntius e foro discessurus erat.
7. femina epistulam mariti acceptura Romae manebat.
8. num servum invenisti villam incensurum?
9. Romani auxilium deorum urbem oppugnaturi petiverunt.
10. senex laetus erat quod ad patriam rediturus erat.

Exercise 8.20

S&C

Translate into Latin (using future participles; no separate words needed for 'when' or 'as'):

1. When I am about to climb a mountain, I am always happy.
2. As he was about to fight, the soldier was afraid.
3. The boys were soon going to eat their dinner.
4. When we were about to hand over the money, we heard a shout.
5. The slave-girl was about to go into the garden

Exercise 8.21

Camillus at Falerii

When the Romans are besieging Falerii, Camillus deals harshly with a teacher who treacherously offers him a chance to take the city (394 BC).

Romani, quos Camillus ducebat, <u>Falerios</u> <u>obsidebant</u>. erat in urbe <u>magister</u> qui filios <u>nobilium</u> <u>docebat</u>. hos pueros in agros saepe ducebat; ibi corpora <u>exercebant</u>. quamquam bellum nunc gerebatur, idem faciebat: periculum non timebat. <u>magister</u> optimus esse videbatur; nunc tamen consilium <u>scelestum</u> cepit. pueros enim ad
5 castra Romana duxit, quod eos hostibus tradere cupiebat. ubi castra intravit, ad imperatorem ipsum adiit. 'ad te veni' inquit 'urbem Falerios Romanis traditurus. si hos pueros accipies, urbem quoque habebis. <u>nam</u> patres eorum magnum imperium habent. quod pacem petere <u>cogentur</u>, urbem tibi tradent.'

Camillus, ubi haec audivit, ira motus est. '<u>sceleste</u>' inquit 'cum dono <u>scelesto</u> <u>frustra</u>
10 venisti. nos Romani cum viris pugnamus, non cum pueris qui se defendere non possunt. ego <u>artibus</u> Romanis, virtute armisque, Falerios superabo.' deinde <u>virgas</u> pueris dedit et iussit eos <u>magistrum</u> punire. pueri <u>magistrum</u> <u>verberaverunt</u>. deinde eum <u>ligatum</u> ducentes in urbem redierunt; cives Faleriorum a muris urbis eos appropinquantes spectabant. mox nuntios ad Camillum miserunt quod pacem facere cupiebant.

	Falerii -orum *m pl*	Falerii (*Etruscan city about 30 miles north of Rome*)
	obsideo -ere	I besiege
	magister -tri *m*	teacher
2	nobiles -ium *m pl*	nobles, aristocrats
	doceo -ere docui doctus	I teach
	exerceo -ere	I exercise
	scelestus -a -um	wicked
	nam	for
8	cogo -ere coegi coactus	I force
	frustra	in vain
	ars artis *f*	art, skill
	virga -ae *f*	rod, stick
	verbero -are -avi -atus	I beat
13	ligo -are -avi -atus	I tie up

- Note here *nam* (for), an alternative to *enim* with the same meaning (giving an explanation), but *nam* starts the sentence (unlike *enim*, which is usually the second word).

ABLATIVE ABSOLUTE (1)

This is a phrase consisting of a noun (or pronoun) and participle in the ablative, not linked grammatically with the rest of the sentence. Its name comes from the old sense of *absolute* as *separated* (rather than its modern meaning of *complete*). It is found most commonly with the perfect passive participle, but it can be used with any participle. It describes circumstances that apply when the main action of the sentence happens.

The literal translation *with* . . . is sometimes acceptable:

omnibus navibus paratis, Romam navigare constituimus.
With all the ships prepared, we decided to sail to Rome.

Sometimes words such as *with* and *having been* can be left out, but the phrase still translated literally:

labore confecto, servi discesserunt.
Their work finished, the slaves left.

More often it is better (as with other participle phrases) to translate an ablative absolute with a clause. As we saw in Chapter Seven, the tense of the participle is in relation to that of the main verb, so if the main verb is past (as it usually is in a passage), the perfect passive participle comes out in English as a clause beginning *After* . . ., *When* . . . or *Because* . . . with a pluperfect verb.

- As we saw in Chapter Seven, *after* . . . is a failsafe translation in a clause representing a perfect passive participle, whereas *when* . . . can also (with an imperfect tense) represent a present participle.

Exercise 8.22

Translate into English:

1. hostibus victis, Romani laeti erant.
2. cibo consumpto, ad tabernam ire constitui.
3. portis urbis oppugnatis, omnes cives timebant.
4. epistula accepta, senex miserior erat.
5. muris deletis, magno in periculo eramus.

When the ablative absolute contains a perfect passive participle, you need to decide whether to make it into an active verb in English, or leave it passive. Consider two examples:

his verbis auditis, puellae laetissimae erant.
lit   With these words having been heard, the girls were very happy.

Latin needs to put it like this because most verbs do not have a perfect active participle (so you cannot normally say *having done* X). But because it is natural to assume from the context that the girls (rather than someone else) heard the words, it is appropriate to translate the ablative absolute as a clause with an active verb:

After (*or* Because) they had heard these words, the girls were very happy.

Contrast this sentence:

urbe capta cives miserrimi erant.
lit   With the city having been captured, the citizens were very miserable.

Here the citizens have obviously not done the capturing (the enemy have), so the translation of the ablative absolute needs to leave it passive:

Because (*or* After) the city had been captured, the citizens were very miserable.

Sometimes the perfect passive participle can be translated not only as active, but as a separate main clause joined by *and*:

pueri cena consumpta discesserunt.
lit   With the dinner having been eaten, the boys left.
i.e.   The boys ate their dinner and left.

- This can also be done with a participle that does not form part of an ablative absolute:

    milites nostri urbem captam incenderunt.
    lit   The soldiers set fire to the having been captured city.
    i.e.   The soldiers captured the city and set fire to it.

- In the less common situation where an ablative absolute is used with a present or future tense main verb, the perfect passive participle comes out in English as *After/because X has been done . . .* (or active equivalent).

Exercise 8.23

Translate into English:

1. his verbis dictis, nuntius discessit.

2. consule necato, cives perterriti erant.

3. puellis conspectis, pueri multo laetiores erant.

4. milites, itinere confecto, dormire poterant.

5. templis deletis, iram deorum timemus.

Exercise 8.24

S&C

Translate into Latin (using ablative absolute; no separate words needed for 'because', 'after' or 'when'):

1. Because the money had been found, the old man was happy.
2. The enemy fled after the fields had been destroyed.
3. When the temple had been built, we praised the gods.
4. When she had read the book, the girl returned to the villa.
5. After hearing the messenger's words, the citizens were afraid

ABLATIVE ABSOLUTE (2)

When a present active participle is used in an ablative absolute, a literal translation is also sometimes acceptable:

navis advenit magna turba spectante.
The ship arrived with a big crowd watching.

- Note that the present active participle has the ablative singular ending *-e* when it is used in an ablative absolute, i.e. in effect acting as a verb. (As we saw in Chapter Seven, it has the ending *-i* when used purely as an adjective.)

More often (as we saw with the perfect passive participle), the ablative absolute is better translated with a clause. If the main verb is past tense, this comes out in English as a clause beginning *While . . ., When . . .* or *Because . . .* with an imperfect verb:

      custode dormiente, captivi effugerunt.
lit With the guard sleeping, the prisoners escaped.
i.e. While (*or* When . . . *or* Because . . .) the guard was sleeping, the prisoners escaped.

Similarly a future active participle with a past tense main verb comes out in English as a clause beginning *When/as . . .* with a 'future in the past' verb *was/were about to . . .*:

      militibus discessuris, nuntius advenit.
lit With the soldiers about to leave, a messenger arrived.
i.e. When the soldiers were about to leave, a messenger arrived.

- In the less common situation where an ablative absolute is used with a present or future tense main verb, the present active participle comes out in English as *While/because X is happening . . .*, and the future active participle as *When/because X is about to happen . . .*.

- The verb *to be* does not have a present participle, so ablative absolute phrases are sometimes found in which *being* needs to be supplied as the literal translation (and there is no actual participle in the sentence):

> Camillo duce hostes vicimus.
> *lit*   With Camillus being leader we conquered the enemy.

or in better English

> With Camillus as leader . . . *or* Under Camillus' leadership . . .

- If a noun referring to a person is used in the ablative without a preposition, it is very likely to be part of an ablative absolute.

- A participle phrase is only put in the ablative absolute if it cannot go into any other case that would relate it to the rest of the sentence. Sometimes a phrase that looks like an ablative absolute is actually dative (the dative and ablative endings being the same for all plurals, and for second declension singulars):

> puellis auxilium petentibus cibum dedi.
> I gave food to the girls who were seeking help.

- On the other hand, a participle phrase may be ablative (for example because it follows a preposition), but not ablative absolute:

> nihil audivi de femina lacrimanti.
> I have heard nothing about the woman who is weeping.

> Note here that the present active participle has the ablative singular ending *-i* because it is being used as an adjective.

Exercise 8.25

Translate into English:

1. servo laborante, dominus in horto dormiebat.
2. Romanis appropinquantibus, dux hostium in castris manere constituit.
3. magnam cenam amicis adventuris paravimus.
4. bello decem annos gesto, urbs tandem capta est.
5. me duce urbem capere poteritis, milites.
6. uxore lacrimante, senex miserrimus erat.
7. quid dicere potes de servo clamanti?
8. heri navibus navigaturis omnes ad mare festinavimus.
9. senator multis audientibus mortem consulis nuntiavit.
10. pueri puellaeque libro lecto omnia intellegent.

Exercise 8.26

Translate into Latin (using ablative absolutes; no separate words needed for 'as', 'with', 'after' or 'when'):

1. The consul walked into the forum as the senator was leaving.
2. As the ship was about to sail, that sailor fell into the sea.
3. The senator was killed with many citizens watching.
4. After the city had been destroyed, we were seeking a new homeland.
5. I arrived when the girls were about to eat their dinner.

REVISION CHECKPOINT

Make sure you know:

- future active participle, e.g. *portaturus* (about to carry)
- ablative absolute (noun and participle, grammatically separate from the rest of the sentence), using perfect passive, present active or future active participle
- translation of the participle as a clause (beginning *when/while/after/because*), moving back a tense if the main verb is past
- when to translate the perfect passive participle with an active verb, and when to leave it passive

Background: the Gauls invade Rome

Rome almost met with disaster when the Gauls crossed the Alps and invaded Italy. Early warnings were ignored. But the defence of the Capitol, the heroic self-sacrifice of the patrician old men, and particularly the raising of the alarm by the sacred geese, all became the stuff of patriotic legend. The Romans were about to surrender on humiliating terms to the Gallic commander Brennus when Camillus came to the rescue. Because the city was in ruins when the Gauls left, some Romans wanted to move the capital to the captured Veii, but Camillus – helped by a timely omen – persuaded them to stay. This was the last time the city was captured by non-Roman forces until Rome fell to the Visigoths in 410 AD, eight centuries later.

Exercise 8.27

The Gauls approach

A warning is ignored as the invading Gauls approach Italy (391 BC).

venerunt ex <u>Alpibus</u> <u>Galli</u>, novi Romanorum hostes. <u>Caedicius</u> <u>pauper</u> erat; nocte dormiens <u>vocem</u> audivit, clariorem <u>voce</u> <u>hominis</u>. 'haec senatoribus nuntia: Galli mox advenient.' his verbis auditis, Caedicius perterritus erat. statim surrexit et ad senatores quam celerrime festinavit. senatores tamen verbis Caedicii non
5   credebant, ridentes quod ille <u>pauper</u> erat et Galli <u>procul</u> habitabant. sic Romani moniti sunt, sed frustra.

deinde Camillus, imperator optimus, ab <u>inimicis</u> de <u>praeda</u> <u>Veiorum</u> <u>accusatus est</u>; <u>nec</u> se defendere poterat, quod de morte filii (qui <u>morbo</u> perierat) miserrimus erat. in <u>exsilium</u> igitur missus est. Camillo hoc modo punito, Romani in maius
10 periculum venerunt. tum nuntii advenerunt, a civibus <u>Clusii</u> missi, auxilium contra Gallos petentes. nam Galli, quamquam <u>procul</u> habitabant, de vino et pecunia <u>Italiae</u> audiverant. Alpes igitur transierunt et Clusium primo oppugnaverunt.

	Alpes -ium *f pl*	the Alps
	Galli -orum *m pl*	Gauls (*from modern France*)
	Caedicius -i *m*	Caedicius
	pauper -eris *m*	poor man
2	vox vocis *f*	voice
	homo -inis *m*	man, human being
	procul	far away
	inimicus -i *m*	(personal) enemy
	praeda -ae *f*	spoil, booty
7	Veii -orum *m pl*	Veii
	accuso -ere -avi -atus	I accuse
	nec	and not, nor
	morbus -i *m*	disease
	exsilium -i *n*	exile
10	Clusium -i *n*	Clusium (*city about 85 miles north of Rome*)
	Italia -ae *f*	Italy

• The proper name *Galli* will not be glossed again in this chapter.

MORE IRREGULAR VERBS

The following three irregular verbs – *volo* (I want), *nolo* (I do not want) and *malo* (I prefer) – should be studied together, and recurrent features noted:

		I want	I do not want	I prefer
present				
sg	*1*	volo	nolo	malo
	2	vis	non vis	mavis
	3	vult	non vult	mavult
pl	*1*	volumus	nolumus	malumus
	2	vultis	non vultis	mavultis
	3	volunt	nolunt	malunt
infinitive		velle	nolle	malle

---

future				
sg	*1*	volam	nolam	malam
	2	voles	noles	males
		etc	*etc*	*etc*

(like regular third conjugation future, e.g. traham*)*

---

imperfect				
sg	*1*	volebam	nolebam	malebam
	2	volebas	nolebas	malebas
		etc	*etc*	*etc*

(like regular third conjugation imperfect, e.g. trahebam*)*

---

perfect				
sg	*1*	volui	nolui	malui
	2	voluisti	noluisti	maluisti
		etc	*etc*	*etc*

(like regular second conjugation perfect, e.g. monui*)*

---

pluperfect				
sg	*1*	volueram	nolueram	malueram
	2	volueras	nolueras	malueras
		etc	*etc*	*etc*

(like regular second conjugation pluperfect, e.g. monueram*)*

Note that *nolo* and *malo* are compounds of *volo*.

- *nolo* is in origin *non volo* (three bits of the present tense remain separated)
- *malo* uses an abbreviated form of the comparative adverb *magis* (= more) attached as a prefix to *volo*: it means *want* something *more* than something else. It is often followed by two infinitives separated by *quam*, which can be translated in various ways:

ambulare quam currere malo.
I prefer to walk (rather) than to run.
or   I prefer walking to running.
or   I would rather walk than run.

Exercise 8.28

Translate into English:

1. novam villam aedificare volo.
2. milites nocte pugnare nolebant.
3. malo sedere quam stare.
4. omnes verba imperatoris audire diu volueramus.
5. cur hoc vinum bibere non vis, pater?
6. nolo de periculo itineris audire.
7. senex viam faciliorem invenire mox volet.
8. ego ad tabernam ire volo; tu dormire mavis.
9. cives, quamquam perterriti erant, fugere noluerunt.
10. hoc consilium malo quod multo melius est.

Exercise 8.29

S&C

Translate into Latin:

1. What do you want to do now, boys?
2. This girl does not want to make the journey to Rome.
3. I had always wanted to see that temple.
4. The old men preferred to stay in Rome.
5. Why do you not want to sail to the island, friends?

The final irregular verb needed for GCSE is *fero* (I carry, I bring, I bear), which is basically third conjugation but loses some vowels from its endings and has unusual principal parts:

fero, ferre, tuli, latus

present			active	passive
			I carry	I am (being) carried
sg	1		fero	feror
	2		fers	ferris
	3		fert	fertur

pl	1	ferimus	ferimur
	2	fertis	ferimini
	3	ferunt	feruntur

imperfect:	ferebam	ferebar
	ferebas	ferebaris
	etc	*etc*

future:	feram	ferar
	feres	fereris
	etc	*etc*

perfect:	tuli	latus sum
	tulisti	latus es
	etc	*etc*

- In Chapter One we met the verb *porto* (carry); *fero* often has the same meaning, but is particularly used for *bring* (carry with you) or *bear* (as in *bearing gifts*, but also in the metaphorical sense *tolerate*, i.e. put up with something unpleasant).

- The following verbs are compounds of *fero*, with similar principal parts:

aufero, auferre, abstuli, ablatus	I take away, I steal	(*au* = *ab*, away)
offero, offerre, obtuli, oblatus	I offer	(*ob* = for)
refero, referre, rettuli, relatus	I bring back, I report	(*re* = back)

- Note the changes of spelling (*ab-* to *au-*, *ob-* to *of-*) to ease pronunciation. The perfect passive participle *ablatus* gives us *ablative*, expressing the idea of separation. The literal meaning of *refero* (I carry back) is extended to mean *bring back news of*, hence *report* or *tell*.

- Note also that the last two parts of *fero* are found with the prefix *sub-* as the last two principal parts of *tollo*, formed as if it had started *subfero*, which would have the same meaning (literally *carry from below*, like a fork-lift truck):

tollo, tollere, sustuli, sublatus	I raise, I lift up

IRREGULAR IMPERATIVES

We saw in Part 1 that a direct command, telling someone to do something, is expressed by the *imperative*:

	carry!	warn!	drag!	listen!	take!
sg	porta	mone	trahe	audi	cape
pl	portate	monete	trahite	audite	capite

Four common third conjugation (or related irregular) verbs drop the *-e* ending in the singular:

from dico   dic   say! speak! tell!
        duco   duc   lead!
        fero   fer   carry!
        facio   fac   make! do!

- The plural of *fer* is *ferte*; the other plurals are regular (*dicite, ducite, facite*).

Exercise 8.30

Translate into English:

1. cur eundem librum semper fers?

2. duc me ad ducem tuum!

3. milites arma gravissima tollere non poterant.

4. dic mihi! quid ibi fecisti?

5. ille servus pecuniam meam abstulit.

6. nuntius verba imperatoris in foro rettulit.

7. amici nostri auxilium offerre possunt.

8. dona optima a puellis ferebantur.

9. vinum fer! cenam fac!

10. pater parvum filium in equum sustulit.

Exercise 8.31

Translate into Latin:

1. The girl always offers food to this old man.

2. Lead us through this land, generals!

3. Bring me my sword, slave!

4. That woman often used to steal food.

5. What are you carrying, boys?

Exercise 8.32

Defending Rome

The Romans debate how to defend their city against the Gauls (390 BC).

Romani <u>legatos</u> <u>Clusium</u> miserunt. illi, quamquam verba nec arma ferre iussi erant, cum Gallis pugnare <u>coeperunt</u>. Galli iratissimi erant; senatores tamen <u>legatos</u> postquam redierunt punire nolebant. Galli igitur Romanos oppugnare constituerunt. Romani, qui hostes ferociores numquam viderant, magno <u>proelio</u>
5 ad <u>Alliam</u> flumen ab eis victi sunt. deinde Galli Romae appropinquaverunt, urbem ipsam oppugnaturi.

cives Romani perterriti et miserrimi erant. in foro igitur convenerunt, consilium petentes. urbem suam omni modo servare volebant, sed labor difficillimus esse videbatur. multi ad alias urbes fugere parabant. iuvenes et viri fortes, inter quos
10 multi senatores erant, <u>Capitolium</u> defendere constituerunt, uxores et filios et filias secum habentes. senes tamen <u>nobiles</u>, qui <u>officia</u> in urbe olim tenuerant, <u>domi</u> manere maluerunt. 'nos' inquiunt '<u>nec</u> arma ferre <u>nec</u> patriam custodire possumus. cibum vestrum consumere nolumus. sed Roma numquam discedemus.' his verbis dictis, <u>domum</u> redierunt.

	legatus -i *m*	envoy, ambassador
	Clusium -i *n*	Clusium
	coepi	I began
	proelium -i *n*	battle
5	Allia -ae *f*	the Allia (*a small river north of Rome*)
	Capitolium -i *n*	the Capitol (*citadel of Rome*)
	nobilis -e	noble, aristocratic
	officium -i *n*	public office, important responsibility
	domi	at home
12	nec . . . nec	neither . . . nor
	domum	home, homewards

- Note that *coepi* is a 'defective' verb, i.e. only some tenses exist – in this case the perfect *coepi* (I began) and the pluperfect *coeperam* (I had begun).

NEGATIVE COMMANDS

A negative direct command, telling someone *not* to do something, is expressed in a distinctive way. It does not (as you might expect) use a negative with the imperative, but uses the imperative of *nolo* (formed as if fourth conjugation) as a sort of auxiliary verb:

	sg	*pl*
imperatives of nolo:	noli	nolite

This is followed by the *infinitive* of the verb expressing what is not to be done:

negative command:	noli festinare nolite festinare
literally	Be unwilling to hurry!
i.e.	Do not hurry!

- The literal translation of *noli/nolite* must be avoided here. A common mistake at GCSE is to write e.g. *I didn't want to hurry*, confusing *noli* with the perfect tense *nolui*.

Exercise 8.33

Translate into English:

1. nolite clamare!
2. noli pecuniam illis hominibus dare!
3. nolite in templo currere, pueri!
4. illos libros movere noli!
5. nolite periculum belli timere!
6. noli consumere cibum quem ibi emisti!
7. nolite verba huius nuntii audire, cives!
8. noli de bello dicere!
9. noli villam prope flumen aedificare!
10. murum delere nolite!

Exercise 8.34

Translate into Latin:

1. Do not hide the money, slave!
2. Don't drink this water, friends!
3. Don't climb that mountain, boy!
4. Do not fear the enemy, citizens!
5. Don't sleep in the garden, girls!

Exercise 8.35

An eerie sight

The Gauls after entering Rome are confronted by a surprising scene.

Galli urbem facile intraverunt. per vias Romae cucurrerunt, <u>praedam</u> petentes.
deinde <u>spectaculum</u> <u>mirum</u> viderunt. nam senes <u>immotos</u> in <u>vestibulis</u> sedentes
invenerunt, animis ad mortem paratis. illi omnes tacebant, <u>trabeas</u> <u>splendidas</u>
<u>gerebant</u> omnes: <u>statuae</u> deorum esse videbantur. hostes primo perterriti erant.
tandem miles <u>Gallus</u> uni seni appropinquavit. 'noli <u>tangere</u>!' clamaverunt ceteri.
5   miles tamen <u>barbam</u> eius <u>mulcere</u> coepit. tum senex, <u>Papirius</u> nomine, iratus surrexit.
militem <u>scipione</u> <u>eburneo</u> <u>pulsavit</u>; ille ad terram cecidit. deinde omnes senes in <u>sellis</u>
suis a Gallis necati sunt.

	praeda -ae *f*	spoil, booty
	spectaculum -i *n*	sight, spectacle
	mirus -a -um	amazing
	immotus -a -um	motionless
2	vestibulum -i *n*	front porch
	trabea -ae *f*	robe
	splendidus -a -um	magnificent
	gero -ere*	(*here*) I wear
	statua -ae *f*	statue
4	Gallus -a -um	Gallic, of the Gauls
	tango -ere	I touch
	barba -ae *f*	beard
	mulceo -ere	I stroke
	Papirius -i *m*	Papirius
6	scipio -onis *m*	staff, rod of office
	eburneus -a -um	(made of) ivory
	pulso -are -avi	I strike
	sella -ae *f*	chair

*As we saw earlier in this chapter, *gero* can mean *I wear* (clothes), as well as *I wage* (war).

Exercise 8.36

Sacred geese

Figure 8.2 *Marble relief of the sacred geese that would raise the alarm on the Capitol.* (Photo By DEA/G. DAGLI ORTI/De Agostini/Getty Images)

As the Gauls attempt to seize the Capitol, the sacred geese raise the alarm.

Galli <u>Capitolium</u> <u>obsidebant</u>: non tamen capere poterant, quod mons <u>altus</u> et <u>praeruptus</u> erat. Romani ridebant et, quamquam minimum cibum habebant, <u>panes</u> ad Gallos <u>deiciebant</u>. cives qui Roma fugerant Camillum de <u>exsilio</u> revocare volebant. nuntium igitur Romam miserunt. ille, ubi in urbem advenit, Capitolium per viam <u>occultam</u> ascendit. senatores qui ibi aderant consilium

5 auditum laudaverunt. 'Camillus' inquiunt '<u>dictator</u> facietur, nam Romam servare solus potest.' nuntius igitur Camillum ad urbem invitaturus discessit.

Galli tamen nuntium Capitolium ascendentem conspexerant; nunc in animo habebant montem eadem via ascendere. paraverunt igitur Capitolium sic oppugnare. media nocte tacentes ascendere coeperunt. Galli nec custodes nec

10 <u>canes</u> excitaverunt. <u>anseres</u> tamen <u>sacros</u>, qui in Capitolio habitabant, nullo modo <u>decipere</u> poterant. nam <u>clangore</u> eorum <u>excitatus est</u> <u>Manlius</u>, vir <u>summae</u> virtutis qui olim consul fuerat. gladio statim rapto, ceteros ad arma vocavit. deinde Gallum qui primus in <u>summo</u> Capitolio steterat <u>deiecit</u>. ille cadens alios quoque <u>deturbavit</u>; omnes necati sunt. hoc modo Roma a Manlio et <u>clangore</u>

15 <u>anserum</u> servata est.

Capitolium -i *n*	the Capitol (*citadel of Rome*)
obsideo -ere	I besiege
altus -a -um	high
praeruptus -a -um	steep

3	panis -is *m*	loaf of bread
	deicio -ere	I throw down
	exsilium -i *n*	exile
	occultus -a -um	secret
	dictator -oris *m*	dictator (*granted sole power to deal with*
5		*an emergency; not a negative term*)
	canis -is *m/f*	dog
	anser -eris *m*	goose
	sacer -cra -crum	sacred
	decipio -ere	I deceive
11	clangor -oris *m*	cackling
	excito -are -avi -atus	I arouse
	Manlius -i *m*	Manlius
	summus -a -um	highest, greatest; top of
	deturbo -are -avi	I dislodge

- Note here the idiom *in animo habeo*, literally *I have in mind*, i.e. *I intend*.

- Translation of the adjective *summus* varies according to context: *vir summae virtutis* means *a man of the highest courage*, but *summus mons* means *the top* (or *the highest part*) *of the mountain* (rather than *the highest mountain* out of several). This is parallel to the use of *medius*, i.e. *media nocte* means *in the middle of the night* (rather than *on the middle night*).

- Translation of the adjective *altus* also varies according to context: it can mean either *high* (e.g. describing a mountain) or *deep* (e.g. describing a river).

MORE QUESTION WORDS

In Chapter Four we met three ways of introducing a question to which the answer will be *yes* or *no*:

-ne (attached to the first word) for an open question (*e.g.* is it . . .?)
nonne expecting the answer *yes* (surely . . .?)
num expecting the answer *no* (surely . . . not?)

We also met the following question words asking for specific information (most of them beginning *qu-*):

cur	why?
quando	when?
ubi	where?
quo	where to?
unde	where from?
quis	who?
quid	what?

In Chapter Seven we met:

quam   how?

The following complete the requirements for GCSE:

quantus -a -um   how big? how much?
quot   how many?
qualis -e   what sort of?
quomodo   how?

The first three of these are adjectives: *quantus* is 2-1-2 like *laetus*; *quot* is indeclinable; *qualis* is third declension like *fortis*. The adverb *quomodo* is in origin a phrase using the ablative of *modus* (*quo modo* = in what way?).

Exercise 8.37

Translate into English:

1. cur semper lente ambulatis?
2. nonne vocem dei audivisti?
3. qualem cibum consumere mavis?
4. quomodo viam ad summum montem invenisti?
5. quando Romam adveniemus?
6. quo festinatis, cives?
7. quis de hoc proelio audivit?
8. quantas et quales naves habes, imperator?
9. unde venit ille nuntius?
10. quid nunc facere vultis?

Exercise 8.38

Translate into Latin:

1. How much money do you have, boy?
2. When did the old man make the journey?
3. How many citizens were in the forum?
4. What sort of battle was fought there?
5. How did you write those books?

REVISION CHECKPOINT

Make sure you know:

- irregular verbs: *volo* (I want), with its compounds *nolo* (I do not want) and *malo* (I prefer); also *fero* (I carry), with its compounds *aufero* (I take away/ steal), *offero* (I offer), *refero* (I bring back), and the irregular *tollo* (I raise)

- irregular imperatives *dic* (say!), *duc* (lead!), *fer* (carry!) and *fac* (make/do!)

- negative commands with *noli/nolite* and the infinitive, e.g. *noli festinare* (do not hurry!)

- question words, including new ones *quantus* (how big?), *quot* (how many?), *qualis* (what sort of?) and *quomodo* (how?)

Exercise 8.39

No surrender

The Romans, hard pressed by the Gauls, are about to surrender on humiliating terms when Camillus intervenes.

Galli, quamquam <u>Capitolium</u> capere non poterant, <u>adhuc</u> Romam <u>obsidebant</u>. agros deleverant, multa <u>aedificia</u> incenderant. tandem senatores, quod cives nullum cibum habentes magno in periculo erant, <u>aurum</u> Gallis offerre volebant. <u>Brennus</u>, dux Gallorum, mille <u>pundo</u> <u>postulavit</u>. Romani igitur <u>aurum</u> tulerunt.
5 Galli tamen <u>pondera</u> <u>iniqua</u> habebant. Romani, ubi hoc intellexerunt, irati erant. sed Brennus ridens gladium suum <u>ponderibus</u> <u>addidit</u>. et verba audita sunt quae Romani ferre non poterant: '<u>vae</u> victis!'

subito tamen Camillus multis cum militibus advenit. et Romanos <u>aurum</u> auferre et Gallos ab urbe discedere iussit. 'Romani' inquit 'patriam <u>ferro</u> non <u>auro</u>
10 defendunt. ego <u>dictator</u> factus sum; pax non facta est. arma vestra parate!' Galli pugnare coacti mox a Romanis victi sunt; fugientes audiverunt haec verba: '<u>vae</u> victis!'

	Capitolium -i *n*	the Capitol
	adhuc	still
	obsideo -ere	I besiege
	aedificium -i *n*	building
3	aurum -i *n*	gold
	Brennus -i *m*	Brennus
	pundo *indecl*	pounds
	postulo -are -avi	I demand
	pondus -eris *n*	weight (*used in a scale*)
5	iniquus -a -um	unfair (*i.e. too heavy, so that what was weighed would seem too light*)
	addo -ere -idi	I add
	vae	woe!
	ferrum -i *n*	iron (*i.e. iron weapons*)
10	dictator -oris *m*	dictator

Exercise 8.40

Home sweet Rome

After the Gauls have left, many Roman citizens want to establish a new city at Veii, but Camillus persuades them to stay.

Roma liberata erat, sed cives per <u>totam</u> urbem <u>ruinas</u> viderunt. magno in
periculo diu fuerant; multi Romae manere timebant. 'locum meliorem' inquiunt
'invenire possumus. <u>Veios</u> captos habemus. novam urbem ibi aedificabimus. <u>tuti</u>
ab hostibus ibi erimus.' Camillus tamen eis respondit: 'cives, <u>Romulus</u> pater
5 noster Romam auxilio deorum <u>condidit</u>. dei ipsi hunc locum sacrum legerunt.
dei urbem nostram semper servaverunt. nolite templa deorum relinquere! ego,
ubi in <u>exsilio</u> eram, Romam redire semper volebam. ego et forum et flumen amo.
novam urbem, si vultis, <u>condere</u> potestis; deos tamen Romae vobiscum non
habebitis.'

10 tum forte venerunt in forum milites, quorum <u>centurio</u> clamavit: '<u>signifer</u>, <u>statue</u>
<u>signum</u>! in hoc loco stare debemus.' hoc <u>signum</u> civibus persuasit; omnes Romae
manere constituerunt. Camillus 'Romulus', 'pater patriae', 'Romae <u>conditor</u>
<u>secundus</u>' a civibus vocabatur.

	totus -a -um	whole
	ruina -ae *f*	ruin
	Veii -orum *m pl*	Veii
	tutus -a -um	safe
4	Romulus -i *m*	Romulus
	condo -ere -idi	I found, I establish
	exsilium -i *n*	exile
	centurio -onis *m*	centurion (*Roman army officer, usually in charge of eighty men*)
10	signifer -eri *m*	standard-bearer
	statuo -ere	I set up, I fix in the ground
	signum -i *n*	military standard; *also* sign, omen
	conditor -oris *m*	founder
	secundus -a -um	second

SUMMARY OF CHAPTER EIGHT GRAMMAR

Principal parts:
Set of four parts of a verb (present active first person singular, infinitive, perfect active first person singular, perfect passive participle), e.g. *porto, portare, portavi, portatus* (I carry, to carry, I [have] carried, having been carried), from which all necessary information about it can be deduced.

Perfect passive:
Made from the perfect passive participle with the present of *to be* as an auxiliary verb, e.g. *portatus sum* (I was carried *or* I have been carried). The nominative participle agrees in gender and number with the subject.

Pluperfect passive:
Made from the perfect passive participle with the imperfect of *to be* as an auxiliary verb, e.g. *portatus eram* (I had been carried). The nominative participle agrees in gender and number with the subject.

If clauses (conditionals):
Use of *si* (if) or negative *nisi* (if not/unless) with present or past tense according to sense; a future condition has a 'hidden future' (a future tense in Latin translated as a present).

Self and Same:
Two important pronouns, often used as adjectives: emphatic *ipse* (-self), agreeing with a noun or with the subject of a verb (any person), and *idem* (the same).

Future active participle:
Made from the perfect passive participle by inserting *-ur-* before the ending, e.g. *portaturus* (about to carry), but is active in meaning.

Ablative absolute:
A noun and participle phrase in the ablative, grammatically separate from the rest of the sentence, describing circumstances (*with X being the case*), often translated by a clause beginning *after, when, while or because*, e.g. *urbe capta* (after the city had been captured).

More irregular verbs:
Irregular verbs *volo* (I want), *nolo* (I do not want), *malo* (I prefer); also *fero* (I carry) and its compounds.

Irregular imperatives:
Singular imperatives *dic* (say!), *duc* (lead!), *fer* (carry!) and *fac* (do!) drop the usual *-e*.

Negative commands:
Use of *noli* (pl *nolite*) with the infinitive, e.g. *noli festinare*, literally *be unwilling to hurry!* but translated *do not hurry!*

More question words:
Question words asking for specific information: *quantus* (how big?), *quot* (how many?), *qualis* (what sort of?) and *quomodo* (how?)

CHAPTER EIGHT VOCABULARY

alii . . . alii	some . . . others
altus -a -um	high; deep
ars artis *f*	art, skill
aufero auferre abstuli ablatus	I take away, I carry off, I steal
ceteri -ae -a	the rest, the others
coepi (*perfect tense*)	I began, I have begun
cogo -ere coegi coactus	I force, I compel
conficio -ere confeci confectus	I finish; I wear out
doceo -ere -ui doctus	I teach
fero ferre tuli latus	I bring, I carry, I bear
frustra	in vain
homo -inis *m*	man, human being
idem eadem idem	the same
imperium -i *n*	empire, power, command
inimicus -i *m*	(personal) enemy
ipse ipsa ipsum	-self (*any person*), himself, herself, itself
labor -oris *m*	work, toil
malo malle malui	I prefer
nam	for
nec/neque	and not, nor, neither
nec/neque . . . nec/neque	neither . . . nor
nisi	if not, unless, except
noli *pl* nolite	don't . . .! (*negative command, + inf*)
nolo nolle nolui	I do not want, I refuse
nullus -a -um	no, not any
offero offerre obtuli oblatus	I offer
ostendo -ere -i ostentus	I show
postea	afterwards
praemium -i *n*	prize, reward, profit
proelium -i *n*	battle
promitto -ere promisi promissus	I promise
qualis -e?	what sort of?
quantus -a -um?	how big? how much?
quomodo?	how? in what way?
quoque	also
quot?	how many?
rapio -ere -ui raptus	I seize, I grab
refero referre rettuli relatus	I bring back, I carry back; I report, I tell
sacer -cra -crum	sacred
scelestus -a -um	wicked
scelus -eris *n*	crime
si	if
sub	under, beneath (+ *acc* [*motion*] or *abl* [*position*])
summus -a -um	highest, greatest; top (of)

surgo -ere surrexi	I get up, I stand up, I rise
tollo -ere sustuli sublatus	I raise, I lift up, I hold up
totus -a -um	whole
videor -eri visus sum	I seem, I appear
volo velle volui	I want, I wish, I am willing
vox vocis *f*	voice, shout

50 words

Chapter Nine

PASSIVE INFINITIVE

As we saw in Chapter Two, the forms of the present *active* infinitive for the four conjugations (and mixed 3rd/4th, met in Chapter Six) are:

1st	*2nd*	*3rd*	*4th*	*mixed 3rd/4th*
to carry	to warn	to drag	to hear	to take
port-are	mon-ere	trah-ere	aud-ire	cap-ere

These are made *passive* by changing the final -*e* to -*i*, except that in the third conjugation (and mixed 3rd/4th) the short -*er*- drops out, so that the passive infinitive ending is just -*i*:

to be carried	to be warned	to be dragged	to be heard	to be taken
port-ari	mon-eri	trah-i	aud-iri	cap-i

- Note carefully the unusual formation for the third (and mixed) conjugation, since with some verbs it may look like the first person singular of the perfect tense (e.g. *legi* = to be read *or* I have read), or like the dative singular of a related third declension noun: e.g. *rego* (I rule) has passive infinitive *regi* (to be ruled), which looks like the dative of *rex* (king).

Exercise 9.1

Translate into English:

1. aedificari
2. mitti
3. deleri
4. faci
5. custodiri

Exercise 9.2

Translate into Latin:

1. to be saved
2. to be punished
3. to be received
4. to be ordered
5. to be placed

Exercise 9.3

Translate into English:

1. haec aqua bibi potest.
2. omnes laudari volumus.
3. dominus omnes servos suos liberari iussit.
4. hic puer puniri debet.
5. deae ab hominibus spectari nolunt.

Exercise 9.4

S&C

Translate into Latin:

1. Surely this food can be eaten?
2. All the horses ought to be sold.
3. Those words could not be heard.
4. The senator wanted to be seen in the forum.
5. I shall order the captives to be guarded.

DEPONENT VERBS

Deponent verbs are *passive* in form but *active* in meaning: they look as if they are passive, but are actually active (the term *deponent* literally means *laying aside*, i.e. *not taking up*, a passive sense). They are formed like the passive equivalent of each tense, according to their conjugation. Their principal parts look like this:

conor, conari, conatus sum   I try

There are only three (present, infinitive, perfect) because the fourth principal part of a normal verb is passive, and a deponent verb has no passive. The perfect participle (itself active in meaning) is incorporated in the perfect tense (formed like the perfect passive of an ordinary verb), so it does not need to be given again separately.

The perfect participle, e.g. *conatus -a -um* (having tried), can also be used independently.

A deponent verb behaves in a sentence just like an ordinary active one. But it cannot be *made* passive: it has only a passive *form*, but only an active *meaning*.

- The verb *videor* (I seem), met in Chapter Eight, is exceptional because it is in origin the passive of *video* (I see), but in practice it can be regarded as a separate deponent verb.

conjugation	*1st*	*2nd*	*3rd*	*mixed 3rd/4th*
	I try	I seem	I speak	I advance
present	conor	videor	loquor	progredior
imperfect	conabar	videbar	loquebar	progrediebar
future	conabor	videbor	loquar	progrediar
perfect	conatus sum	visus sum	locutus sum	progressus sum
pluperfect	conatus eram	visus eram	locutus eram	progressus eram
infinitive	conari	videri	loqui	progredi

(There are also 4th conjugation deponent verbs, but none are needed for GCSE.)

- All these are formed like the equivalent passive tenses of an ordinary verb. Deponent verbs have present active and future active participles like other verbs, e.g. *conans -antis* (trying) and *conaturus -a -um* (about to try).

Other deponent verbs:

hortor, hortari, hortatus sum	I encourage, I urge
in/e/re-gredior, -gredi, -gressus sum	I go in/out/back
miror, mirari, miratus sum	I wonder at, I admire
morior, mori, mortuus sum	I die
patior, pati, passus sum	I suffer, I endure
proficiscor, proficisci, profectus sum	I set out
sequor, sequi, secutus sum	I follow

- Note the several compounds of *-gredior* (go), which is not used on its own but only with a prefix.

Exercise 9.5

Translate into English:

1. sequitur
2. patiebamur
3. locuti sunt
4. proficiscar
5. regrediebamini

Exercise 9.6

S&C

Translate into Latin:

1. We encourage.
2. You (*pl*) were admiring.
3. He died.
4. You (*f sg*) set out.
5. They will go out.

Exercise 9.7

Translate into English:

1. viam invenire diu conabamur.
2. senex tandem e templo egressus est.
3. imperator milites pugnaturos diu hortabatur.
4. mons altus esse videbatur.
5. per terram hostium progrediebamur.
6. omnes novam villam senatoris mirati estis?
7. amici multas horas in taberna loquebantur.
8. ille nauta, qui <u>vulnera</u> gravissima passus erat, mox mortuus est.
9. pueri turbam puellarum sequebantur.
10. heri profecti sumus; hodie iter <u>lentum</u> facimus; cras regrediemur.

vulnus -eris *n*	wound
lentus -a -um	slow

Exercise 9.8

S&C

Translate into Latin (using deponent verbs):

1. The senator was speaking for a long time.
2. I shall try to advise these boys.
3. The slaves did not want to follow their master.
4. The general was encouraging the messengers.
5. All the citizens went out of the forum.

PERFECT ACTIVE PARTICIPLE

The perfect active participle that deponent verbs have (instead of the usual passive one, though like it in form) is an important and useful feature, which ordinary Latin verbs do not have.

present tense	*perfect active participle*	*meaning*
conor	conatus -a -um*	having tried
hortor	hortatus	having encouraged
in/e/re-gredior	in/e/re-gressus	having gone in/out/back
progredior	progressus	having advanced
loquor	locutus	having spoken
miror	miratus	having admired
morior	mortuus	having died
patior	passus	having suffered
proficiscor	profectus	having set out
sequor	secutus	having followed

* all are regular 2-1-2 in declension

- Note that English derivatives (e.g. *progress, passive, consecutive, elocution*) often come from the perfect active participle.

As with other participles, the literal translation (here *having done* X) often sounds artificial, and a translation such as *after doing* X or *when/because they had done* X is more appropriate. A perfect participle always describes an action preceding that of the main verb. If that verb is in a past tense (as it usually is in a passage), any perfect participle when translated as a clause (*after/because* . . .) comes out like a pluperfect tense:

> milites, ducem multas horas secuti, dormire volebant.
lit   The soldiers, having followed their leader for many hours, wanted to sleep.
i.e. Because the soldiers had followed their leader for many hours, they wanted to sleep.

A perfect active participle agreeing with the subject can sometimes be used instead of an ablative absolute using a perfect passive participle:

> haec verba locutus, nuntius discessit. *or* his verbis dictis, nuntius discessit.
> *lit* Having spoken these words, . . . With these words having been spoken, . . .
> *i.e.* After the messenger had spoken these words, he departed.

Exercise 9.9

Translate into English:

1. puella saepe conata optimam epistulam scripsit.
2. amici nostri heri profecti mox advenient.
3. viri in taberna clamantes feminam ingressam non viderunt.
4. Romam regressi de morte senatoris audivimus.
5. imperator milites hortatus statim pugnare constituit.
6. senex e taberna egressus viam invenire frustra conatus est.
7. nuntius in terram hostium duo horas progressus redire constituit.
8. milites malum imperatorem secuti magnum in periculum ducebantur.
9. servum multa vulnera passum in via inveni.
10. cives novas portas mirati abierunt.

Exercise 9.10

Translate into Latin (using perfect active participles; no separate words needed for 'after' or 'because'):

1. Having spoken for a long time, the senator was now silent.
2. After admiring the temple, we walked into the forum.
3. Because the master had encouraged the slaves, he was expecting better work.
4. The soldiers, having advanced slowly, caught sight of the enemy.
5. After going back to Rome, I tried to find my brother.

Background: Carthage and Hannibal

In the third century BC Rome began to expand overseas as well as in Italy. Her main rival was Carthage, the North African city founded according to tradition by Dido (and visited by Aeneas) about 900 years earlier. Rome and Carthage fought the First Punic War (264–241 BC), clashing initially in Sicily; both powers coveted the rich agricultural land there, and Rome saw a potential threat to southern Italy. The Romans quickly built a fleet, defeated the established naval power of Carthage, and made Sicily the first province of the Roman Empire. Carthage then tried to recoup its losses by expanding into Spain, a land rich in minerals. Both in Sicily and in Spain the Carthaginians were led by Hamilcar. Further war was inevitable, and tradition recorded that his nine-year-old son Hannibal was made to swear an oath of undying hostility to Rome. Hannibal succeeded his father in Spain and captured the city of Saguntum, which was allied to Rome. This sparked off the Second Punic War (218–201 BC). Hannibal decided to attack Rome, but could not do so directly because the Roman fleet controlled the sea. So, with the daring imagination that made him one of the greatest generals of all time, he decided to march through Spain and Provence, then cross the Alps and come down like an unexpected thunderbolt into northern Italy. He set off with about 50,000 men and thirty-seven fighting elephants. Various delays meant he had to cross the Alps in winter: hostile tribes and difficult conditions caused heavy losses. It is uncertain what route he took, but he made it to Italy.

Exercise 9.11

Hannibal's oath

Echoing the dying wish of Dido long ago, the boy Hannibal vows undying hostility to Rome.

urbs <u>antiqua</u> fuit, quam <u>Dido</u> regina olim aedificaverat, <u>Carthago</u>. postea <u>Poeni</u>
magnum imperium habebant: et mare et terras regere volebant. <u>Hannibal</u>, puer
novem annos <u>natus</u> qui in hac urbe habitabat, cum patre ad templum ivit.
<u>Hamilcar</u> enim, qui imperator Poenorum erat, in <u>Hispaniam</u> proficisci parabat,
5   cum <u>sociis</u> Romanorum ibi pugnaturus. auxilium igitur deorum petere volebat.
filius quoque, et templum et virtutem patris miratus, iter facere volebat. pater
eum rogavit: 'visne mecum ad castra proficisci? te mecum ducam si <u>iurabis</u>.'
deinde puerum ad <u>aram</u> duxit eamque tenentem <u>iurare</u> iussit: 'Romanos semper
<u>detestabor</u>.' Hannibal haec verba locutus per totam <u>vitam</u> in animo servabat.

	antiquus -a -um	ancient
	Dido -onis *f*	Dido
	Carthago -inis *f*	Carthage (*city in north Africa*)
	Poeni -orum *m pl*	Carthaginians
2	Hannibal -alis *m*	Hannibal
	natus -a -um*	old, aged
	Hamilcar -aris *m*	Hamilcar (*father of Hannibal*)
	Hispania -ae *f*	Spain
	socius -i *m*	ally

7	iuro -are	I swear an oath
	ara -ae *f*	altar
	detestor -ari	I hate intensely
	vita -ae *f*	life

*The adjective *natus* (literally *born*, translated *old* or *aged*) is used with an accusative expression of *time how long* to give someone's age.

- The proper names *Hannibal* and *Poeni* will not be glossed again in this chapter. The Carthaginians were called *Poeni* because their ancestors were settlers from Phoenicia (modern Lebanon).

Exercise 9.12

War with Rome

Hannibal succeeds his father and captures the Spanish town of Saguntum, allied to Rome (219 BC). Diplomacy fails and the Romans declare war.

Hamilcar bellum in Hispania multos annos gessit multasque gentes superavit. tandem pugnans mortuus est. Hannibal post mortem patris in castra venit. milites mirati sunt. 'Hamilcar' inquiunt 'nobis redditus est iuvenis.' Hannibal enim eandem formam, eandem virtutem habebat. mox imperator factus est, et

5 ipse in Hispania bellum gessit. ubi urbem Saguntum obsidere coepit, cives auxilium Romanorum petiverunt, quorum socii erant. Romani legatos misit; Hannibal tamen eos accipere noluit. legati igitur Carthaginem missi sunt. unus eorum, sicut dona sub toga ferens, 'et pacem et bellum' inquit 'vobis tulimus. utrum legitis?' Poeni 'date utrum vultis!' audacter responderunt. Romanus

10 'bellum' inquit 'igitur damus.' et Poeni iterum responderunt: 'donum vestrum libenter accipimus.'

	Hamilcar -aris *m*	Hamilcar (*father of Hannibal*)
	Hispania -ae *f*	Spain
	gens gentis *f*	tribe, people
	reddo -ere reddidi redditus	I give back, I restore
4	forma -ae *f*	appearance
	Saguntum -i *n*	Saguntum (*a city in Spain*)
	obsideo -ere	I besiege
	socius -i *m*	ally
	legatus -i *m*	envoy, ambassador
8	sicut	as if
	toga -ae *f*	toga
	uter -tra -trum	which of the two
	iterum	again
	libenter	willingly, gladly

SEMI-DEPONENT VERBS

Semi-deponent verbs are active in form in the present, imperfect and future tenses, but become deponent (i.e. use the passive forms but still have an active meaning) in the perfect and pluperfect. There are only a few of them. All three needed for GCSE are second conjugation. Their principal parts look like this:

	gaudeo, gaudere, gavisus sum	I rejoice, I am pleased

	2nd conjugation
	I rejoice
present	gaudeo
imperfect	gaudebam
future	gaudebo
perfect	gavisus sum
pluperfect	gavisus eram

Similarly:

audeo, audere, ausus sum	I dare
soleo, solere, solitus sum	I am accustomed

Semi-deponent verbs, like deponent ones, have the useful perfect active participle:

gavisus -a -um	having rejoiced
ausus	having dared
solitus	having become accustomed

- Semi-deponent verbs, like deponent ones, have present active and future active participles formed in the usual way, e.g. *gaudens -entis* (rejoicing) and *gavisurus -a -um* (about to rejoice).

- It is important not to confuse *audeo* with *audio* (I hear): see the list of words easily confused (Appendix 5, p. 269).

- The literal translation of *soleo* (I am accustomed) often sounds clumsy. *I am in the habit of* is an improvement, but a translation such as *usually* is often preferable, with the following infinitive made into an ordinary verb in English:

	aquam bibere soleo.
lit	I am accustomed to drink water
i.e.	I am in the habit of drinking water.
or	I usually drink water.

Exercise 9.13

Translate into English:

1. senex lente ambulare solebat.
2. labore confecto, omnes gavisi sumus.
3. quis in castra hostium ingredi audebit?
4. quando iterum gaudere poterimus?
5. puer, qui tacere solitus erat, consilium offerre ausus est.

Exercise 9.14

S&C

Translate into Latin:

1. I am in the habit of reading many books.
2. This soldier dared to attack the gate.
3. You will soon rejoice, friends!
4. The children had never dared to speak.
5. The citizens rejoiced because the enemy had fled.

REVISION CHECKPOINT

Make sure you know:

- how the passive infinitive is formed
- deponent verbs (passive in form but active in meaning), e.g. *conor* (I try)
- perfect active participle (a unique and useful feature of deponent verbs), e.g. *conatus* (having tried)
- semi-deponent verbs (active form and meaning in the present, future and imperfect tenses; passive form but active meaning in the perfect and pluperfect), e.g. *gaudeo*, *gaudere*, *gavisus sum* (I rejoice)

Exercise 9.15

Hannibal's dream

Hannibal has a dream while planning his invasion of Italy.

Hannibal igitur, postquam <u>Saguntum</u> cepit, <u>copias</u> in <u>Italiam</u> ducere et bellum
cum Romanis gerere constituit. 'Romanos' inquit 'timere non soleo. malo enim
perire quam patriam ab eis victam videre.' illa nocte Hannibal in <u>somnio</u>
videbatur in <u>concilium</u> deorum vocari. ubi de itinere rogavit, <u>Iuppiter</u> '<u>ducem</u>'
5 inquit 'dabo qui te in Italiam ducet.' statim aderat iuvenis, qui Hannibali 'me'
inquit 'sequi debes. noli in itinere <u>respicere</u>.' et in <u>somnio</u> profecti sunt. Hannibal
tamen, non longe progressus, quod milites suos spectare volebat, subito <u>respicere</u>
ausus est. tum post se vidit <u>monstrum</u> ingens, quod agros et silvas et villas
delebat. Hannibal miratus ducem de <u>monstro</u> rogavit; iuvenis ei respondit:
10 '<u>vastitas</u> Italiae est.' deinde Hannibal progredi iussus est, nec plura quaerere.

	Saguntum -i *n*	Saguntum (*a city in Spain*)
	copiae -arum *f pl*	forces, troops
	Italia -ae *f*	Italy
	somnium -i *n*	dream
4	concilium -i *n*	council, meeting
	Iuppiter Iovis *m*	Jupiter (*king of the gods*)
	dux ducis *m*	(*here*) guide
	respicio -ere	look back
	monstrum -i *n*	monster
10	vastitas -atis *f*	devastation, destruction

* The proper name *Italia* will not be glossed again in this chapter.

Exercise 9.16

Crossing the Rhone

*Hannibal plans to cross the Alps and invade Italy from the north. With his troops and
elephants he travels through Spain and crosses the Rhone despite local opposition.*

Hannibal, ubi omnia parata sunt, mox profectus est. trans mare non navigavit,
quod naves Romanorum <u>litora</u> Italiae custodiebant. in animo habebat <u>Alpes</u>
transire et in Italiam descendere, ubi Romani hostes <u>invadentes</u> non exspectabant.
maximas igitur copias in <u>Hispaniam</u> duxit, inter quas multi <u>elephanti</u> erant: his
5 enim, non <u>antea</u> in media Italia visis, hostes terrere volebat. deinde in terram
<u>Volcarum</u> venit, ubi <u>Rhodanum</u> transire debebat. illi tamen, qui <u>socii</u>
Romanorum erant, <u>ripam</u> <u>ulteriorem</u> contra Poenos nunc tenebant.

Hannibal igitur <u>Hannonem</u> cum parte copiarum per <u>ripam</u> <u>adverso flumine</u> iter
facere iussit, deinde flumen transgressum <u>signum</u> <u>fumo</u> sibi mittere. Hannibal
10 hoc <u>signo</u> mox accepto gavisus est; deinde ceteros milites flumen transire iussit.
<u>elephanti</u> in magnis <u>ratibus</u> portati sunt: quamquam <u>nonnulli</u> perterriti in aquam

ceciderunt, omnes ad <u>ripam</u> advenerunt. ibi Volcae Poenos clamoribus exspectantes stabant. tum tamen maior clamor erat: Hanno <u>interea</u> hostes a <u>tergo</u> oppugnaverat. Volcae, <u>utrimque</u> <u>oppressi</u>, fugerunt.

	litus -oris *n*	shore, coast
	Alpes -ium *f pl*	the Alps
	invado -ere	I invade
	Hispania -ae *f*	Spain
4	elephantus -i *m*	elephant
	antea	previously, before
	Volcae -arum *m*	the Volcae (*a Gallic tribe allied to Rome*)
	Rhodanus -i *m*	the Rhone (*a major river in modern France*)
	socius -i *m*	ally
7	ripa -ae *f*	bank, riverbank
	ulterior -us	further, far
	Hanno -onis *m*	Hanno (*an officer in Hannibal's army*)
	adverso flumine	upstream
	signum -i *n*	signal
9	fumus -i *m*	smoke
	ratis -is *f*	raft
	nonnulli -ae -a	some, several, a few
	interea	meanwhile
	tergum -i *n*	back
14	utrimque	from both sides
	opprimo -ere oppressi	
	oppressus	I crush, I overwhelm

- Note that the plural adjective *nonnulli* is literally a double negative: *not no . . .* (plural of *nullus*).

Figure 9.1 *Hannibal crosses the Rhone with elephants.* (Photo by Stock Montage/Getty Images)

INDIRECT STATEMENT (1)

A statement is any ordinary sentence which is not a question or command. A *direct* statement may be the actual quoted words of a speaker:

The messenger said 'The Romans are winning the war'.

Or it may be simply something the narrator tells us:

In the next year, the Romans began winning the war.

An *indirect* statement *reports* someone's words or thoughts (hence it is also called a *reported* statement):

The messenger said that the Romans were winning the war.

This historian claims that in the next year the Romans began winning the war.

English inserts the word *that* (though it can be omitted), then in effect starts a new sentence with its own subject and verb. Latin does it in a different way: the subject of the indirect statement becomes *accusative*, and the verb becomes *infinitive*. Hence this construction is commonly referred to as *accusative and infinitive*.
    An accusative and infinitive is possible in English with some verbs:

I consider the story to be true.

This sentence reports my original thought *The story is true*. It may seem strange that a subject should be accusative, but imagine this sentence cut short: in *I consider the story* it should be obvious that *story* cannot be nominative.

- In this example *I* is nominative: a sentence can only introduce a *second* nominative (after the main subject) if it has a second *finite* verb, with a person ending: the *infinitive* as its name implies is not finite.

In English the accusative and infinitive is not found very often, but in Latin it is used for *all* indirect statements. It is one of the most common of all constructions, and failure to recognise it is one of the main sources of confusion and error in GCSE. Both active and passive infinitives can be used. You need to think about the literal meaning, then put it into natural English using *that*:

	nuntius dicit navem appropinquare.
lit	The messenger says the ship <u>to be</u> approaching.
i.e.	The messenger says <u>that</u> the ship <u>is</u> approaching.

	ancilla laborem suum a domino laudari dicit.
lit	The slave-girl says her work <u>to be</u> praised by the master.
i.e.	The slave-girl says <u>that</u> her work <u>is</u> praised by the master

- In Latin there is no separate word for *that* to introduce an indirect statement: this meaning is given by the infinitive.

- The use of *that* to introduce an indirect statement in English must not be confused with *ille* (that one there), though *ille* might happen to occur *within* an indirect statement in Latin.

Exercise 9.17

Translate into English:

1. senex dicit liberos timere.
2. cur hunc servum stultum esse dicis?
3. nuntius dicit milites nostros nunc bene pugnare.
4. pueri dicunt illum cibum optimum esse.
5. femina dicit cenam a servis nunc parari.

In the accusative and infinitive construction, <u>the tense of the infinitive is always that of the original direct statement</u>. If the introductory verb (usually a verb of *saying*) is present tense, this is straightforward. If the introductory verb is past tense (as in practice it usually is), the infinitive still has the tense of what was originally said or thought, but the English translation <u>moves back a tense</u>, so an ordinary (present) infinitive is translated as an imperfect tense:

nuntius dixit navem appropinquare.

lit   The messenger <u>said</u> the ship <u>to be</u> approaching.
i.e. The messenger <u>said that</u> the ship <u>was</u> approaching.

- This rule is of crucial importance: getting the tense wrong when translating an indirect statement is one of the most common of all mistakes at GCSE.

Exercise 9.18

Translate into English:

1. nuntius dicit turbam in foro adesse.
2. nuntius dixit turbam in foro adesse.
3. senatores dixerunt Romam in periculo esse.
4. cur dicis hunc puerum stultum esse?
5. femina dixit cenam a servis parari.

Exercise 9.19

Translate into Latin (using accusative and infinitive; no separate word for 'that' is needed)

1. The woman says that the slaves are sleeping.
2. The general said that the enemy were approaching.
3. The soldiers said that their leader was very brave.
4. Who says that this temple is beautiful?
5. The messenger said that the city was being attacked.

INDIRECT STATEMENT (2)

Because this construction is used to report original direct statements, which might have verbs in any tense (active or passive), Latin needs to use a range of infinitives. From Chapter Two onwards we have frequently met the present active infinitive:

1st	portare	to carry
2nd	monere	to warn
3rd	trahere	to drag
4th	audire	to hear
mixed 3rd/4th	capere	to take

And earlier in this chapter we met the present passive infinitive:

1st	portari	to be carried
2nd	moneri	to be warned
3rd	trahi	to be dragged
4th	audiri	to be heard
mixed 3rd/4th	capi	to be taken

As we have seen, these present infinitives are common in various contexts. Other infinitives are found mainly in indirect statements.

Perfect active infinitive

The *perfect active infinitive* (literally *to have X-ed*) is formed from the *perfect stem* (third principal part less -*i*) plus -*isse*:

1st	portavisse	to have carried
2nd	monuisse	to have warned
3rd	traxisse	to have dragged
4th	audivisse	to have heard
mixed 3rd/4th	cepisse	to have taken

- This formula also works for irregular and defective verbs:

fuisse   to have been
potuisse   to have been able
ivisse   to have gone (*in compounds* -iisse, *e.g.* abiise [to have gone away])
coepisse   to have begun

If the introductory verb is present tense, the perfect infinitive is translated as a perfect tense:

nuntius dicit hostes fugisse.
lit   The messenger says the enemy <u>to have fled</u>.
i.e. The messenger says <u>that</u> the enemy <u>have fled</u>.

If the introductory verb is past tense (as it usually is), English again moves back a tense, so the perfect infinitive is translated as a pluperfect tense:

nuntius dixit hostes fugisse.
lit   The messenger said the enemy <u>to have fled</u>.
i.e. The messenger said <u>that</u> the enemy <u>had</u> fled.

Exercise 9.20

Translate into Latin:

1. to have guarded
2. to have seen
3. to have promised
4. to have received
5. to have walked

Exercise 9.21

Translate into English:

1. dominus dicit servos bene laboravisse.
2. dominus dixit servos bene laboravisse.
3. pueri dixerunt puellas risisse.
4. cives dicunt senatorem e foro exiisse.
5. senator dixit milites fortiter pugnavisse.

Verbs introducing indirect statements

An indirect statement is commonly introduced by a verb of *saying*. But this construction is used with verbs describing any 'above the neck' process: the use of words, the mind, or the feelings (the 'statement' reported need not have been spoken aloud). Look out for the accusative and infinitive after the following:

dico	I say
narro	I tell
nuntio	I announce
refero	I report
respondeo	I reply
promitto	I promise
audio	I hear
video	I see
invenio	I find
cognosco	I get to know, I find out
intellego	I understand, I realise
puto	I think
scio	I know
credo*	I believe
sentio	I feel

* In this construction, *credo* like other verbs is followed by the accusative and infinitive (overriding the usual rule that it takes a dative). So *credo ei* (I believe him) but *credo eum stultum esse* (I believe that he is stupid).

Exercise 9.22

Translate into English:

1. imperator nuntiavit copias hostium appropinquare.
2. scio milites Romanos fortes esse.
3. puellae laborem suum facilem esse putabant.
4. cives nuntium discessisse audiverunt.
5. domina dixit ancillas multas horas laboravisse.
6. omnes urbem in periculo esse sentiebant.
7. amicos nostros advenisse invenimus.
8. pueri flumen altum esse credebant.
9. senator captivos a militibus custodiri cognovit.
10. audivimus bellum ferocissimum ibi geri.

Exercise 9.23

Translate into Latin (first working out which tense of the infinitive to use):

1. This girl says that the horse is afraid.
2. I saw that three ships were approaching.
3. The citizens believed that the king had fled.
4. I think that the book is being written.
5. The master replied that the slaves had always worked carefully.

Exercise 9.24

A short pep talk

Hannibal encourages his troops as they prepare to cross the Alps.

Hannibal nunc <u>Alpes</u> transire parabat. Poeni tamen et hostes et iter timebant. Hannibal igitur eos sic hortatus est: 'milites, scio vos multos per annos hostes semper vicisse, montes et pericula saepe superavisse. video vos arma, cibum, <u>saga</u> habere. puto nullum montem caelum <u>tangere</u>. audio multos viros antea cum
5 <u>liberis</u> uxoribusque Alpes ascendisse. nonne milites arma ferentes idem facere possunt? nisi nomen Poenorum deleri vultis, credite vos omnia ferre, omnia facere posse!'

Alpes -ium *f pl*	the Alps
sagum -i *n*	thick military cloak
tango -ere	I touch
liberi -orum *m pl*	children

- Note that *liberi* (children) should not be confused with *liber* (book), plural *libri*, or with *libertus* (freedman, ex-slave), plural *liberti*: see the list of words easily confused (Appendix 5, p. 269). It originally meant *freeborn ones*, as distinct from slave children.

INDIRECT STATEMENT (3)

Accusative subjects and objects

The accusative subject of the infinitive cannot be missed out, and indeed is one way of recognising an indirect statement. If the subject of the infinitive is the same as that of the introductory verb, a *reflexive* pronoun is used:

nuntius dixit <u>se</u> quam celerrime cucurrisse.
lit   The messenger said <u>himself</u> to have run as quickly as possible.
i.e.   The messenger said that <u>he</u> had run as quickly as possible.

- When translating a reflexive pronoun in indirect statement, there is no need to say e.g. *he himself.*
- Remember that a reflexive pronoun refers back to the subject of the verb, so *se* in an indirect statement might need to be translated *she* or *they.*
- The third person *se* is most commonly found, but first and second person pronouns (*me, nos, te, vos*) can also be used reflexively as the subject of an infinitive.

If *he* had referred to someone else, i.e. had not been reflexive, *eum* would have been used instead:

femina, quae servum amabat, dixit <u>eum</u> bene laboravisse.
The woman, who liked the slave, said that <u>he</u> had worked well.

Because the infinitive has an accusative subject and may also have a direct object, two different accusatives may come one after the other. In such a sentence the first accusative will be the subject, the second one the object:

credo senem pueros laudavisse.
I believe that the old man praised the boys.

Exercise 9.25

Translate into English:

1.   puella dixit se pecuniam in via invenisse.
2.   milites portam fortiter custodire credimus.
3.   servus respondit se <u>nihil</u> de hoc scelere scire.
4.   magnam turbam in foro adesse vidi.
5.   puto me nullos inimicos habere.
6.   nuntius dixit gentem ferocem in insula habitare.
7.   dominus intellexit servos <u>fideles</u> fuisse.
8.   imperator, qui militem bene cognoverat, dixit eum fortem esse.
9.   novam villam prope mare aedificari vidi.
10. miles nuntiavit hostes iter per montes fecisse.

nihil *n*   nothing
fidelis -e   faithful, loyal

Exercise 9.26

S&C

Translate into Latin:

1. The general announced that the enemy had finally fled.
2. The woman replied that she was waiting for her husband.
3. I believe that the senator praised the girls.
4. We heard that the captives were being guarded in the camp.
5. The boys realised that the work was very easy.

The remaining two infinitives should be studied together, and similarities noted.

Perfect passive infinitive

The *perfect passive infinitive* (literally *to have been X-ed*) is formed from the *perfect passive participle* with the infinitive of the verb *to be*:

1st	portatus* esse	to have been carried
2nd	monitus* esse	to have been warned
3rd	tractus* esse	to have been dragged
4th	auditus* esse	to have been heard
mixed 3rd/4th	captus* esse	to have been taken

Future active infinitive

The future active infinitive (literally *to be about to X*) is formed from the future active participle, again with the infinitive of the verb *to be*:

1st	portaturus* esse	to be about to carry
2nd	moniturus* esse	to be about to warn
3rd	tracturus* esse	to be about to drag
4th	auditurus* esse	to be about to hear
mixed 3rd/4th	capturus* esse	to be about to take

* The participle (with normal 2-1-2 endings) is normally accusative in indirect statement, but can be any gender, singular or plural, agreeing with the subject of the infinitive. In the accusative and infinitive construction, the possibilities are as follows (using the perfect passive infinitive of *porto* as an example, but the pattern of endings applies to all perfect passive and future active infinitives):

	m	*f*	*n*
sg	portatum esse	portatam esse	portatum esse
pl	portatos esse	portatas esse	portata esse

- Remember that the participles from which these infinitives are made are *perfect passive* (e.g. *portatus*) and *future active* (e.g. *portaturus*). Latin does have a future passive infinitive, but it is rare, formed in a different way, and not needed for GCSE.

Exercise 9.27

Translate into English:

1. laudatus esse
2. discessurus esse
3. missus esse
4. iacturus esse
5. factus esse

In an indirect statement where the introductory verb is past tense, the rule about moving back a tense in translation applies as usual. The perfect passive infinitive comes out in English as a pluperfect passive:

> audivi urbem captam esse.

lit I heard the city <u>to have been</u> captured.

i.e. I heard <u>that</u> the city <u>had been</u> captured

The future active infinitive in this situation is translated as a 'future in the past' (*was/ were going to* or *would*):

> sciebam has ancillas bene laboraturas esse.

lit I knew these slave-girls <u>to be going to</u> work well.

i.e. I knew <u>that</u> these slave-girls <u>were going to</u> (*or* <u>would</u>) work well.

As usual the secret is first to think what the Latin says literally, then to recast this as natural English.

- Note two verbs that, to reinforce their meaning, are followed by a *future* infinitive in indirect statement:

  promitto   I promise
  spero -are -avi -atus   I hope

  promitto me epistulam scripturum esse.
  I promise that I shall write the letter.

This can be translated simply *I promise to write the letter*, but Latin has to use the accusative and infinitive. The same applies to the following example (where the literal *I hope that I shall . . .* sounds awkward):

spero me cras venturum esse.
I hope to come tomorrow.

- Note that deponent verbs have a perfect infinitive (active in meaning) formed like a perfect passive one, and a future active infinitive formed in the usual way:

conatus esse   to have tried
conaturus esse   to be going to try

- The indirect statement can continue with another infinitive after a semi-colon (representing an original direct statement consisting of more than a single sentence):

nuntius dixit bellum confectum esse; hostes fugisse; se haec a rege ipso audivisse.

The messenger said that the war was finished, that the enemy had fled, and that he had heard these things from the king himself.

- A passive version of the indirect statement can be used. In this case the subject (of both the passive introductory verb and the infinitive) is nominative:

servus dicitur stultus esse.
The slave is said to be stupid.

If a perfect passive or future active infinitive is used like this, the participle forming part of it will be nominative:

epistula dicitur missa esse.
The letter is said to have been sent.

Exercise 9.28

Translate into English:

1. senator scelus ibi factum esse cognovit.
2. vidistine muros iam deletos esse?
3. cives ex agris fugere coactos esse audio.
4. puer promisit se pecuniam mox traditurum esse.
5. cives milites de <u>victoria</u> maxime gavisos esse audiverunt.
6. credimus amicos auxilium mox missuros esse.
7. miles narravit hostes tandem superatos esse.
8. senex se mox moriturum esse sensit.
9. liber puellae ablatus esse dicitur.
10. speramus nos Romam mox adventuros esse.

victoria -ae *f*   victory

Exercise 9.29

S&C

Translate into Latin:

1. The girl found out that the money had been hidden.
2. We were hoping that the Romans would save us.
3. The general announced that the city had been captured.
4. The slave promised that he would finish the work.
5. I saw that the soldier had suffered many wounds.

Exercise 9.30

Crossing the Alps

Treacherous local guides and hostile inhabitants make the ascent of the Alps difficult, but the elephants prove useful and the Carthaginians are finally rewarded with a prospect of Italy.

ubi Hannibal <u>Alpibus</u> <u>nivosis</u> appropinquabat, dux gentis <u>Gallicae</u> ad eum venit. 'homines' inquit 'tibi offero qui copias tuas per montes ducent.' Hannibal, quamquam verbis ducis non <u>omnino</u> credebat, homines accepit. mox tamen cognovit eos <u>falsos</u> esse. nam Poeni in <u>angustias</u> ducti sunt; subito <u>montani</u>
5   ingentia <u>saxa</u> in eos de loco altiore <u>devolverunt</u>. Poeni maximo in periculo nunc erant: multi necati, multi <u>vulnerati sunt</u>.

Hannibal ipse cum ceteris effugit. <u>elephanti</u> enim, quamquam lente
progrediebantur, <u>montanos</u> terruerunt: sic magnum auxilium Hannibali
dederunt. tandem Poeni ad summum montem advenerunt. Hannibal militibus
10 suis terram Italiae ostendit. Poeni agros, silvas, flumina videre poterant.
Hannibal dixit eos muros Italiae, muros <u>etiam</u> Romae, iam transire; <u>reliquam</u>
partem itineris facilem futuram esse; eos post unum <u>vel</u> duo proelia <u>arcem</u> Italiae
habituros esse.

	Alpes -ium *f pl*	the Alps
	nivosus -a -um	covered in snow
	Gallicus -a -um	Gallic, of the Gauls
	omnino	completely
4	falsus -a -um	false, treacherous
	angustiae -arum *f pl*	narrow pass
	montani -orum *m pl*	mountain-dwellers
	saxum -i *n*	rock
	devolvo -ere -i	I roll (something) down
6	vulnero -are -avi -atus	I wound
	elephantus -i *m*	elephant
	etiam	even
	reliquus -a -um	remaining
	vel	or
12	arx arcis *f*	citadel (*here referring to Rome*)

REVISION CHECKPOINT

Make sure you know:

- how the accusative and infinitive construction works
- the infinitive always keeps the tense of the original direct statement
- if the introductory verb is past tense, the infinitive is translated one tense back in English, so e.g. a present infinitive comes out as an imperfect
- Latin has a range of infinitives
- indirect statement is introduced by verbs describing speech, thoughts or feelings
- if the subject of the infinitive is also the subject of the introductory verb, a reflexive pronoun (e.g. *se*) is used
- if the infinitive has two accusatives (subject and object), the subject comes first

Background: Hannibal in Italy

In Italy Hannibal seemed initially to carry all before him; he won a series of victories, most spectacularly at Lake Trasimene where he trapped the Roman army in a narrow pass in thick mist. The Romans then tried different tactics; under Fabius, they avoided pitched battle but followed Hannibal as he marched southwards. Roman opinion turned against Fabius when Hannibal outwitted him in crossing the Apennines. The consuls decided to fight another pitched battle, but the Romans were again defeated at Cannae: this was the last time they fought Hannibal on Italian soil. Yet despite these victories, Hannibal never broke the power of Rome. Rome's allies did not desert as he had hoped. Hannibal had several opportunities to attack the city directly, but did not do so because he knew its fortifications would make it difficult to capture. Roman naval supremacy prevented him receiving reinforcements direct from Carthage. His brother Hasdrubal crossed the Alps with a relief army, but he was captured and killed by the Romans. Eventually the Romans under Scipio attacked the Carthaginians in Africa and Hannibal was recalled to defend his country. Scipio defeated him at Zama. The Romans respected their determined opponent, and there were later several statues of Hannibal in Rome. In the Third Punic War (149–146 BC) the Romans destroyed Carthage.

Exercise 9.31

Down into Italy

The descent from the Alps proves even more difficult than the ascent. Hannibal suffers heavy losses but wins two battles on Italian soil (218 BC).

Poeni, postquam descendere coeperunt, putabant se pessimum laborem iam confecisse. iter tamen quod de montibus facere debuerunt multo difficilius erat. via enim angusta et lubrica erat. milites igitur iterum atque iterum cadebant. saepe viam per saxa sibi facere coacti sunt. tandem ad campos advenerunt.
5 quamquam Hannibal dimidium copiarum in itinere amiserat, Poeni in Italia nunc aderant.

ibi tamen quiescere non poterant. Hannibal 'milites,' inquit 'si eundem animum habebitis quem semper habuistis, vincetis. hoc anno magna itinera per flumina montesque fecistis. mox labor conficietur. dei praemia vobis dabunt quae nullis
10 hominibus antea dederunt.' Hannibal cum Romanis in hac parte Italiae pugnavit et duobus proeliis vicit. deinde Romam iter facere conatus est. iterum per montes ire debebat. saevae tempestates in itinere fuerunt. equi Hannibalis labore confecti erant et elephanti, qui longum iter fecerant, omnes praeter unum mortui erant. Poeni igitur castra posuerunt et ibi hiemare parabant.

Figure 9.2 *Hannibal looks down into Italy after his journey across the Alps.* (Photo by Archive Photos/Getty Images)

	angustus -a -um	narrow
	lubricus -a -um	slippery
	atque	and
	saxum -i *n*	rock
4	campus -i *m*	plain, flat place
	dimidium -i *n*	half
	amitto -ere amisi	I lose
	quiesco -ere	I rest
	tempestas -atis *f*	storm
13	elephantus -i *m*	elephant
	praeter	except, apart from (+ *acc*)
	hiemo -are	I spend the winter

- Note here *atque* (also spelled *ac*), yet another word for *and*, often used to link two nouns or two similar words.

PREPOSITIONS (3)

From Chapter One onwards we have seen a range of prepositions. They are followed by a noun (or pronoun) in either the accusative or the ablative case, and they often serve to focus a meaning the case has already. Those with the accusative often have the idea of *motion towards* or *through*, and those with the ablative the idea either of *motion away from*, or of *position* (being or staying in a place). Here is a complete list, including two new ones.

(1)   Prepositions with the accusative:

ad	to, towards, at
circum	around
contra	against
in	into, onto
inter	among, between
per	through, along
post	after, behind
prope	near
propter	on account of, because of
sub	(going) under, beneath
trans	across

newer in blue → propter, sub

(2)   Prepositions with the ablative:

a/ab*	from, away from, by
cum	with
de	from, down from, about
e/ex*	from, out of
in	in, on
pro	in front of, for, in return for, *on behalf of*
sine	without
sub	under, beneath

(* the forms *ab* and *ex* are used if the next word begins with a vowel or *h*)

- Note that *in* and *sub* can be used with either accusative or the ablative according to meaning.
- When a preposition has several meanings, you need to judge the most appropriate one from the context in the sentence.
- Note that the adverbs *antea* (before, previously), *postea* (afterwards) and *interea* (meanwhile) are in origin the prepositions *ante* (= before [but not needed for GCSE]), *post* and *inter* with the neuter accusative plural pronoun *ea* (those things).

We saw in Part 1 that *time how long* is expressed by the accusative, and *time when* or *within which* by the ablative, usually without a preposition:

time how long:	decem annos pugnabamus. We were fighting for ten years.
time when:	illo anno urbem cepimus. In that year we captured the city.
time within which:	amici nostri tribus horis advenient. Our friends will arrive within three hours.

Sometimes a preposition is added for emphasis, especially *per* with the accusative:

per decem annos pugnabamus.
We were fighting for ten whole years *or* throughout ten years.

There is a special idiom for expressions such as *after many years*:

multis post annis urbem cepimus.
After many years we captured the city.

Here *post* is not doing its usual job as a preposition with the accusative, but is used as an adverb (like *postea*) with the ablative, literally *afterwards by many years*.

Note the distinction between:

post cenam	after dinner	*preposition* ~acting as adverb.
multis post annis	after many years	*special idiom*
postea	afterwards	*adverb*
postquam	after (X happened), . . .	*conjunction*

- The conjunction *postquam* is literally *after than*, introducing a time clause: at a later time *than* one thing happened, something else happened.

- As we saw in Chapter Six, many prepositions are also used as prefixes to form compounds verbs: *a/ab-, ad-, e/ex-, in-, trans-*. Note, however, that the prefix *re-* (back) is not found as a preposition. In GCSE papers you are expected to be able to work out the meaning of a compound verb from knowledge of the simple verb and its prefix.

Exercise 9.32

Translate into English:

1. hostes trans mare fugere coacti sunt. *perfect passive*
2. scio milites a duce in periculum missos esse.
3. postquam rediimus, senem pro ianua villae sedentem conspeximus.
4. ille scelestus multis post annis contra patriam suam pugnare constituit.
5. dei omnia quae sub caelo accidunt videre possunt.
6. fratrem meum inter captivos postea inventum esse cognovi.
7. propter hoc vulnus puer per totam vitam currere non poterit.
8. nonne haec sine magno labore facere potestis?
9. donum pro auxilio tuo mittam, amice.
10. maritus sub terram iter fecit quod uxorem suam quaerere cupiebat.

accido -ere accidi   I happen

Exercise 9.33

S&C

Translate into Latin:

1. Did you find the book in the street, father?
2. After dinner we wanted to go into the city.
3. All the citizens departed from the forum.
4. I believe the letter was written by a slave.
5. Those tribes came down from the mountains some time ago.

Exercise 9.34

Trasimene

Flaminius is provoked into fighting, despite bad omens. The Romans are led into a trap and suffer a crushing defeat at Lake Trasimene (217 BC).

Romani, quod in duobus proeliis victi erant, cum Poenis pugnare nunc timebant. Hannibal tamen, qui sciebat <u>Flaminium</u>, consulem Romanum, virum audacem et <u>gloriosum</u> esse, eum <u>provocare</u> constituit. <u>fundos</u> igitur incendit, agros delevit. Flaminius, ubi haec vidit, statim pugnare volebat. in equum ascendit; equus cecidit,
5 cecidit Flaminius quoque, <u>super</u> caput equi iactus. <u>signa</u> moveri iussit; <u>signa</u> in terra <u>haeserunt</u>. dei Flaminium de periculo monere videbantur. ceteri duces Romani eum monere conati sunt. Flaminius tamen audire nolebat. tandem cum militibus suis profectus est. Romani Hannibalem ad <u>Trasumenum</u> secuti sunt. ibi via inter montes et aquam erat; Romani in <u>angustias</u> a Poenis ducti sunt, qui <u>equites</u> in montibus
10 celaverant. Hannibal Romanos in <u>nebula</u> subito oppugnavit; plurimi perierunt et consul ipse. multi qui effugerunt postea ab hostibus capti sunt. Romani <u>cladem</u> gravissimam passi erant.

	Flaminius -i *m*	Flaminius
	gloriosus -a -um	boastful
	provoco -are	I provoke
	fundus -i *m*	farm
5	super (+ *acc*)	over
	signa -orum *n pl*	military standards
	haereo -ere haesi	I stick fast
	Trasumenus -i *m*	Lake Trasimene (*in northern Italy*)
	angustiae -arum *f pl*	narrow pass
9	equites -um *m pl*	cavalry, mounted troops
	nebula -ae *f*	mist
	clades -is *f*	disaster

Figure 9.3 *The Battle of Lake Trasimene during the Second Punic War.* (Photo by Time Life Pictures/Mansell/The LIFE Picture Collection/Getty Images)

LESS COMMON PRONOUNS (1)

a certain, a, one *pl* some

		m	*f*	
sg	*nom*	quidam	quaedam	quoddam
	acc	quendam	quandam	quoddam
	gen	cuiusdam	cuiusdam	cuiusdam
	dat	cuidam	cuidam	cuidam
	abl	quodam	quadam	quodam
pl	*nom*	quidam	quaedam	quaedam
	acc	quosdam	quasdam	quaedam
	gen	quorundam	quarundam	quorundam
	dat	quibusdam	quibusdam	quibusdam
	abl	quibusdam	quibusdam	quibusdam

- This is the relative pronoun *qui, quae, quod* with *-dam* stuck on the end, and minor adjustments. Again note the distinctive genitive and dative singular endings (underlined), which many prepositions have, this time with *-dam* added.

- Compare how *idem* (the same) is the pronoun *is, ea, id* with *-dem* stuck on the end. In forming parts of *quidam* too, any part of the original pronoun ending *-m* changes it to *-n* before *-dam* is added, to ease pronunciation (so masculine accusative singular *quendam*, not *quemdam*). Here the neuter ending *-d* is kept, producing *quoddam*.

Any part of *quidam* can be used alone (supplying e.g. *man, woman, thing, people*) or with a noun (which it usually follows):

quosdam in summo monte conspexi.
I caught sight of some people on the top of the mountain.

librum quendam quaero.
I am looking for a certain book.

puellae quaedam in via stabant.
Some girls were standing in the street.

Exercise 9.35

Translate into English:

1. nuntius quidam victoriam nobis rettulit.

2. quaedam ex matribus locutura surrexit.

3. sensi quendam me sequi.

4. senex servis quibusdam semper credebat.

5. pecuniam cuiusdam in via inveni.

Exercise 9.36

Despondency and a dictator

News of the defeat at Trasimene causes alarm in Rome. Fabius is appointed dictator, but his new policy of watching and waiting does not prevent Hannibal outwitting him.

ubi <u>rumor</u> de proelio Romae auditus est, cives perterriti in forum festinaverunt. primo nihil clarum cognoscere poterant. tum <u>praetor</u>, nomine <u>M. Pomponianus</u>, '<u>pugna</u>' inquit 'magna victi sumus.' nec plura dixit. verbis tamen eius auditis, urbs subito <u>rumorum</u> <u>plena</u> erat. alii dicebant omnes milites ab hostibus captos
5 esse, alii consulem ipsum cum maxima parte copiarum interfectum esse. mox turba feminarum ad portas urbis convenit. omnes enim de filiis timebant. ubi nuntii tandem advenerunt, nonnullae matres, ubi filios suos <u>vivere</u> cognoverunt, gavisae sunt; ceterae miserrimae erant.

senatores, quod Hannibali resistere volebant, consilium diu petebant. tandem
10 <u>Q. Fabium Maximum</u> <u>dictatorem</u> fecerunt. ille postea '<u>Cunctator</u>' vocatus est quod novum consilium belli cepit: proelium <u>vitare</u> hostesque lentius vincere volebat. Fabius Hannibalem per Italiam progredientem secutus est. ubi Poeni montes in media Italia transire parabant, Fabius omnes <u>calles</u> <u>clausit</u> <u>praeter</u> unum; ibi Hannibalem exspectabat. ille tamen <u>boves</u> <u>cornigeros</u> invenit, <u>faces</u> eis <u>fixit</u>,
15 <u>aliquo</u> nocte <u>egit</u>. custodes Romani <u>boves</u>, quos Poenos esse putabant, secuti sunt; Hannibal igitur montes facile transiit.

	rumor -oris *m*	rumour
	praetor -oris *m*	praetor (*Roman magistrate*)
	M. Pomponianus -i *m*	Marcus Pomponianus
	pugna -ae *f*	fight
4	plenus -a -um	full
	vivo -ere vixi	I live, I am alive
	Q. Fabius -i Maximus -i *m*	Quintus Fabius Maximus (*also called just* Fabius)
	dictator -oris *m*	dictator
10	Cunctator -oris *m*	'Delayer'
	vito -are	I avoid
	callis -is *m*	mountain path
	claudo -ere clausi	I block
	praeter (+ *acc*)	except
14	boves boum *m pl*	oxen, cattle
	cornigerus -a -um	with horns
	fax facis *f*	torch, firebrand
	figo -ere fixi	I attach
	aliquo	in a different direction
15	ago -ere egi actus	I drive

- Note *ago*, here *I drive* (e.g. animals), which can also mean *I do* or *I act*, e.g. *quid agis* (what are you doing?).

LESS COMMON PRONOUNS (2)

one . . . the other (*of two*), another, a/the second

		m	*f*	*n*
sg	nom	alter	altera	alterum
	acc	alterum	alteram	alterum
	gen	<u>alterius</u>	<u>alterius</u>	<u>alterius</u>
	dat	<u>alteri</u>	<u>alteri</u>	<u>alteri</u>
	abl	altero	altera	altero
pl	nom	alteri	alterae	altera
	acc	alteros	alteras	altera
	gen	alterorum	alterarum	alterorum
	dat	alteris	alteris	alteris
	abl	alteris	alteris	alteris

(regular 2-1-2 plural)

- Again note the distinctive genitive and dative singular forms. This gives us the English word *alternate*. It is often used in a pair, requiring a different translation each time (*one . . . the other*):

    alter liber difficilis est, alter facilis.
    One book is difficult, the other easy.

The use of *alter . . . alter* implies that just two are involved. If there are more than two, *alius . . . alius* (see below) is used. In the singular this is translated *one . . . another*, but (as we saw in Chapter Eight) it is more often found in the plural as *some . . . others*:

    alii servorum laborabant, alii in taberna sedebant.
    Some of the slaves were working, others were sitting in the pub.

- If forms of *alius* different from each other in gender and/or case are paired, a double statement is made (abbreviated in Latin, as it can be in English):

	alii alia dicunt.
short for	alii[1] alia[1], alii[2] alia[2] dicunt.
	(*where 1 = some people/things, 2 = other people/things*)
literally	Some people say some things, others say other things.
i.e.	Different people say different things.

- Compare other paired words that we have already met:

et . . . et	both . . . and
nec/neque . . . nec/neque	neither . . . nor

		no-one *m/f*	nothing *n*
sg	*nom*	nemo	nihil (*indeclinable*)
	acc	neminem	
	gen	nullius	
	dat	nemini	
	abl	nullo	

- This is formed like a third declension noun (stem *nemin-*), but its genitive and ablative are borrowed from the adjective *nullus* (no . . ., not any).

- Note that the distinctive singular endings used by most pronouns (genitive *-ius*, dative *-i* across all three genders) are also used for the following adjectives, which are otherwise regular 2-1-2 in declension:

	alius*	other, another, else
	nullus	no . . ., not any
	solus	alone, only
	totus	whole
also	unus	one (*met in Chapter Six*)

* Note that *alius* has neuter nominative and accusative singular *aliud* rather than the expected *alium* (compare *illud*).

Exercise 9.37

Translate into English:

1. alter consul fidelis erat, alter scelestus.
2. nihil sine auxilio amicorum facere possum.
3. cives perterriti nec discedere nec in foro manere volebant.
4. nemo pecuniam in terra celatam inveniet.
5. senator uni civi persuasit.
6. consilium totius belli, a nullo antea visum, tandem cognovimus.
7. alii alia de scelere dicebant.
8. tibi soli credo, amice.
9. equis nostris in proelio necatis, alios emere debemus.
10. inimicus nullius volo esse.

Exercise 9.38

Translate into Latin:

1. No-one knows the name of the prisoner.
2. We caught sight of certain women in the street.
3. I have heard nothing about the battle.
4. One soldier was wounded, the other was killed.
5. Some of the slaves are happy, others are sad.

> ## REVISION CHECKPOINT
>
> Make sure you know:
>
> - prepositions that take the accusative (often indicating motion towards or through)
>
> - prepositions that take the ablative (often indicating motion away from, or position in a place)
>
> - less common pronouns: *quidam* (a certain), *alter* (one/the other), *nemo* (no-one)
>
> - the use of *alter . . . alter* (one . . . the other), *alii . . . alii* (some . . . others) and the idiom *alii alia dicunt* (different people say different things)

Exercise 9.39

Enter Scipio

Abandoning the policy of Fabius, the Romans suffer another defeat at Cannae (216 BC). Hannibal resists advice to make a direct assault on Rome. The young Scipio vows to save the city.

cives consilium <u>Fabii</u> non laudaverunt: proelium cum Hannibale facere malebant. <u>proximo</u> anno igitur Romani, a consulibus iterum ducti, cum Hannibale <u>Cannis</u> pugnaverunt. alter consul consilium <u>Fabii</u> in animo tenebat; alter audacior erat. Romani tamen iterum victi sunt. alii ab hostibus interfecti
5 sunt, alii capti. post proelium <u>Maharbal</u> Hannibali 'si Romam oppugnabis' inquit 'cenam in <u>Capitolio</u> mox consumes. si festinabis, Romani te venisse, non venturum esse, cognoscent.' haec tamen non acciderunt. Hannibal consilium eius laudavit sed accipere noluit. multi postea credebant illam <u>moram</u> Romam servavisse.

10 postea nonnulli milites qui e proelio effugerant <u>Canusium</u> advenerunt. ibi aderant alii duces Romani et <u>P. Scipio</u> iuvenis. ubi victoria Hannibalis eis relata est, ceteri Romam ipsam confectam esse dixerunt; trans mare fugere volebant. Scipio tamen 'audere' inquit 'et sperare debetis. si urbem servare vultis, me arma ferentes sequi debetis. ego Romam numquam relinquam.'

Fabius -i *m*	Fabius
proximus -a -um	next
Cannae -is (*locative* Cannis) *f pl*	Cannae (*a town in south-east Italy*)
Maharbal -alis *m*	Maharbal (*an officer in Hannibal's*
5	*army*)
Capitolium -i *n*	the Capitol (*citadel of Rome*)
mora -ae *f*	delay
Canusium -i *n*	Canusium (*a town in southern Italy*)
P. Scipio -onis *m*	Publius Scipio (*also called just* Scipio)

Exercise 9.40

Hannibal and Scipio

Hannibal approaches Rome but does not attack. His brother is captured and killed.
When Scipio fights successfully in Spain and Africa, Hannibal is recalled to Carthage.
The two great generals finally face off at Zama (202 BC).

Hannibal <u>Capuae</u> diu manebat; copiae quaedam Romanae urbem diu
<u>obsidebant</u>. ubi Poeni ab eo loco tandem profecti sunt, castra prope Romam
ipsam posuerunt. Hannibal ad portas <u>equitavit</u>, urbem clarissimam spectare
volens. Romam tamen oppugnare non potuit, quod urbs bene custodiebatur.
5   interea <u>Hasdrubal</u>, qui in <u>Hispania</u> pugnabat, trans <u>Alpes</u> iter fecit, auxilium
Hannibali fratri laturus. ubi tamen in Italiam advenit, a Romanis captus et
interfectus est. caput eius in castra Hannibalis iactum est. Hannibal, ubi caput
invenit, dixit se <u>fatum</u> <u>Carthaginis</u> in <u>ore</u> fratris videre.

P. <u>Scipio</u> imperator factus in Hispaniam missus est. cum Poenis bellum gerebat,
10 qui maiorem partem terrae tenebant. mox <u>Carthaginem Novam</u> cepit et Poenos
superavit. deinde in <u>Africam</u> transiit. Romani cum Poenis in <u>Sicilia</u> quoque
pugnabant. Poeni, qui bellum multis in locis gerere non poterant, perterriti erant.
tandem igitur Hannibal Carthaginem revocatus est. quod redire coactus erat,
credebat se a Poenis ipsis, non a Romanis, victum esse.

15 Scipio de pace loqui conabatur, sed frustra. Romani igitur cum Hannibale
<u>Zamae</u> pugnaverunt. Hannibal <u>elephantos</u> iterum habuit; illi tamen, <u>tubis</u>
Romanorum perterriti, Poenos ipsos oppugnatos oppresserunt. Romani
Hannibalem tandem vicerunt. Scipioni postea propter hanc victoriam nomen
'Africanus' datum est.

	Capua -ae (*locative* Capuae) *f*	Capua (*a city in southern Italy*)
	obsideo -ere	I besiege
	equito -are -avi	I ride on horseback
	Hasdrubal -alis *m*	Hasdrubal (*brother of Hannibal*)
5	Hispania -ae *f*	Spain
	Alpes -ium *f pl*	the Alps
	fatum -i *n*	fate
	Carthago -inis *f*	Carthage
	os oris *m*	face
9	P. Scipio *m*	Publius Scipio (*also called just* Scipio)
	Carthago -inis Nova -ae *f*	New Carthage (*a city in Spain, modern* *Cartagena*)
	Africa -ae *f*	Africa
	Sicilia -ae *f*	Sicily
16	Zama -ae (*locative* Zamae) *f*	Zama (*a town in north Africa*)
	elephantus -i *m*	elephant
	tuba -ae *f*	war-trumpet
	Africanus -a -um	'African'

SUMMARY OF CHAPTER NINE GRAMMAR

Passive infinitive:
Changes the final vowel of the active infinitive from *-e* to *-i*, e.g. *portari* (to be carried), except that third conjugation has just *-i* instead of the expected *-eri*, e.g. *trahi* (to be dragged).

Deponent verbs:
Verbs that are passive in form but active in meaning. They have three principal parts: first person singular present tense, infinitive, first person singular perfect tense, e.g. *conor, conari, conatus sum* (I try). The perfect participle (here active) forms part of the perfect tense.

Perfect active participle:
Deponent verbs have this useful feature lacking in ordinary verbs, e.g. *conatus* (having tried).

Semi-deponent verbs:
Verbs that are active in the present, future and imperfect, but deponent (i.e. passive form) in the perfect and pluperfect. Like deponents, they have three principal parts, e.g. *gaudeo, gaudere, gavisus sum* (I rejoice).

Indirect statement:
Latin always uses the accusative and infinitive construction (like *I believe the story to be true*), not a clause with a separate word for *that*, but it is usually better translated as a *that* clause in English, e.g. *I believe that the story is true*.

If the introductory verb is past, the tense of the Latin infinitive (which preserves that of the original direct speech or thought) needs be moved a tense back in English, e.g. *nuntiavit hostes appropinquare* becomes *he said that the enemy were approaching*.

A wide range of verbs describing speech acts, mental processes and perceptions can introduce indirect statement.

If the subject of the infinitive is the same as that of the introductory verb, a reflexive pronoun (e.g. *se*) is used. If the infinitive has two accusatives (subject and object), the subject comes first.

In addition to the present active and passive infinitives already familiar, e.g. *portare* (to carry) and *portari* (to be carried), other infinitives are used in indirect statement.

The perfect active infinitive is formed from the perfect stem (third principal part less *-i*) and *-isse*, e.g. *portavisse* (to have carried).

The perfect passive infinitive is formed from the perfect passive participle with *esse*, e.g. *portatus esse* (to have been carried).

The future active infinitive is formed from the future active participle with *esse*, e.g. *portaturus esse* (to be about to carry).

The participle in these last two infinitives is normally accusative in indirect statement.

Prepositions:

Round-up of prepositions taking the accusative (often for motion towards or through) and the ablative (often for position or motion from), including two new ones: *propter* + acc (on account of) and *pro* + abl (in front of, for, in return for).

Less common pronouns:

Use of *quidam* (a certain), *alter* (one/the other, another, the second); paired *alii . . . alii* (some . . . others) and *alter . . . alter* (one . . . the other); *nemo* (no-one) and *nihil* (nothing); adjectives with gen and dat sg *-ius -i* like pronouns (*alius, nullus, solus, totus,* and numeral *unus*).

CHAPTER NINE VOCABULARY

ac/atque	and
accido -ere -i	I happen
ago -ere egi actus	I do, I act, I drive
alius -a -ud	other, another, else
alter -era -erum	the other, another, one (of two), the second (of two)
alter . . . alter	one . . . the other
antea	before, previously
audeo -ere ausus sum	I dare
cognosco -ere cognovi cognitus	I get to know, I find out
conor -ari conatus sum	I try
copiae -arum *f pl*	forces, troops
egredior egredi egressus sum	I go out
etiam	even, also
fidelis -e	faithful, loyal
gaudeo -ere gavisus sum	I rejoice, I am pleased
gens gentis *f*	family, tribe, race, people
hortor -ari hortatus sum	I encourage, I urge
ingredior ingredi ingressus sum	I enter
interea	meanwhile
iterum	again
lentus -a -um	slow
libenter	willingly, gladly
liberi -orum *m pl*	children
loquor loqui locutus sum	I speak
miror -ari miratus sum	I wonder at, I admire
morior mori mortuus sum	I die
nemo neminis *m/f*	no-one, nobody
nonnulli -ae -a *pl*	some, several
opprimo -ere oppressi oppressus	I crush, I overwhelm
patior pati passus sum	I suffer, I endure
pro (+ *abl*)	in front of, for, in return for
proficiscor proficisci profectus sum	I set out
progredior progredi progressus sum	I advance
propter (+ *acc*)	on account of, because of
proximus -a -um	next, next to
puto -are -avi -atus	I think
quidam quaedam quoddam	a certain, a, one, some
reddo -ere reddidi redditus	I give back, I restore
regredior regredi regressus sum	I go back, I return
scio -ire -ivi -itus	I know
sentio -ire sensi sensus	I feel, I notice
sequor sequi secutus sum	I follow
soleo -ere solitus sum	I am accustomed

spero -are -avi -atus	I hope, I expect
tempestas -atis *f*	storm
victoria -ae *f*	victory
vita -ae *f*	life
vivo -ere vixi	I live, I am alive
vulnero -are -avi -atus	I wound, I injure
vulnus -eris *n*	wound

50 words

Chapter Ten

IMPERFECT SUBJUNCTIVE

The subjunctive is a form of a verb that typically expresses a *possibility* rather than a fact (something that *might* happen, or *might* be the reason for something else). The term *subjunctive* means *joined under*, i.e. *bolted on*, as an alternative form.

- All verb forms met so far with a tense and person ending are in contrast called *indicative* because they do state or *indicate* a fact.

- The imperfect is the most common tense of the subjunctive (only one other, the pluperfect, is needed for GCSE).

- Translation of the imperfect subjunctive varies according to the construction it is in (it does not have one single meaning), but it is very easy to form and recognise. For the active, the basic person endings (*-m, -s, -t, -mus, -tis, -nt*) are stuck onto the present active infinitive (the second principal part).

conjugation		*1st*	*2nd*	*3rd*	*4th*
sg	*1*	portare-m	monere-m	trahere-m	audire-m
	2	portare-s	monere-s	trahere-s	audire-s
	3	portare-t	*etc*	*etc*	*etc*
pl	*1*	portare-mus			
	2	portare-tis			
	3	portare-nt			

similarly for mixed 3rd/4th conjugation: capere-m, capere-s, *etc*

This also applies to irregular verbs:

	infinitive	*imperfect subjunctive*
sum	esse	essem -es -et *etc*
possum	posse	possem
eo	ire	irem
volo	velle	vellem
nolo	nolle	nollem
malo	malle	mallem
fero	ferre	ferrem

The passive form of the imperfect subjunctive is made by changing the active endings to passive ones (*-r, -ris, -tur, -mur, -mini, -ntur*) in the usual way:

sg	*1*	portare-r	monere-r	trahere-r	audire-r
	2	portare-ris	monere-ris	trahere-ris	audire-ris
	3	portare-tur	*etc*	*etc*	*etc*
pl	*1*	portare-mur			
	2	portare-mini			
	3	portare-ntur			

similarly for mixed 3rd/4th conjugation: capere-r, capere-ris, *etc*

- The imperfect subjunctive of a deponent verb is like the passive imperfect subjunctive of an ordinary verb, i.e. formed as if from an active infinitive of the equivalent conjugation. So *conor* (I try) is first conjugation: its actual (passive form) infinitive is *conari*, but an active infinitive of the same conjugation would end *-are*, so the imperfect subjunctive is *conarer*.

Exercise 10.1

Using the rules above, give the following forms:

1. active imperfect subjunctive of *festino*, third person singular
2. active imperfect subjunctive of *venio*, first person plural
3. passive imperfect subjunctive of *capio*, second person singular
4. active imperfect subjunctive of *sum*, third person plural
5. passive imperfect subjunctive of *rego*, second person plural

---

PURPOSE CLAUSES

One of the most common uses of the imperfect subjunctive is in a purpose clause, explaining the aim with which something was done.

I went to Rome to see the emperor.

The girl worked hard in order to get a top grade.

Latin does not use the infinitive for this as you might expect from English, but instead uses the word *ut* (= in order to) with the imperfect subjunctive.

Translation as an infinitive in English (*to do X*) often works if the subject of the purpose clause is the same as the subject of the main verb of the sentence:

> senex ad urbem ambulavit ut librum emeret.
>
> *lit*   The old man walked to the city in order that he might buy a book.
>
> *i.e.*   The old man walked to the city to buy a book.

If the purpose clause has a new subject, a translation such as *in order that* or *so that* is needed, putting *might* or *would* (expressing a *possibility*) with the verb:

> femina diu laborabat ut liberi cibum haberent.
> The woman was working for a long time so that her children would have food.

A negative purpose clause uses *ne* (= in order not to) instead of *ut*:

> noctem exspectavimus ne ab hostibus videremur.
> We waited for night in order not to be seen by the enemy.

- A purpose clause is sometimes called a *final* clause, not because it comes last thing in the sentence (though it often does) but because it tells us the *end* in view, in the old sense of *aim*.

- Note that *ut* with an indicative verb (or no verb at all) means *as* or *when*.

Exercise 10.2

Translate into English:

1. pueri in via stabant ut puellas salutarent.
2. Romam ire volebam ut templa forumque viderem.
3. hi mortui sunt ut nos viveremus.
4. ancilla tabernam iniit ut cibum emeret.
5. captivus clamabat ut ab omnibus audiretur.
6. amici ad villam advenerunt ut nobiscum loquerentur.
7. cives ad portas urbis festinaverunt ut verba nuntii audirent.
8. nonne custodiebaris ne ab inimicis necareris?
9. milites per noctem laborabant ut nova castra conficerent.
10. servus fugisse videbatur, ut saepe accidit, ne a domino puniretur.

Exercise 10.3

Translate into Latin:

1. I walked to the city in order to find my friends.
2. The old man stayed in the inn in order not to be seen by his wife.
3. The women were standing in the street in order to look at the queen.
4. We sent more soldiers so that the city would not be captured.
5. A slave arrived to show us the way.

Background: The young Caesar

The republican government of Rome had been designed to run a city-state, not an empire. As Rome expanded overseas in the last two centuries BC, the system was increasingly unable to cope. Rome was dominated by a sequence of ambitious men who had experienced great power as military commanders or provincial governors, and were unwilling to give it up when they returned to Rome. The last and greatest of these was Julius Caesar. Born in 100 BC into a patrician family claiming descent from Iulus (another name for Ascanius, the son of Aeneas), Caesar became head of his family at the age of sixteen and showed early signs of great ambition. He cultivated rich and powerful friends, and connections that would help him later, though he also made enemies.

Exercise 10.4

Caesar captured by pirates

The young Caesar is captured by pirates (75 BC). Acting with relaxed confidence, he reveals his good opinion of himself and enjoys a bantering relationship with them, but is in the end ruthless.

Caesar ubi iuvenis erat ad Graeciam navigabat ut oratores claros audiret et ab eis doceretur. subito navis a praedonibus oppugnata est. Caesar et nonnulli servi capti sunt. deinde ad parvam insulam ducti sunt. praedones eos ibi captivos tenebant, ut pecuniam sibi facerent. Caesar tamen, ubi praedones pretium viginti
5 talentorum pro vita sua petiverunt, vehementer risit. 'pretium multo maius' inquit 'pro tanto homine petere debetis.' et promisit se quinquaginta talenta eis daturum esse. deinde servos quosdam Romam misit ut hanc pecuniam referrent.

interea multa iocosa cum praedonibus loquebatur; olim dixit se mox eos puniturum esse. praedones verbis iuvenis auditis riserunt; ubi tamen servi
10 redierunt, ut ille promiserat, pecuniam libenter acceperunt. Caesar sic liberatus naves atque comites quaerere coepit. brevi tempore ad insulam rediit ut praedones

puniret: pecunia eorum rapta, omnes saevissime <u>occidit</u>. sic <u>praedones</u> pro sceleribus <u>poenas dederunt</u>. sic Caesar omnia fecit quae se facturum esse dixerat.

	Caesar -aris *m*	Caesar
	Graecia -ae *f*	Greece
	orator -oris *m*	orator, public speaker
	praedo -onis *m*	pirate
4	pretium -i *n*	price, ransom
	viginti	twenty
	talentum -i *n*	talent (*large unit of money*)
	vehementer	loudly
	tantus -a -um	so great, such a great
6	quinquaginta	fifty
	iocosus -a -um	in jest, as a joke
	brevis -e	brief, short
	tempus -oris *n*	time
	occido -ere -i occisus	I kill
13	poenas do dare dedi	I pay the penalty, I am punished

- Note here *occido* (literally *I cut down*), yet another word (alongside *neco* and *interficio*) for *I kill*.

- Note too the idiom *poenas do*, which means *I pay the penalty* or *I am punished* (not *impose penalties on other people*, as you might think from the literal meaning *give penalites.*)

- The proper name *Caesar* will not be glossed again in this chapter.

FOURTH AND FIFTH DECLENSION NOUNS

These are much less common than the first three declensions. There are only a few of each, but they include some important words. The fourth declension can be thought of as a variant of the second, and the fifth as a variant of the third.

		fourth declension	*fifth declension*
		hand, *or* group of people	day
		f	*m*
sg	nom	man-us	di-es
	acc	man-um	di-em
	gen	man-us	di-ei
	dat	man-ui	di-ei
	abl	man-u	di-e
pl	nom	man-us	di-es
	acc	man-us	di-es
	gen	man-uum	di-erum
	dat	man-ibus	di-ebus
	abl	man-ibus	di-ebus

- The two different meanings of *manus* are linked by the idea of a group of people as a *handful*.

- There are both masculine and feminine nouns in both the fourth and the fifth declension (there is also a neuter version of fourth, but there are no examples in the GCSE vocabulary).

- Four different bits of a word like *manus* (nominative and genitive singular, nominative and accusative plural) are spelled in the same way (but the *u* in the nominative singular is pronounced short, the others long). The number and case have to be worked out from the context. Note in particular that if the word is accusative, it must also be plural:

  hic servus magnas manus habet.
  This slave has big hands.

- Note the following adverb formed from *dies*:

  postridie   on the next day

  This is in origin a contraction of *posteriore* (= following) *die*, an ablative expression of *time when*.

The other fourth and fifth declension nouns needed for GCSE are:

fourth:		*fifth:*	
domus -us *f*	house, home	res rei *f*	thing, matter, event
exercitus -us *m*	army	spes spei *f*	hope

- Note that *domus* (house) has the ablative singular *domo* (and usually the accusative plural *domos*) as if it were second declension. The accusative *domum* is used without a preposition to mean *home* or *homewards*, with a verb of motion (compare *Romam* = to Rome). Also formed as if second declension is the common locative *domi* (= at home).

  senex domum festinavit. postridie domi manere constituit.
  The old man hurried home. On the next day he decided to stay at home.

- Note that *res* has a range of meanings: *thing, matter, event*. Sometimes *story* is the appropriate translation:

  nuntius totam rem narravit.
  The messenger told the whole story.

- Unfamiliar words of these declensions may be used in a GCSE passage: they will be glossed with the genitive singular (given in full), which as usual enables you to work out the declension, e.g.

gradus, gradus *m*	footstep	*(fourth)*
acies, aciei *f*	battle-line	*(fifth)*

Exercise 10.5

Translate into English:

1. domum redii ut cenam consumerem.
2. senatores de re gravissima loquebantur.
3. quis exercitum Romanum tum ducebat?
4. haec victoria spem pacis nobis dat.
5. altera puella Romam ire volebat, altera domi manere malebat.
6. magnam manum captivorum in castris invenimus.
7. naves multis post diebus navigare potuerunt.
8. quid in manu tenes, serve?
9. haec ancilla in omnibus rebus fidelis erat.
10. dux exercitus nostri postridie ab urbe profectus est.

Exercise 10.6

Translate into Latin:

1. Did you see a group of soldiers near the temple, master?
2. The army was advancing for four days.
3. The soldier's hand had been wounded.
4. In this matter I have the hope of a reward.
5. We returned home in order to look for the book.

REVISION CHECKPOINT

Make sure you know:

- formation of the imperfect subjunctive from the present active infinitive with basic person endings, active (e.g. *portarem*) or passive (e.g. *portarer*)
- construction for purpose clauses using *ut* (in order to) and the imperfect subjunctive; negative version uses *ne* (in order not to) instead of *ut*
- fourth declension (e.g. *manus* = hand) and fifth declension (e.g. *dies* = day) nouns

Exercise 10.7

Caesar's ambition

Caesar travels to Spain on military service (69 BC). He offers and is offered some thoughts about ambition.

Caesar exercitum suum ad <u>Hispaniam</u> ducebat. per montes multos dies iter faciebant. mox ad parvum <u>vicum</u> advenerunt; omnes qui ibi habitabant <u>pauperes</u> erant. Caesar militesque de <u>vico</u> loquebantur. miles quidam '<u>fortasse</u>' inquit 'viri etiam in hoc <u>vico</u> saepe pugnant quod <u>quisque</u> rex esse vult. quam stulti sunt!'
5   tum ceteri milites riserunt. Caesar tamen '<u>vero</u> pugnant' inquit 'sed stulti non sunt. ego enim malo minimo in <u>vico</u> primus esse quam <u>secundus</u> Romae.' omnes qui haec verba audiverunt in animo tenebant. postea in Hispania Caesar <u>statuam</u> <u>Alexandri Magni</u> in templo conspexit. hac visa, maxime motus lacrimare coepit. 'Alexander' inquit '<u>adhuc</u> iuvenis <u>mundum</u> vicerat; ego nihil magnum <u>umquam</u>
10 feci.' <u>itaque</u> Romam rediit seque ad res maiores paravit.

	Hispania -ae *f*	Spain
	vicus -i *m*	village
	pauper -eris *m*	poor man, peasant
	fortasse	perhaps
4	quisque	each
	vero	indeed, certainly
	secundus -a -um	second
	statua -ae *f*	statue
	Alexander -dri Magnus -i *m*	Alexander the Great (*356-323 BC*,
8		*Greek king who created vast empire*)
	adhuc	still
	mundus -i *m*	world
	umquam	ever
	itaque	and so, therefore

Exercise 10.8

Politics not pomp

After successful campaigning during a second period in Spain, Caesar has the chance of celebrating a triumph, the great procession into Rome of a victorious general, but foregoes this temporary publicity in favour of furthering his ambitions by standing for office as consul (60 BC).

Caesar postea in <u>Hispania</u> iterum bellum gessit. multis Romanorum hostibus ibi victis, Romam redire volebat ut consul esset. sperabat se quoque urbem in <u>triumpho</u> intraturum esse, cum captivis militibusque suis. senatores tamen '<u>officium</u> consulis' inquiunt 'petere non potes nisi urbem <u>privatus</u> intrabis.'

5 Caesar igitur imperium unum annum habere maluit quam a turba unum diem laudari. alter consul eodem anno <u>Bibulus</u> erat: hic tamen <u>paene</u> nihil fecit, Caesar <u>paene</u> omnia. postea ex omnibus <u>provinciis</u> <u>Galliam</u> legit. gentes feroces ibi habitabant; Romani primo parvam partem terrae habebant. mox tamen Caesare duce Romani omnem Galliam superaturi erant.

	Hispania -ae *f*	Spain
	triumphus -i *m*	triumphal procession
	officium -i *n*	office, position
	privatus -i *m*	private citizen
6	Bibulus -i *m*	Bibulus
	paene	almost
	provincia -ae *f*	province
	Gallia -ae *f*	Gaul (*modern France and surrounding area*)

Background: Caesar in Gaul and Britain

After his consulship Caesar was given a special command as proconsul in Gaul. He saw that he could gain wealth by conquest, and prestige by extending Roman territory. He took four legions with him, and raised two more. He defeated several tribes and secured the borders of the expanded province. By a show of strength he deterred German tribes from crossing them. After finding out as much as he could about Britain (with which the Gauls were in close contact), he twice crossed the Channel and invaded, but did not make a permanent conquest. Finally he defeated the rebel Gallic leader Vercingetorix, his most dangerous opponent. Caesar was now virtually sovereign of a very large and wealthy province. He wrote about all this in his *Gallic Wars*, a detailed and extensive war diary. He always refers to himself in the third person as 'Caesar', which makes the trumpet-blowing a bit less obvious.

Exercise 10.9

Caesar in Gaul

Caesar makes conquests in Gaul and a show of Roman strength in Germany.

Caesar in <u>Gallia</u> et pecuniam et <u>gloriam</u> sibi petebat. quattuor <u>legiones</u> ducens, multas gentes ibi vicit. <u>Helvetii</u> e terra sua discesserunt et trans Galliam iter facere coeperunt; Caesar eos redire coegit, quamquam domos suas antea incenderant. Caesar saepe crudelis erat: olim pugnaturus diu manebat, ut hostes
5   nullam aquam haberent; deinde, postquam eos facile vicit, manus omnium <u>praecidi</u> iussit. ubi cognovit gentes <u>Germaniae</u> Galliam <u>invasuros esse</u>, <u>pontem</u> trans <u>Rhenum</u> flumen fecit. legiones in Germaniam duxit, ut copiae suae ab omnibus viderentur. deinde, sine proelio, legiones in Galliam reduxit et <u>pontem</u> deleri iussit. <u>Germani</u> nuntium celatum intellexerunt; Galliam non <u>invaserunt</u>.

	Gallia -ae *f*	Gaul
	gloria -ae *f*	glory
	legio -onis *f*	legion (*army division of up to 6000 men*)
2	Helvetii -orum *m pl*	the Helvetii (*a tribe in modern Switzerland*)
	praecido -ere	I cut off
	Germania -ae *f*	Germany
	invado -ere invasi invasus	I invade
6	pons pontis *m*	bridge
	Rhenus -i *m*	the Rhine (*major river dividing Gaul and Germany*)
	Germani -orum *m pl*	Germans

INDIRECT COMMANDS

As we saw in Part 1, a *direct* command uses the imperative, e.g. *festinate* (hurry!). An *indirect* command reports a command:

direct: Hurry!
indirect: I told the children to hurry.

The verb *iubeo* (I order) uses the infinitive for an indirect command just as English does (we have seen numerous examples of this already, as it translates naturally):

senator cives audire iussit.
The senator ordered to citizens to listen.

All other verbs met at GCSE use instead a clause with *ut* and the imperfect subjunctive. This construction is the same as the one for a purpose clause, but in an indirect command *ut* with the imperfect subjunctive is translated *to do X* (just like the infinitive after *iubeo*) or *that X should happen*.

senator cives rogavit ut audirent.
The senator asked the citizens to listen.

- The constructions for a purpose clause and an indirect command are the same because the underlying thought (of wanting to get some aim achieved) is the same. But in practice they are quite separate. If you are dealing with an indirect command, the translation *in order to* must be avoided (it is penalised at GCSE).

A *command* in the grammatical sense can be a polite request or suggestion, rather than an actual order. Thus indirect commands with *ut* can be introduced by a wide range of verbs, most of which we have met before:

hortor	I encourage, I urge
impero -are -avi -atus	I order (+ *dat*)
moneo	I warn, I advise
oro	I beg
persuadeo	I persuade (+ *dat*)
rogo	I ask

Note that *impero* and *persuadeo* take a dative, because the idea is of giving an order or applying persuasion *to* someone:

senator civibus imperavit ut audirent.
The senator ordered the citizens to listen.

- The presence of one of these verbs should enable you to distinguish an indirect command from a purpose clause.

The translation *to* works for *ut* in an indirect command addressed to the person or people who are to do the action:

senex pueros oravit ut tacerent.
The old man begged the boys to be quiet.

Otherwise (e.g. with a passive verb and/or if no-one specific is addressed) the translation *that* is needed, putting *should* with the verb:

dux hostium imperavit ut urbs deleretur.
The enemy leader ordered that the city should be destroyed.

A negative indirect command uses *ne* instead of *ut*, just as a negative purpose clause does:

feminas monui ne in foro manerent.
I advised the women not to stay in the forum.

A command that something should *never* be done uses *ne . . . umquam* (not . . . ever) rather than *numquam*:

> imperator milites hortatus est ne umquam fugerent.
> The general urged the soldiers never to run away.

This also applies to *never* in a purpose clause.

- It is not possible to use *iubeo* and the infinitive for a negative indirect command.

Exercise 10.10

Translate into English:

1. domina ancillis imperavit ut cenam optimam pararent.
2. senex liberos tacere iussit.
3. pater filium monuit ne pecuniam auferret.
4. dux militibus imperavit ut prope flumen castra ponerent.
5. servus dominum rogavit ut statim liberaretur.
6. captivi orabant ut cibus sibi daretur.
7. civibus persuasi ne huic senatori <u>faverent</u>.
8. pueri celerius laborare iussi sunt.
9. deos oravimus ut urbem nostram servarent.
10. imperator nos hortatus est ut per montes lente progrederemur.

faveo -ere favi   I favour, I support (+ *dat*)

Exercise 10.11

S&C

Translate into Latin (remember that the infinitive can be used only with iubeo):

1. The master ordered the slaves to build a wall.
2. The general was urging the soldiers to fight bravely.
3. The old man asked the children not to shout in the temple.
4. I persuaded my mother to give me more money.
5. The senator warned the citizens to stay at home on the next day.

Exercise 10.12

Translate into English (mixed purpose clauses and indirect commands):

1. dominus servis imperavit ut laborem conficerent.
2. prima <u>luce</u> profecti sumus ut eodem die adveniremus.
3. domina iussit ancillas cenam parare.
4. manebatisne in horto ne a me videremini?
5. senex ad forum rediit ut pecuniam inveniret.
6. dux suos hortatus est ut celerius progrederentur.
7. feminae festinabant ut maritos a bello regressos salutarent.
8. quis vobis persuasit ut domi maneretis?
9. captivi in forum ducti sunt ut ab omnibus spectarentur.
10. consul nos oravit ut in foro taceremus.

lux lucis *f*   light

• Note here the idiom *prima luce* = at first light, at dawn.

Exercise 10.13

Britain in prospect

During his campaign in Gaul, Caesar decides to invade Britain (55 BC).

Caesar, quamquam parva pars <u>aestatis</u> manebat, in <u>Britanniam</u> proficisci constituit. insulam enim superare volebat quod <u>Britannos</u> auxilium <u>Gallis</u> in bello mittere cognoverat. <u>mercatores</u> igitur invenit qui in Britanniam iter facere solebant. illos ad se vocatos hortatus est ut de loco, gentibus, modo belli loquerentur. quamquam
5   <u>tam</u> <u>diligens</u> erat, paene nihil tamen ab eis cognoscere poterat. deinde <u>Voluseno</u> imperavit ut una nave ad insulam transiret et de his rebus quaerere conaretur.

	aestas -atis *f*	summer
	Britannia -ae *f*	Britain
	Britanni -orum *m pl*	Britons, people of Britain
	Galli -orum *m pl*	Gauls
3	mercator -oris *m*	merchant
	tam	so
	diligens -entis	careful
	Volusenus -i *m*	Volusenus (*an officer in Caesar's army*)

ipse interea cum omnibus copiis in eam partem <u>Galliae</u> <u>processit</u> <u>unde</u> <u>traiectus</u>
brevissimus erat. ibi naves ex aliis partibus convenire iussit. ubi Britanni per
<u>mercatores</u> de consilio Caesaris audiverunt, nonnullae gentes nuntios ei
10 miserunt: se imperium Romanorum accepturos esse dixerunt. eos auditos Caesar
hortatus est ut in eadem <u>sententia</u> manerent; deinde domum misit. tum Volusenus
rediit; sed non multa referre poterat quod e nave non egressus erat. plurimi
tamen Britanni patriam defendere parabant.

	Gallia -ae *f*	Gaul
	procedo -ere processi	I advance, I proceed
	unde	(*not a question*) from where
	traiectus -us *m*	crossing
11	sententia -ae *f*	opinion

- The proper names *Gallia*, *Galli*, *Britannia* and *Britanni* will not be glossed
  again in this chapter.

RESULT CLAUSES (1)

A result clause focuses on the *outcome* of an action:

The boy ran <u>so</u> fast <u>that</u> he won the prize.

It is recognised by a signpost word (*so* etc) in the first half of the sentence, then *ut*
for *that* introducing the second half (the actual result clause), with the verb in the
imperfect subjunctive to describe a result in the past.
    The most common signpost words are:

tam	so	(*with an adjective or adverb*)
adeo	so much, to such an extent	(*with a verb*)
ita	in such a way	(*with a verb*)

haec puella tam fortis erat ut omnes eam laudarent.
This girl was so brave that everyone praised her.

puer adeo clamabat ut omnes eum audirent.
The boy was shouting so much that everyone heard him.

senator ita loquebatur ut omnes ei crederent.
The senator used to speak in such a way that everyone trusted him.

There are also some more specialised signpost words:

tantus	so great, so big	(*used instead of* tam magnus)
tot	so many	(*used instead of* tam multi)
talis	such, of such a sort	(*used with nouns*)

- Of these, *tantus* is normal 2-1-2 in declension (*tantus -a -um*) and *talis* is a
  third declension adjective like *fortis* (*talis -e*); *tot* is indeclinable.

- Note the distinction between *tot* and the plural of *tantus*:

tot equi	so many horses
tanti equi	such big horses

- Note the similarity of these signpost words beginning *t-* to the question words beginning *qu-*, which they can also be used to answer:

question		*answer*	
quantus	how big?	tantus	so big
quot	how many?	tot	so many
qualis	what sort?	talis	of such a sort, this sort

- Because a result clause depends so importantly on the signpost word in the first half of the sentence, it is sometimes also called a *consecutive* (= following on) clause.

Exercise 10.14

Translate into English:

1. hic miles tam fortis erat ut in castra hostium solus iniret.
2. puella ita locuta est ut ab omnibus laudaretur.
3. servi tam lente laborabant ut dominus eos saepe puniret.
4. femina adeo lacrimabat ut domum redire vellet.
5. cives tam stulti erant ut huic senatori crederent.
6. tempestas tanta erat ut multas naves deleret.
7. vinum tale erat ut omnes bibere vellent.
8. scelera illius hominis tanta erant ut Roma expelleretur.
9. nuntius tam clare dixit ut omnes eum audiremus.
10. miles tot vulnera accepisset ut mox moreretur.

Exercise 10.15

Translate into Latin:

1. The book was so short that the children read it easily.
2. The slave was laughing so much that he fell into the water.
3. The noise was so great that it could be heard in the street.
4. The boy received so many prizes that everyone admired him.
5. Our men fought so well that they conquered the enemy.

RESULT CLAUSES (2)

A result clause must be carefully distinguished from a purpose clause (which also uses *ut* and the subjunctive). It has a different emphasis:

purpose clause:

The girl worked hard in order to get a top grade.

That was the aim, but might not have been the result: she could have been unlucky, or not worked quite hard enough.

result clause:

The girl worked so hard that she got a top grade.

That was the result, but might not have been the aim: she could have been unduly modest and aiming only for a pass.

A purpose clause and a result clause both normally use *ut* and (in the examples you will meet in GCSE) the imperfect subjunctive. But if the clause contains a negative, there is an important difference: a negative purpose clause uses *ne* instead of *ut*, but a negative result clause uses <u>*non* as well as *ut*</u> (this is the only place where *ut* and *non* are used together with the subjunctive).

cibus talis erat ut eum consumere non possem.
The food was such (*or* so bad) that I could not eat it.

Note here that flexibility is needed in translation of *talis* according to context.

Another negative (e.g. *nihil* or *numquam*) can take the place of *non* in a result clause, but still with *ut* as well:

cives adeo clamabant ut nihil audirem.
The citizens were shouting so much that I heard nothing.

- We saw above that a purpose clause must also be distinguished from an indirect command. It is important to be absolutely clear about the distinction between the three different constructions – purpose clause, indirect command and result clause – that use *ut* and the imperfect subjunctive:

purpose clause	I went home <u>in order to</u> sleep.
indirect command	The master ordered the slaves <u>to</u> work quickly.
result clause	The boy ran <u>so</u> fast <u>that</u> he won the prize.

Exercise 10.16

Translate into English (mixed purpose clause, indirect command and result clause):

1. prima luce profecti sumus ut Romam quam celerrime adveniremus.
2. tempestas tam saeva erat ut navigare non possemus.
3. dominus servis imperavit ut totum diem in agris laborarent.
4. equos in agrum agebamus ne turba clamantium eos terreret.
5. liberi tam stulti erant ut nihil intellegerent.
6. imperator quosdam emisit ut castra hostium invenirent.
7. senex tot epistulas accepit ut omnibus respondere non posset.
8. femina pueros monuit ne in templo clamarent.
9. adeo timebam ut nihil dicere possem.
10. cives iussi sunt arma rapere ut portas urbis defenderent.

Exercise 10.17

S&C

Translate into Latin (mixed purpose clause, indirect command and result clause):

1. These soldiers were so daring that they were never afraid.
2. I wanted to return home in order to eat dinner with my friends.
3. The senator persuaded the citizens to listen to the messenger.
4. The citizens were so much afraid that they could do nothing.
5. The boys were running in order not to be seen by the girls.

Exercise 10.18

A difficult landing

Landing in Britain proves difficult, but a brave standard-bearer sets a good example.

omnibus rebus paratis, Caesar tempus <u>idoneum</u> esse <u>ratus</u> ad Britanniam
navigavit. ubi insulae appropinquabat, copias Britannorum in <u>collibus</u> arma
ferentes conspexit. locus talis erat ut <u>tela</u> e terra altiore facile iaci possent. itaque
Caesar ad aliam partem <u>litoris</u> progressus est. Britanni tamen secuti celeriter ad
5 eundem locum advenerunt. milites igitur, quod <u>simul</u> de navibus in aquam altam
<u>desilire</u> et cum hostibus pugnare debebant, perterriti erant. is tamen qui <u>decimae</u>
legionis <u>aquilam</u> ferebat 'desilite,' inquit 'milites, nisi <u>aquilam</u> hostibus <u>prodere</u>
vultis. ego <u>officium</u> meum pro patria atque imperatore faciam.' his verbis magna
voce dictis, in aquam <u>desiluit</u> et in hostes <u>aquilam</u> ferre coepit. ceteri igitur,
10 <u>simulac</u> hoc viderunt, virtutem eius adeo mirati sunt ut omnes e navibus
<u>desilirent</u>. Britannos de <u>litore pulsos</u> tandem superaverunt.

	idoneus -a -um	suitable
	ratus -a -um	thinking
	collis -is *m*	hill
	telum -i *n*	missile
4	litus -oris *n*	shore
	simul	at the same time
	desilio -ire	I leap down
	decimus -a -um	tenth
	aquila -ae *f*	eagle, legionary standard
7	prodo -ere	I betray
	officium -i *n*	duty
	simulac	as soon as
	pello -ere pepuli pulsus	I drive

- Note the distinction between the adverb *simul* (at the same time) and the
  conjunction *simul ac* or *simulatque* (as soon as), i.e. as soon as X happened,
  Y happened (lit *at the same time and*, because X and Y happened almost
  simultaneously).

VERBS OF FEARING

The verb *timeo* (I fear) can take a direct object or an infinitive, as in English:

omnes nautae periculum maris timebant.
All the sailors feared the danger of the sea.

cur templum intrare times?
Why are you afraid to enter the temple?

But it also commonly takes a clause using *ne* and the imperfect subjunctive, expressing what someone feared might happen. In form this construction is like a negative purpose clause (or indirect command) but here *ne is not negative in English*. The old-fashioned word *lest* gives the sense exactly, but because it is no longer in common use it is better avoided. Modern English just says *that*, or misses it out completely:

> timebamus ne urbs nostra caperetur.
> We feared that our city would be captured.
>
> *or* We feared our city would be captured.

- The reason a negative was used in the first place (though it is not translated as such) is that fearing is thought of as *hoping that something would not happen*. Translating *ne* after a verb of fearing as *not* is a common mistake at GCSE.

- Note that *timeo* means *I fear*; *terreo* means *I frighten* (someone). The English *I am frightened* (describing a state of mind) would normally be represented in Latin by *timeo*, used in the active. Note, however, that *perterritus* (the perfect passive participle of the compound *perterreo*, literally *I frighten thoroughly*) is used as an adjective meaning *terrified*.

It is also possible (though much less common) to express a negative fear, that something might *not* happen (i.e. you *hoped it would* happen). For this Latin uses *ne* followed by *non* (the only place where *ne* and *non* are found together):

> timebam ne custos clamores non audiret.
> I feared that the guard might not hear the shouts.

Exercise 10.19

Translate into English:

1. cives timebant ne urbs ab hostibus caperetur.
2. periculum belli omnes timemus.
3. servus timebat ne a domino inveniretur.
4. captivus timebat ne cibum non acciperet.
5. cur silvam intrare times?

Exercise 10.20

Translate into Latin:

1. I was afraid that the horse would escape.
2. Surely you are not afraid of the enemy's army, soldiers?
3. The slaves were afraid that they would be punished.
4. The boy was afraid to ask for money.
5. The prisoners were afraid they would not be heard.

REVISION CHECKPOINT

Make sure you know:

- indirect commands – *iubeo* (I order) takes an infinitive, other verbs need *ut* and the imperfect subjunctive, negative version *ne* (like purpose clause, but 'in order to' must be avoided here)
- result clauses (focusing on outcome) – signpost word (e.g. *tam* = so) in first half, then a clause with *ut* and the imperfect subjunctive; negative version *ut non*
- how to distinguish between purpose clause, indirect command, and result clause
- verbs of fearing can be followed by direct object, infinitive or clause with *ne* (*here* = that) and the imperfect subjunctive; negative version *ne non*

Exercise 10.21

Legionaries under attack

Soldiers of the Seventh Legion are attacked while repairing ships damaged in a storm, but Caesar comes to the rescue and defeats the Britons, who then seek peace.

eadem nocte multae naves tempestate deletae sunt. hiems iam appropinquabat:
Romani igitur timebant ne in Britannia manere cogerentur. principes Britannorum,
quod sciebant eos paucas naves et nullum cibum habere, etiam hieme pugnare
constituerunt. itaque Romanos, cura confectos, iterum oppugnare parabant. Caesar
5 interea milites septimae legionis et cibum quaerere et naves reliquas reficere iusserat.

subito ei qui portas castrorum custodiebant nuntiaverunt magnam pulveris
nubem videri. Caesar intellexit milites laborantes ab hostibus oppugnatos esse.
statim igitur, quod timebat ne omnes occiderentur, cum exercitu profectus est.
auxilio eius milites septimae legionis se defendere poterant. Caesar tamen propter
10 tempestates diutius pugnare non poterat; postea Britannos in magno proelio
terga vertere coegit. eodem die nuntii ab hostibus missi ad Caesarem venerunt ut
de pace loquerentur. ille imperavit ut obsides darentur; deinde in Galliam rediit.

	hiems hiemis *f*	winter
	princeps -cipis *m*	chief
	pauci -ae -a	few
	cura -ae *f*	care, worry
5	septimus -a -um	seventh
	reliquus -a -um	remaining
	reficio -ere	I repair
	pulvis -eris *m*	dust

	nubes -is *f*	cloud
10	diutius	any longer
	tergum -i *n*	back
	verto -ere verti versus	I turn (something)
	obses -idis *m*	hostage

PLUPERFECT SUBJUNCTIVE

This is the second most common tense of the subjunctive after the imperfect, and the only other one needed for GCSE. We have seen that the *imperfect* subjunctive is formed by adding the basic person endings to the *present* active infinitive. By a similar process the *pluperfect* subjunctive in the active is formed by adding the same basic person endings to the *perfect* active infinitive (perfect stem plus -*isse*), again producing a tense one back from the infinitive involved.

We saw that the imperfect subjunctive cannot be translated in isolation because it depends on its job in a construction. The pluperfect subjunctive in contrast translates just like a normal pluperfect.

conjugation		*1st*	*2nd*	*3rd*	*4th*
sg	1	portavisse-m	monuisse-m	traxisse-m	audivisse-m
	2	portavisse-s	monuisse-s	traxisse-s	audivisse-s
	3	portavisse-t	*etc*	*etc*	*etc*
pl	1	portavisse-mus			
	2	portavisse-tis			
	3	portavisse-nt			

similarly for mixed 3rd/4th conjugation: cepisse-m, cepisse-s, *etc*

Again this also applies to irregular verbs:

verb	*perfect tense*	*perfect infinitive*	*pluperfect subjunctive*
sum	fui	fuisse	fuissem
possum	potui	potuisse	potuissem
eo	i(v)i	i(v)isse	i(v)issem
volo	volui	voluisse	voluissem
nolo	nolui	noluisse	noluissem
malo	malui	maluisse	maluissem
fero	tuli	tulisse	tulissem

The passive form of the pluperfect subjunctive simply takes the ordinary pluperfect passive and puts the auxiliary verb, which is the imperfect of *to be*, into its own subjunctive form:

1st conjugation

sg	1	portatus essem
	2	portatus esses
	3	portatus esset

pl	*1*	portati essemus
	2	portati essetis
	3	portati essent

Similarly for the other conjugations:

2nd	monitus essem
3rd	tractus essem
4th	auditus essem
mixed 3rd/4th	captus essem

The pluperfect subjunctive of a deponent or semi-deponent verb is formed in the same way, but is active in meaning:

conatus essem	(I had tried)
ausus essem	(I had dared)

- As with the ordinary pluperfect passive, the perfect passive participle forming the first part of this tense agrees in number and gender with the subject of the sentence.

Exercise 10.22

Translate into Latin (all subjunctive, using the rules above):

1. He had walked.
2. They had arrived.
3. She had been seen.
4. We had set out.
5. I had departed.

CUM CLAUSES

Clauses telling us *when* or *why* something happened commonly have a word such as *ubi* (when) or *quod* (because) with an ordinary indicative verb:

ubi Romam adveni, de morte imperatoris audivi.
When I (had) arrived in Rome, I heard about the death of the emperor.

servus, quod dormiebat, nihil audivit.
The slave, because he was asleep, heard nothing.

The first example states that two things happened one after the other. The second tells us one thing that is definitely the reason for the other. Indicative verbs are appropriate because facts are being stated.

In either of these sentences *cum* (translated *when* or *since*) with the appropriate tense of the subjunctive could be used instead:

cum Romam advenissem, de morte imperatoris audivi.

servus, cum dormiret, nihil audivit.

In practice the meaning is virtually the same as in the previous versions. The slight difference of emphasis is to convey a *suggested reason*: it was *only* by arriving then that I heard the news (and so not just a coincidence of time); it was *presumably* because the slave was asleep (rather than that he was stone deaf or very drunk).

- Note in the first example above that *ubi* is used with a perfect tense indicative verb (though this can be translated as a pluperfect in English), because the thought is 'after X happened, Y happened', but the *cum* version uses the pluperfect subjunctive, because the thought here is 'in a situation when X had happened, Y happened'.

Cum clauses are very common. The imperfect or pluperfect subjunctive here (in contrast to other subjunctive clauses we have met) translates according to sense, coming out as the same tense in English. The word *since* is favoured as a translation of *cum* because it suggests 'a *when* that is also a *because*' (this use of *since* must be distinguished from its other meaning *from the time that*), though *when* sometimes sounds better.

- Sometimes a *cum* clause is used when an ablative absolute would also have been possible (e.g. *cum urbs capta esset* . . . or *urbe capta* . . . for *when the city had been captured*): Latin often has several ways of saying the same thing.
- Note that this *cum* is a completely separate word from the preposition *cum* used with the ablative and meaning *with*. These are *homonyms*: see the list of words with more than one meaning (Appendix 6, p. 271).

Exercise 10.23

Translate into English:

1. cum Romam advenissem, domum amici petere coepi.
2. cives, cum de victoria audivissent, diu gaudebant.
3. cum ceteri iam discessissent, nos quoque domum redire constituimus.
4. senator, cum ad forum ambularet, ab inimico oppugnatus est.
5. cum senex epistulam filiae legisset, multo laetior erat.
6. pueri, cum montem ascenderent, corpus invenerunt.
7. cum custos dormiret, captivi effugere poterant.
8. dominus, cum totam rem intellexisset, servum liberari iussit.
9. cum pater iratus esse videretur, liberi tacite laborabant.
10. miles, cum tot vulnera passus esset, mox mortuus est.

Exercise 10.24

Translate into Latin (using cum clauses):

1. Since it was night, we could not find the way.
2. When they had heard the messenger's words, the citizens were very sad.
3. Since they had worked well, the girls received prizes.
4. When we were guarding the gate, we saw an army approaching.
5. Since I had read the book, I immediately understood everything.

Exercise 10.25

Vercingetorix

Late in his time in Gaul, Caesar faces a rebellion led by Vercingetorix.

Vercingetorix princeps Arvernorum erat. alias gentes convocatas ducens, exercitum
Caesaris proelio vicit. multi milites Romani occisi sunt. Galli tamen inter se semper
vehementer pugnabant: Vercingetorix non poterat omnibus persuadere ut unum
animum haberent. Caesar igitur altero proelio Vercingetorigem superavit. ille
5   victus se Caesari scaenice dedit: nam circum castra Romana in equo pulcherrimo
equitavit; arma sua deposuit; pro pedibus imperatoris Romani tacite sedebat.
deinde abductus est. postea Romae captivus quinque annos tenebatur; tandem in
triumpho Caesaris civibus ostentus est. tum in carcere interfectus est; Caesar
interea in templo dona deis dabat.

	Vercingetorix -igis *m*	Vercingetorix
	Arverni -orum *m pl*	the Arverni (*a tribe in Gaul*)
	convoco -are -avi -atus	I call together, I gather
	vehementer	(*here*) violently
5	scaenice	dramatically
	equito -are -avi	I ride
	pes pedis *m*	foot
	triumphus -i *m*	triumphal procession
	carcer -eris *m*	prison

Figure 10.1 *Vercingetorix surrenders to Caesar.* (Photo by MPI/Getty Images)

INDIRECT QUESTIONS (1)

This construction reports a direct question, just as an indirect statement reports a statement and an indirect command reports a command:

direct:	cur taces?	(*present*)
	Why are you silent?	
indirect:	servum rogavi cur taceret.	
	I asked the slave why he was silent.	
direct:	quis epistulam scripsit?	(*past*)
	Who wrote the letter?	
indirect:	senex filiam rogavit quis epistulam scripsisset.	
	The old man asked his daughter who had written the letter.	
direct:	quid facies?	(*future*)
	What will you do?	
indirect:	puellam rogavi quid factura esset.	
	I asked the girl what she was going to (*or* would) do.	

Latin moves a tense back in changing from the direct to the reported form, just like English does, but makes the verb subjunctive. A present tense in the direct question comes out as an imperfect, a past tense as a pluperfect, and a future as a 'future in the past' (made up of the imperfect subjunctive of *to be* with a future participle). Each translates naturally into English ('tense by sense').

The question words asking for specific information (e.g. *who, what, where, how* – see p. 71 for a complete list) are used in indirect questions just as in direct ones. An indirect question is often used when the original direct question is only implied rather than actually asked:

difficile erat nobis cognoscere quid accidisset.
It was difficult for us to find out what had happened.

Here the direct question *What happened?* might have existed only in our minds. A verb suggesting *asking* need not be involved at all:

puer nuntiavit quid fecisset.
The boy reported what he had done.

Here the idea is that he said *what it was* that he had done, again answering an implied question *What did you do?*

- Note the difference between an indirect question and a relative clause:

    (1) *indirect question*
        puellam rogavi quem ibi vidisset.
        I asked the girl whom she had seen there.

(2) *relative clause*

puella nihil dicere poterat de homine quem ibi viderat.
The girl could say nothing about the man whom she had seen there.

• The key identifier of an indirect question is the presence of a question word with the subjunctive.

Exercise 10.26

Translate into English:

1. puellam rogavi quot libros portaret.

2. dominus servos rogavit unde cibum emissent.

3. cognovistine quid senatores de hac re constituissent?

4. nemo nobis dicere poterat ubi captivus nunc esset.

5. imperator rogatus est quot milites in proelio occisi essent.

6. senem rogavimus quis equos in agrum pepulisset.

7. rogati sumus quo festinaremus.

8. omnes cognoscere conabantur quantum praemium iuvenis accepisset.

9. difficile erat intellegere quales essent dei.

10. ancilla <u>nesciebat</u> quomodo pecunia ablata esset.

nescio -ire -ivi   I do not know

Exercise 10.27

S&C

Translate into Latin:

1. We asked the girl where she had come from.

2. The citizens did not know who was in the temple.

3. I was asking the soldiers what sort of horses they had.

4. The senator asked the messenger what he had heard about the war.

5. No-one was able to find out how the walls had been destroyed.

INDIRECT QUESTIONS (2)

With questions asking if something is the case (to which the answer will be *yes* or *no*), there is a very important difference between direct and indirect ones. *Direct* questions can be slanted according to the answer the questioner hopes for:

-ne (*added to first word*)	is it the case?	(*open*)
nonne	surely . . .?	(*hoping for the answer* yes)
num	surely . . . not?	(*hoping for the answer* no)

In an *indirect* question this distinction cannot be shown, and <u>any</u> question to which the answer will be *yes* or *no* is (rather confusingly) introduced by *num*, here meaning *whether*. Note therefore the important rule:

| num | *in a* <u>direct</u> *question* | surely . . . not? |
| | *in an* <u>indirect</u> *question* | whether |

servum rogavi num fratrem meum vidisset.
I asked the slave whether he had seen my brother.

The original direct question reported here might have been a *-ne, nonne,* or *num* type: all come out the same in the indirect form.

- Note that *if* is another possible translation of *num* in an indirect question, but it should not be confused with *si* (if), which is used only in a conditional clause.

Exercise 10.28

Translate into English:

1. liberos rogavi num laeti essent.
2. dominus servum rogavit num laborem confecisset.
3. cognoscere non poteramus num consul adesset.
4. puer rogatus est num pecuniam invenisset.
5. mater filiam rogavit num Romam ire vellet.

Exercise 10.29

Translate into Latin:

1. The woman asked the girl whether she had seen the horse.
2. The father often used to ask his son whether he was working well.
3. I asked the old man whether he wanted to return home.
4. We wanted to find out whether the woman had heard a shout.
5. Nobody knew whether the ship had arrived.

REVISION CHECKPOINT

Make sure you know:

- formation of the pluperfect subjunctive – active from the perfect active infinitive with basic person endings (e.g. *portavissem*), passive from the indicative equivalent, making the auxiliary verb subjunctive (e.g. *portatus essem*)
- *cum* (when *or* since) clauses using the imperfect or pluperfect subjunctive according to sense, used to explain the time and/or reason something happened
- indirect questions using the imperfect or pluperfect according to sense (one tense back from the direct question, as in English), introduced by a question word asking for specific information, or *num* (here = *whether*)

Exercise 10.30

Crossing the Rubicon

After his successful campaigns as proconsul in Gaul, Caesar decides not to disband his army and return to Rome as a private citizen but to march on Rome with his troops in defiance of the law (49 BC). His crossing of the Rubicon has become proverbial for passing a point of no return.

Caesar, cum in Gallia ac Britannia octo annos iam pugnavisset, Romam redire volebat ut consul iterum esset. sed nesciebat quomodo hoc facere posset. multos enim inimicos in urbe habebat, inter quos erant <u>Pompeius</u> et plurimi senatores. itaque, quod periculum timebat, sine exercitu regredi nolebat. imperatores tamen
5   Romani copias in <u>Italiam</u> ducere <u>legibus</u> <u>vetabantur</u>.

Pompeius -i *m*	Pompey
Italia -ae *f*	Italy
lex legis *f*	law
veto -are	I forbid

Caesar igitur, cum ad <u>Rubiconem</u> advenisset (flumen enim Galliam ab Italia
<u>dividebat</u>), de bello futuro diu <u>cogitabat</u>. militibus suis 'etiam nunc' inquit 'redire
possumus. si tamen hoc flumen transibimus, contra patriam pugnare cogemur.'
tandem voce magna clamavit: '<u>alea</u> iacta est. nunc ibimus <u>quo</u> inimici nos
10 vocant.' deinde cum exercitu flumen transiit. cum Caesar urbi appropinquaret,
Pompeius fugere paravit: 'omnes' inquit 'qui patriam et <u>libertatem</u> habere malunt
quam imperium <u>tyranni</u> ferre, me sequi debent.'

6	Rubico -onis *m*	the Rubicon (*a small river dividing Gaul and Roman territory*)
	divido -ere	I divide
	cogito -are -avi -atus	I think, I consider
9	alea -ae *f*	die (*pl* dice)
	quo	(*not a question*) to where
	libertas -atis *f*	freedom
	tyrannus -i *m*	tyrant

Figure 10.2 *Caesar crosses the Rubicon.* (Photo by Bob Thomas/Popperfoto/Getty Images)

Exercise 10.31

Civil war

After returning to Rome, Caesar fights a civil war. His rival Pompey flees to Greece but is defeated there, then to Egypt, where he is killed (48 BC).

Caesar postquam Romam rediit bellum <u>civile</u> gerebat. <u>Pompeius</u>, quamquam multi senatores ei favebant, ad <u>Graeciam</u> fugit: ibi cum copiis Caesaris diu pugnabat. Pompeius multas naves et exercitum <u>validum</u> habebat, sed <u>felix</u> non erat. olim Caesar in proelio <u>cedere</u> coactus est. quod tamen Pompeius non <u>institit</u>, Caesar

5 'Pompeius' inquit '<u>infelix</u> est'. credebat enim inimicum nescire quomodo vincere posset. tandem ad <u>Pharsalum</u> Caesar eum magno proelio vicit. postea Pompeius ad <u>Aegyptum</u> fugit. cum advenisset, occisus est a militibus <u>Ptolemaei</u>, qui caput eius Caesari misit; <u>iacebat</u> prope mare <u>truncus</u>. Ptolemaeus hoc fecit ut a Caesare laudaretur. ille tamen iratus erat, quod <u>clementiam</u> hostibus victis ostendere volebat.

	civilis -e	civil, within the state
	Pompeius -i *m*	Pompey
	Graecia -ae *f*	Greece
	validus -a -um	strong
3	felix -icis	fortunate, happy
	cedo -ere	I give way
	insto -are institi	I press forward, I follow up an advantage
	infelix -icis	unlucky, unhappy
6	Pharsalus -i *f*	Pharsalus (*a town in central Greece*)
	Aegyptus -i *f*	Egypt
	Ptolemaeus -i *m*	Ptolemy (*XIII, ruler of Egypt 51-about 47 BC*)
	iaceo -ere iacui	lie
8	truncus -i *m*	headless body
	clementia -ae *f*	mercy

CONNECTING RELATIVE

A connecting relative is the relative pronoun (*qui, quae, quod*) used to start a new sentence (or a new clause after a semi-colon, which is virtually a new sentence). The pronoun refers back to someone or something mentioned in the previous sentence, thus connecting the content of the two sentences. The appropriate translation here is not the usual *who/which* but (according to number, gender and context) for example *he, she, it, they, these things*: the trick is to identify the part of the relative pronoun that is being used, then think of and translate the equivalent bit of *is, ea, id* or *hic, haec, hoc*.

ancilla tandem advenit. quam ubi vidi, laetissimus eram.

lit   The slave-girl finally arrived. When I saw whom, I was very happy. (quam *here doing the job of* eam)

i.e.   The slave-girl finally arrived. When I saw <u>her</u>, I was very happy.

rex nuntios misit; qui cum advenissent totam rem nobis narraverunt.

lit   The king sent messengers. Who, when they had arrived, told us the whole story.
(qui *here doing the job of* ei)

i.e.   The king sent messengers. When <u>they</u> had arrived, they told us the whole story.

victoria tandem Romae relata est. quibus verbis auditis, omnes gavisi sumus.

lit   The victory finally was reported in Rome. With which words having been heard, we all rejoiced.
(quibus *here doing the job of* his)

i.e.   The victory finally was reported in Rome. When <u>these</u> words had been heard (*or* When we had heard <u>these</u> words), we all rejoiced.

The connecting relative is very common and it is important to be able to recognise it. It is often found as part of an ablative absolute or a *cum* clause beginning the new sentence. Because the relative pronoun needs to be the first word in the new sentence, some adjustment of word order may be needed in English.

Particular care is needed with *quam* and *quod* because they have several different meanings: see the list of words with more than one meaning (Appendix 6, p. 271). Only context and sense enable you to tell whether *quod* starting a sentence is a connecting relative or *because*. Note also that *quod* as a connecting relative can be used without a particular neuter word as the antecedent, instead referring more loosely to the whole of the previous sentence:

milites nostri omnes effugerunt. quod ubi vidimus, laetissimi eramus.

lit   Our soldiers all escaped. Which (thing) when we saw, we were very happy.
(quod *here doing the job of* id *or* hoc)

i.e.   Our soldiers all escaped. When we saw <u>this</u>, we were very happy.

- The adverb *quo* (to where) in its non-question sense can also be used as a connecting relative, translated as *to there* or just *there*:

turba in foro antea convenerat. quo cum advenissem, nihil inveni.

lit   A crowd had previously gathered in the form. To where when I (had) arrived, I found nothing.

i.e.   A crowd had previously gathered in the forum. When I (had) arrived <u>there</u>, I found nothing.

Exercise 10.32

Translate into English:

1. equum validum olim vendideram. quem iterum visum libenter emi.

2. senator multa promisit. quibus factis, erat <u>gaudium</u> in urbe.

3. miles manum hostium solus repulsit; quod ubi vidimus, mirati sumus.

4. nuntius res <u>diras</u> rettulit. quibus verbis dictis, omnes tacuerunt.

5. ille captivus Romam fugit. quo eum secuti tandem cepimus.

gaudium -i   *n*   joy
dirus -a -um   dreadful

Exercise 10.33

S&C

Translate into Latin (using connecting relatives):

1. I had once loved that girl. When I caught sight of her again, I happily greeted her.
2. Our army was crushed. When we had heard this, we were terrified.
3. For a long time I used to admire that villa. Finally I was able to buy it.
4. The soldiers heard shouts in the wood. Having advanced to there, they found a body.
5. The mistress was saved from danger by her slave. When she had praised him, she set him free on account of his courage.

Exercise 10.34

Triumph and mortality

Caesar celebrates a speedy victory with a slogan that became famous (46 BC). He offers some thoughts on ambition and death.

olim Caesar cum exercitu valido ad <u>Pontum</u> profectus est, ubi rex <u>Pompeio</u>
faverat. quo cum advenisset, hostes quattuor horis vicit. postea Romae in
<u>triumpho</u> <u>titulus</u> trium verborum ferebatur: 'veni, vidi, vici'. quod tamen multos
inimicos in urbe habebat, comites ei persuadere conabantur ut custodes haberet;
5 quibus Caesar 'malo' inquit '<u>semel</u> mori quam mortem semper timere.' ubi cives
quidam eum ut regem salutaverunt, dixit se nolle sic vocari: 'Caesar sum, non
rex.' postea cum amicis cenabat, quorum unus eum rogavit 'qualem mortem
optimam esse putas?' cui Caesar respondit '<u>inopinatam</u>'; quod postea accidit.

	Pontus -i *m*	Pontus (*the Black Sea region*)
	Pompeius -i *m*	Pompey
	triumphus -i *m*	triumphal procession
	titulus -i *m*	notice, placard
5	semel	once
	inopinatus -a -um	unexpected

AD WITH THE GERUNDIVE TO EXPRESS PURPOSE

This is another way of expressing purpose: a less common alternative to a clause with *ut* and the imperfect subjunctive. A *gerundive* is an adjective made from a verb (not counted as a participle, but with similar characteristics). Its literal meaning is *needing to be X-ed*: it is *passive* and has the idea of *necessity*. It does not have a tense, but refers to a sort of possible future (just as an imperative does): something that has not happened yet, but should. It is formed from the verb stem, the characteristic vowel(s) for the conjugation (as in the imperfect tense or present participle) and *-ndus* (with normal 2-1-2 endings). Thus:

gerundive:

portandus -a -um	needing to be carried
monendus -a -um	needing to be warned
trahendus -a -um	needing to be dragged
audiendus -a -um	needing to be heard
capiendus -a -um	needing to be taken

It is easy to recognise because few other Latin words have the combination of letters *-nd-* with vowels either side. The gerundive has various jobs in more advanced Latin, but the only use of it met at GCSE is with *ad* to express purpose. This use of *ad* for an aim or purpose is an extension of its normal idea of *motion towards*.

> misit nuntios ad regem necandum.
> *lit*   He sent messengers (with a view) to the king needing to be killed.
> *i.e.* He sent messengers to kill the king.

- This sentence means the same as *misit nuntios ut regem necarent*.

The English translation of the gerundive used after *ad* should get away both from the passive and from the idea of necessity. This may seem a complex change, but if you think of the basic sense of each word (*ad* = to, *necare* = kill, *rex* = king), taking the noun as the object of the verb expressed by the gerundive, the meaning should be obvious.

Further examples:

Romam festinavi ad fratrem inveniendum.
I hurried home to find my brother.

imperator nuntium misit ad cives monendos.
The general sent the messenger to warn the citizens.

visne ad villam meam venire ad vinum bibendum?
Do you want to come to my house to drink wine?

- Note in each of these sentences how the gerundive agrees (in number and gender) with the accusative noun.

USES OF *DUM*

In a time clause with an indicative verb *dum* means *while*, and is used with a present tense verb (usually translated as an imperfect) to express the idea of one thing going on when another thing interrupts it.

> dum per silvam ambulo, pecuniam inveni.
> *lit*   While I am walking through the wood, I found some money.
> *i.e.* While I was walking through the wood, I found some money.

- This is an example of the present tense used of past events for vividness (as we do in English when telling a joke: 'There are these three men on a desert island . . .'), or it could be compared to the way a present participle is used, its tense expressing relationship to that of the main verb.

But *dum* can also (less commonly) be used as yet another way of expressing purpose. With an imperfect subjunctive it means *until*, implying purpose as well as time:

> cives in foro manebant dum senator adveniret.
> The citizens waited in the forum until the senator arrived (*or* could arrive).
> *or*   The citizens waited in the forum for the senator to arrive.

This is in effect a disguised purpose clause: they waited *so that he could* arrive with them still there (he may or may not actually have done so); as usual, the subjunctive here emphasises a possibility rather than a fact.

Exercise 10.35

Translate into English:

1. puer ad urbem ambulavit ad librum emendum.
2. milites dum montem ascendunt ab hostibus conspecti sunt.
3. femina domi manere iussa est dum epistulam acciperet.
4. iuvenes ad tabernam ambulaverunt ad vinum bibendum.
5. dum custos dormit, captivi effugerunt.
6. pueri in via manebant dum puellae redirent.
7. Romam cras iter faciam ad novum templum videndum.
8. imperator exspectabat dum naves advenirent.
9. servus dum in agro laborat gladium in terra celatum invenit.
10. cives in foro aderant ad verba nuntii audienda.

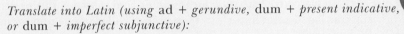

Exercise 10.36

Translate into Latin (using ad + *gerundive,* dum + *present indicative, or* dum + *imperfect subjunctive):*

1. I went home to prepare dinner.
2. While the girls were waiting, the boys arrived.
3. The old man was shouting in order to warn the children.
4. We decided to remain in the forum until we saw the senator.
5. The army was sent to capture the city.

Background: Caesar reigns supreme

After several stints as consul and dictator, Caesar finally had himself declared 'perpetual dictator' (a contradiction in terms, by traditional standards, as the appointment of a dictator was usually a temporary measure). His increasingly monarchical style (despite his show of reluctance to be called a king), and the ill-feeling aroused by his affair with the Egyptian queen Cleopatra, led to discontent among some members of the Senate, and plots against his life began to be made.

Exercise 10.37

Plotting against Caesar

Caesar now holds supreme power in Rome, but his affair with Cleopatra provokes suspicion and his enemies in the senate discuss how he might be killed.

Caesar summum imperium Romae iam tenebat. omnibus enim hostibus in bello necatis, multa praemia accepit: 'pater patriae' vocatus est; in curia supra ceteros senatores sedebat; nomen 'Iulius' septimo mensi anni datum est; coronam lauream semper gerere poterat. dictator in perpetuum factus erat. alii tamen
5 senatores timebant ne rex esse vellet; alii credebant eum Alexandriam caput imperii Romani facturum esse, ut cum Cleopatra regina Romanos regeret.

itaque nonnulli senatores consilium ad Caesarem necandum capere volebant. M. Brutum optimum ducem futurum esse putabant. quod tamen palam loqui non audebant, nuntium ei miserunt: 'dormis, Brute'; quibus verbis ei
10 persuaserunt. de modo mortis alii alia dicebant. alius senator eum per Viam Sacram ambulantem oppugnare volebat, alius de ponte in flumen trudere. tandem Caesarem in curia Idibus Martiis necare constituerunt, ut libertatem civium et dignitatem Romae defenderent.

	curia -ae *f*	senate-house
	supra (+ *acc*)	above
	Iulius -i *m*	Julius (*i.e.* July)
	septimus -a -um	seventh
3	mensis -is *m*	month
	corona -ae *f*	wreath
	laureus -a -um	of laurel leaves (*usually worn by generals in triumphal procession*)
	dictator -oris *m*	dictator
4	in perpetuum	for life, permanently
	Alexandria -ae *f*	Alexandria (*a large coastal city in Egypt*)
	caput -itis *n*	(*here*) capital
	Cleopatra -ae *f*	Cleopatra (*queen of Egypt*)
8	M. Brutus -i *m*	Marcus Brutus
	palam	openly
	Via Sacra *f*	Sacred Way (*a main street in Rome*)
	pons pontis *m*	bridge
	trudo -ere	I push
12	Idus -uum Martiae -arum *f pl*	the Ides (*i.e.* 15th) of March (*the Roman calendar had landmark days in each month*)
	libertas -atis *f*	freedom
	dignitas -atis *f*	dignity

TRANSLATING COMPLEX SENTENCES

Latin typically does not tell a story in a series of short sentences (or clauses equivalent to separate sentences, joined by *and* or *but*); it prefers instead more complex sentences with one *main* clause (which could stand alone) and one or more *subordinate* clauses (which would not make sense in isolation). Here are some typical examples of subordinate clauses:

(1)   When we arrived in Rome . . .
(2)   . . . to find the book
(3)   If you give me the money . . .
(4)   . . . in order to guard the walls
(5)   . . . whom I saw yesterday
(6)   Although I had heard nothing . . .
(7)   . . . that she understood everything
(8)   Since he had said this . . .
(9)   . . . who had sent the letter
(10) . . . where they had been before

Try identifying which type of clause each one is (some could be more than one). Many of the constructions described in this book count as subordinate clauses.

To find your way through a difficult sentence, try to identify the main clause; bracket off (mentally or on paper) the subordinate bit or bits; then decide how to put the whole thing together.

Thought needs to be given to appropriate expression in English:

>   milites, postquam in castra advenerunt, cibum quaesiverunt.
> *lit*   The soldiers, after they arrived in the camp, looked for food.

A very common mistake in GCSE is to write:

> The soldiers, after they arrived in the camp, they looked for food.

This is wrong because it puts in too many subjects (*The soldiers . . . they . . . they*). There are two verbs, and two clauses, so there can only be two subjects. But the candidate who made this mistake sensed rightly that the literal translation sounds awkward. The best solution here is to put *the soldiers* inside the subordinate clause:

> After the soldiers arrived in the camp, they looked for food.

A participle often needs to be translated as a subordinate clause. A perfect passive participle can be translated as an active verb if it is clear from the context that the action has been done by the person who is subject of the sentence:

>   puer puellam conspectam salutavit.
> *lit*   The boy greeted the having been caught sight of girl.
> *i.e.* The boy greeted the girl he had caught sight of.

An ablative absolute is often translated as a subordinate clause:

> his verbis dictis nuntius discessit.
> When he had said these words the messenger left.

But it is also acceptable to make two main clauses, joined by *and*: the clauses are now *co-ordinated* (i.e. both of equal importance):

> The messenger said these words and left.

Double subordination is when one subordinate clause has another clause (or an ablative absolute, or other participle phrase) inside it. It is usually better in English to make the two subordinate elements parallel to each other:

>   milites misi ut rege interfecto urbem caperent.
> *lit*   I sent soldiers in order that, with the king having been killed, they could capture the city.
> *i.e.* I sent soldiers to kill the king and capture the city.

Here the ablative absolute has been treated like another purpose clause.

> cum senator epistula lecta surrexisset, omnes tacuerunt.
>
> *lit* When the senator, with the letter having been read, had stood up, everyone was silent.
>
> *i.e.* When the senator had read the letter and stood up, everyone was silent.

Here the ablative absolute has been treated like another *cum* clause.

> deus dixit hunc hominem, Romam ingressum, regem futurum esse.
>
> *lit* The god said that this man, having entered Rome, would be king.
>
> *i.e.* The god said that this man would enter Rome and be king.

Here the participle phrase has been treated like another indirect statement.

Sometimes a double subordination can be retained in English:

> cum omnes qui audire volebant advenissent, senator loqui coepit.
>
> When everyone who wanted to listen had arrived, the senator began to speak.

Here the relative clause has been translated literally, inside the *cum* clause.

The following exercises are deliberately designed to illustrate the most difficult sentences you could find in a GCSE paper.

Exercise 10.38

Translate into English:

1. cum hostes urbe incensa discessissent, cives nesciebant ubi habitare possent.

2. ubi est puella quae promisit se epistula scripta cenam paraturam esse?

3. liberos convocatos rogavi quid postridie agere vellent.

4. nomen huius pueri olim auditum in animo tenere non poteram.

5. omnes timebamus ne templum tempestate deleretur; quod cum accidisset, novum templum aedificare constituimus.

6. nonnullis militibus relictis ad portas castrorum custodiendas, imperator cum ceteris profectus est.

7. servus dixit se in via manere dum ancilla ad tabernam missa rediret.

8. nuntius, ubi patres quorum filii aberant in foro vidit, de proelio loqui coepit.

9. nautis imperavi ut labore confecto navem ad mare portarent.

10. miles qui multa vulnera iam acceperat gladio rapto egressus est ut iterum pugnaret.

Exercise 10.39

Translate into Latin:

1. The boy said that when he had read the book he would finish his work.
2. The senator persuaded everyone who was in the forum to wait until the messenger arrived.
3. The citizens were afraid that the city would be captured and they would all be killed.
4. I decided to ask the old man, who was present yesterday, what he had seen in the street.
5. The slave wanted to find the stolen money so he would not be punished by the master.

REVISION CHECKPOINT

Make sure you know:

- how to recognise a connecting relative – the relative pronoun (*qui, quae, quod*) starting a sentence, translated not *who/which*, but e.g. *he, she, it, they*
- the use of *ad* with the gerundive to express purpose (e.g. *ad regem necandum* = to kill the king)
- the use of *dum* (= while) with a present indicative (translated as an imperfect) to describe an action in the course of which something else happened
- the use of *dum* (= until) with an imperfect subjunctive as yet another way of expressing purpose
- how to handle complex sentences, especially ones involving double subordination

Exercise 10.40

Death on the Ides

Ignoring several warnings, Caesar goes to the senate-house and is assassinated by Brutus and others (44 BC). The event was later to be immortalised in Shakespeare's play Julius Caesar.

dum Caesar deis <u>sacrificat</u>, <u>Spurinna haruspex</u> eum monuit: '<u>cave Idus Martias</u>.'
deinde equus qui Caesarem trans <u>Rubiconem</u> portaverat nuntiatus est in agro

Figure 10.3 *Medieval woodcut showing Caesar's assassination.* (Photo by: Leemage/UIG via Getty Images)

lacrimans cibum consumere nolle. pridie Idus Calpurnia, uxor Caesaris, in somnio domum deletam maritumque necatum vidit. itaque eo die Caesar prima

5 luce domi manere constituit. coniurati igitur D. Brutum miserunt ut Caesarem ad curiam adduceret. ille Caesari 'senatores' inquit 'te exspectant, quod rem magnam in manibus habent.' Caesar igitur, iam audacior, quinta hora profectus est.

	sacrifico -are	I make a sacrifice
	Spurinna -ae *m*	Spurinna
	haruspex -icis *m*	soothsayer (*examined innards of sacrificed animals to foretell future*)
1	cave	beware of!
	Idus -uum Martiae -arum *f pl*	the Ides (i.e. 15th) March
	Rubico -onis *m*	the Rubicon
	pridie	on the day before (+ *acc*)
	Calpurnia -ae *f*	Calpurnia
4	somnium -i *n*	dream
	coniuratus -i *m*	conspirator
	D. Brutus -i *m*	Decimus Brutus (*cousin of M. Brutus*)
	curia -ae *f*	senate-house
	quintus -a -um	fifth (*the fifth hour was mid/late morning*)
7		

dum <u>curiam</u> intrat Spurinnam prope <u>ianuam</u> conspectum <u>derisit</u>, cum <u>Idus</u>
10 <u>Martiae</u> sine periculo venissent. <u>haruspex</u> tamen respondit eas venisse, sed non
<u>praeteriisse</u>. postquam Caesar <u>curiam</u> intravit, <u>circumventus est</u> a <u>coniuratis</u> qui
<u>pugiones</u> habebant. inter quos <u>M. Brutum</u>, qui amicus fuerat, conspexit; 'et tu,
Brute?' rogavit. deinde <u>togam</u> pro <u>vultu</u> traxit. coniurati Caesarem <u>foderunt</u>, qui
et ad pedes <u>statuae</u> <u>Pompeii</u> cecidit: vulneribus <u>viginti tribus</u> interfectus erat.

15 in hac re M. Brutus et D. Brutus <u>exemplum</u> <u>proavi</u> clarissimi sequebantur. nam
<u>L. Brutus</u> regem <u>Tarquinium Superbum</u> Roma olim expulerat.

	ianua -ae *f*	door
	derideo -ere derisi	I laugh at, I ridicule
	praetereo -ire -ii	I pass, I go past
	circumvenio -ire circumveni	
11	circumventus	I surround
	pugio -onis *m*	dagger
	M. Brutus -i *m*	Marcus Brutus
	toga -ae *f*	toga
	vultus -us *m*	face
13	fodio -ire fodi	I stab
	statua -ae *f*	statue
	Pompeius -i *m*	Pompey (*former rival of Caesar*)
	viginti tres	twenty-three
	exemplum -i *n*	example
15	proavus -i *m*	ancestor, forefather
	L. Brutus -i *m*	Lucius Brutus (*traditionally one of the first two consuls in 509* BC: *see Exercise 6.38 in Part 1*)
	Tarquinius -i Superbus -i *m*	Tarquinius Superbus ('the Proud')

SUMMARY OF CHAPTER TEN GRAMMAR

Imperfect subjunctive:
Formed from present active infinitive with basic person endings (active *-m, -s, -t, -mus, -tis, -nt*, passive *-r, -ris, -tur, -mur, -mini, -ntur*), e.g *portarem, portarer*. Translation depends on construction, but the subjunctive basically expresses possibility rather than fact.

Purpose clauses:
Latin does not use the infinitive for purpose as English does, but a clause with *ut* and the imperfect subjunctive, e.g. *Romam festanavi ut imperatorem viderem* (I hurried to Rome in order to see the emperor). A negative purpose clause uses *ne* instead of *ut*.

Fourth and fifth declension nouns:
A few nouns belong to the fourth declension, e.g. *manus* (hand) and a few to the fifth, e.g. *dies* (day).

Indirect commands:
iubeo (I order) takes an infinitive like English; other verbs take an *ut* clause (like a purpose clause, but translation *in order to* must be avoided here). A negative version uses *ne* instead of *ut*. Some verbs take the dative, e.g. *imperavi puero ut festinaret* (I ordered the boy to hurry).

Result clauses:
After a signpost word for *so . . . in* the first half (*tam, adeo* or a more specialised alternative), a result clause uses *ut* and the imperfect subjunctive, e.g. *tam iratus erat ut servos puniret* (he was so angry that he punished the slaves). A negative version uses *ut . . . non*. Distinguish a result clause (focusing on the outcome) from a purpose clause (focusing on the intention).

Verbs of fearing:
A verb of fearing may be followed by a direct object, an infinitive or (most often) a clause using *ne* (= that) and the imperfect subjunctive, e.g. *servus timebat ne puniretur* (the slave feared that he would be punished); *ne* here is not a negative. A negative version uses *ne . . . non*.

Pluperfect subjunctive:
The active pluperfect subjunctive is formed from the perfect active infinitive with basic person endings (*-m, -s, -t, -mus, -tis, -nt*), e.g. *portavissem*. The passive makes the auxiliary verb subjunctive, e.g. *portatus essem*. Unlike the imperfect subjunctive, the pluperfect is always translated like the equivalent indicative, e.g. *I had carried, I had been carried*.

Cum clauses:
Clauses using *cum* (when/since) with the subjunctive (imperfect or pluperfect according to sense), express time, reason or supposed reason (often much like a clause with *ubi* or *quod* and the indicative).

Indirect questions:
An indirect question has a subjunctive verb (imperfect or pluperfect according to sense, in either case a tense back from the original direct question). The normal question words are used, except that any question to which the answer will be *yes* or *no* uses *num* (whether).

Connecting relative:
If the relative pronoun (*qui*) starts a sentence (referring back to someone/something mentioned in the previous one), it needs to be translated not as *who/which* but like the equivalent part of *is* or *hic*, e.g. *quos ubi vidi, laetus eram* (when I saw them, I was happy).

Ad with the gerundive to express purpose:
Verb stem with characteristic vowel(s) and *-ndus -a -um* forms the gerundive (literally *needing to be X-ed*). It is used as an adjective with a noun after *ad* to express purpose, e.g. *ad urbem capiendam* (to capture the city), as an alternative to a clause with *ut* and the subjunctive.

Uses of *dum*:
With a present indicative (translated as an imperfect), *dum* means *while* and describes an action during which something else happened, e.g. *dum domum ambulo, pecuniam inveni* (while I was walking home I found some money). With an imperfect subjunctive it means *until*, e.g. *manebam dum imperator adveniret* (I was waiting until the emperor arrived).

Translating complex sentences:
In a Latin sentence with several subordinate elements, first identify the main clause, then decide how best to accommodate the other parts in English. Double subordination (e.g. an ablative absolute inside a purpose clause, e.g. *so that, with X done, they could do Y*) can sometimes be preserved, but is often better made into two parallel elements (*so that they could do X and then Y*).

CHAPTER TEN VOCABULARY

adeo	so much, so greatly, to such an extent
brevis -e	short, brief
cogito -are -avi -atus	I think, I consider
cum	when, since (+ *subj*)
cura -ae *f*	care, worry
dies -ei *m*	day
diligens -entis	careful
dirus -a -um	dreadful
domus -us (domum = home[wards], domi = at home) *f*	house, home
dum	while (+ *present tense translated as imperfect*); until (+ *subj*)
exercitus -us *m*	army
faveo -ere favi fautus	I favour, I support (+ *dat*)
felix -icis	fortunate, happy
gaudium -i *n*	joy, pleasure
iaceo -ere iacui	I lie, I am lying down
ianua -ae *f*	door
impero -are -avi -atus	I order, I command (+ *dat*)
infelix -icis	unlucky, unhappy
ita	so, in this way, in such a way, to such an extent
itaque	and so, therefore
legio -onis *f*	legion
lux lucis *f*	light
manus -us *f*	hand; group of people
ne	that . . . not, so that . . . not; (*after verb of fearing*) that, lest
nescio -ire -ivi	I do not know
num	whether (*in indirect question*)
occido -ere -i occisus	I kill
oro -are -avi -atus	I beg
paene	almost
pello -ere pepuli pulsus	I drive
pes pedis *m*	foot
poena -ae *f*	punishment
poenas do	I pay the penalty, I am punished
postridie	on the next day
princeps -cipis *m*	chief; emperor
procedo -ere processi	I advance, I proceed
quo	(*not question*) to where
res rei *f*	thing, matter, event
simul	at the same time
simulac/simulatque	as soon as

spes spei *f*	hope
talis -e	such, of such a kind
tam	so
tantus -a -um	so great, such a great
tempus -oris *n*	time
tot	so many
umquam	ever
unde	(*not question*) from where
ut	(+ *subj*) that, so that, in order to;
	(+ *indicative, or no verb*) as, when
validus -a -um	strong
vehementer	violently; loudly
verto -ere verti versus	I turn (something)

49 new words

Coverage of all GCSE grammar and vocabulary is now complete.

Chapter Eleven

REVISION PASSAGES

The twenty passages in this chapter describe the reigns of the first five Roman emperors, called the 'Julio-Claudians', all of whom were related to each other. They are Augustus (ruled 27 BC–AD 14), Tiberius (AD 14–37), Caligula (AD 37–41), Claudius (AD 41–54) and Nero (AD 54–68).

Exercise 11.1

Antony and Octavian

After the death of Julius Caesar, Antony and Octavian, Caesar's heir, fight for power.

Antonius post mortem Caesaris cives Romanos incitavit contra Brutum comitesque, qui eum occiderant. illi igitur ex urbe fugerunt. imperium exercitus Romani Antonio a senatoribus datum est. Caesar tamen, qui nullum filium habebat, Octavianum filium filiae sororis adoptaverat. ille in Graecia tum erat;
5 ubi de Caesare interfecto audivisset, Romam quam celerrime rediit ut imperium sibi peteret. duo legiones Caesaris se Octaviano tradiderunt; cum quibus ille bellum civile cum Antonio gessit. pace tandem facta, Octavianus et Antonius inimicos Caesaris proelio oppresserunt. deinde tamen Antonius, ad provinciam suam profectus, apud Cleopatram reginam Aegypti diu manebat, quam antea
10 Caesar ipse amaverat; uxorem suam, Octaviani sororem, dimisit. quidam e civibus Romanis timebant ne Antonius Cleopatram reginam Romae quoque faceret. Octavianus igitur iterum cum Antonio bellum gessit.

	Antonius -i *m*	Antony
	Caesar -aris *m*	Caesar
	incito -are -avi	I urge on, I rouse
	Brutus -i *m*	Brutus
4	Octavianus -i *m*	Octavian
	soror -oris *f*	sister
	adopto -are -avi	I adopt
	Graecia -ae *f*	Greece
	civilis -e	civil
8	provincia -ae *f*	province
	apud (+ *acc*)	with, at the house of
	Cleopatra -ae *f*	Cleopatra
	Aegyptus -i *f*	Egypt
	dimitto -ere dimisi	I dismiss, I divorce

Figure 11.1 *Roman marble bust of Cleopatra. 50–30* BC. *Berlin, Pergamonmuseum* (Archaeological Museum) (Photo by DeAgostini/Getty Images)

Exercise 11.2

Actium

Octavian defeats Antony and Cleopatra in a sea-battle at Actium in 31 BC.

proelium <u>navale</u> quod ad <u>Actium</u> pugnatum est bellum confecit. <u>uterque</u>
imperator plurimas naves paraverat. <u>uterque</u> in nave alta stabat, armis <u>insignis</u>.
<u>Octavianus</u> populos <u>Italiae</u> in pugnam duxit. contra eum <u>Antonius</u> <u>Aegyptum</u>
populosque <u>Orientis</u> duxit; quem secuta est <u>Cleopatra</u>, Aegypti regina et domina
5 Antonii. <u>classis</u> contra <u>classem</u> navigavit; multa <u>tela</u> iaciebantur; mare sanguine
<u>fluebat</u>. Cleopatra omnes deos Aegypti contra deos Romanos <u>invocavit</u>. <u>Mars</u>
navem contra navem vertit. tandem tota <u>classis</u> Aegypti timore superata flumen
<u>Nilum</u> petivit. ipsa regina prima e proelio fugit; quam Antonius mox secutus est.
deinde, miser quod victus erat, Antonius se necavit. libertus quidam Cleopatram
10 custodiebat ne idem faceret. <u>calathus</u> tamen <u>ficorum</u> reginae datus est; sub <u>ficis</u>
erat <u>aspis</u>, cuius <u>morsu</u> Cleopatra mortua est.

	navalis -e	naval
	Actium -i *n*	Actium (*port in north-west Greece*)
	uterque utraque utrumque	each (of two)
	insignis -e	conspicuous
3	Octavianus -i *m*	Octavian
	Italia -ae *f*	Italy
	Antonius -i *m*	Antony
	Aegyptus -i *f*	Egypt
	Oriens -entis *m*	the East, the Orient
4	Cleopatra -ae *f*	Cleopatra
	classis -is *f*	fleet
	telum -i *n*	missile
	fluo -ere	I flow
	invoco -are -avi	I call upon
6	Mars Martis *m*	Mars (*Roman god of war*)
	Nilus -i *m*	the Nile
	calathus -i *m*	basket
	ficus -i *f*	fig
	aspis -idis *f*	viper
11	morsus -us *m*	bite

Exercise 11.3

Tell-tale birds

Octavian is flattered by a talking bird and amused when he discovers its owner has hedged his bets.

Octavianus, postquam ad Actium Antonium proelio superavit, Romam rediit. cum in urbem advenisset, senem in via conspexit qui corvum in cavea habebat. corvus 'salve,' inquit 'Caesar, victor, imperator!' Octavianus miratus dixit se corvum emere velle. senex respondit se corvum magno pretio venditurum esse.
5 Octavianus corvum emit; senex laetus discessit. postridie tamen vicinus quidam dixit illum senem alterum corvum habere. 'hic corvus' inquit 'melius loqui potest.' Octavianus respondit se libenter auditurum esse illum corvum; quem senex statim ferre iussus est. corvus statim 'salve' inquit 'Antoni, victor, imperator!' senex perterritus dixit se ad utramque rem paratum esse. Octavianus
10 ridens promisit se alterum corvum eodem pretio empturum esse.

	Octavianus -i *m*	Octavian
	Actium -i *n*	Actium (*port in north-west Greece*)
	Antonius -i *m*	Antony
	corvus -i *m*	raven
2	cavea -ae *f*	cage
	salve!	greetings!
	Caesar -aris *m*	Caesar
	victor -oris *m*	victor, winner
	pretium -i *n*	price (*here ablative of price, translated*
4		for/at)
	vicinus -i *m*	neighbour
	uterque utraque utrumque	either

Exercise 11.4

Augustus established

Octavian celebrates his victory and, with the name 'Augustus', establishes himself as emperor (29–27 BC).

postea Octavianus Romam in triumpho intravit. ante omnia templa deis sacrificabat; per omnes vias cives laeti imperatorem suum salutabant. captivi ex omnibus terris quas Romani superaverant in ordine ducebantur. Octavianus ipse non modo victor in bello sed etiam princeps totius imperii Romani nunc erat.
5 de novo nomine cogitabat: 'Romulus' aptus videbatur, sed 'Augustus' (id est, veneratus) lectus est. Augustus laetus erat si primus civis, princeps, imperator, Caesar vocatus est. nolebat rex vocari, quod Romani reges olim detestati erant. nolebat deus vocari, sed sperabat se post mortem inter deos locum habiturum esse. quamquam nomen Romuli non legerat, mores Romae antiquae in omnibus
10 rebus restituere constituit.

	Octavianus -i *m*	Octavian
	triumphus -i *m*	triumphal procession
	ante (+ *acc*)	in front of
	sacrifico -are	I offer a sacrifice
3	ordo -inis *m*	line
	modo	only
	victor -oris *m*	victor, winner
	Romulus -i *m*	Romulus
	aptus -a -um	suitable
5	Augustus -i *m*	Augustus
	veneratus -a -um	revered
	Caesar -aris *m*	Caesar (*the name was taken as a title by Augustus and later emperors*)
	detestor -ari -atus sum	I hate intensely
9	mos moris *m*	custom
	antiquus -a -um	ancient
	restituo -ere	I restore

- The proper name *Augustus* will not be glossed again in this chapter.
- From the time of Augustus, the words *imperator* (originally *general* or *leader*) and *princeps* (originally *chief*, e.g. of a tribe) were commonly used to mean *emperor*.

Exercise 11.5

Augustus and Pollio

Augustus puts an arrogant host in his place.

Pollio in magna villa habitabat. multas lampetras in piscina ibi habebat. olim Augustum ad cenam invitavit. dum cenam consumunt, servus quidam Pollionis crystallum forte fregit. Pollio, qui dominus crudelissimus erat, statim iussit eum in piscinam iaci, ut a lampetris consumeretur. servus perterritus ad pedes Augusti
5 cecidit et oravit ne tali modo puniretur. Augustus Pollioni persuadere conabatur, sed frustra. tum igitur omnia crystalla quae in villa erant ferri et frangi iussit. Pollio, quamquam iratus erat, servum pro crystallo fracto punire non poterat, quod imperator idem fecerat; servum etiam liberavit. ubi Pollio mortuus est, villam suam Augusto reliquit; qui tamen eam deleri iussit, ne Pollio
10 monumentum haberet.

	Pollio -onis *m*	Pollio
	lampetra -ae *f*	lamprey (*flesh-eating eel-like fish*)
	piscina -ae *f*	fish-pond
	crystallum -i *n*	crystal drinking cup
3	frango -ere fregi fractus	I break
	monumentum -i *n*	memorial

Exercise 11.6

Lost legions

Varus loses three legions, to the great distress of Augustus.

Varus copias Romanas in Germania ducebat. ubi audivit gentes quasdam
imperio Romano resistere parare, Arminio principi Cheruscorum stulte credebat;
qui Romanos in insidias duxit. nam tres legiones, in silva et in tempestate
pugnare coactae, a Germanis deletae sunt. tres aquilae ab hostibus captae sunt.
5 Varus se necavit; corpore invento, caput Romam missum est. Augustus, ubi et
caput Vari et nuntium cladis accepit, capite suo ianuam iterum atque iterum
tundebat, misere clamans 'Vare, legiones mihi redde!' postea umbrae militum
Romanorum per silvam ambulantes videbantur. sex post annis, ubi Augustus
mortuus est, Germanicus cum quattuor legionibus missus est ut ultor huius
10 cladis esset. in silva arma, ossa, membra et hominum et equorum invenit. quae
cum sepelivisset, aquilas a Germanis rettulit.

	Varus -i *m*	Varus (*a Roman officer*)
	Germania -ae *f*	Germany
	Arminius -i *m*	Arminius
	Cherusci -orum *m pl*	the Cherusci (*a German tribe*)
3	insidiae -arum *f pl*	ambush, trap
	Germani -orum *m pl*	Germans
	aquila -ae *f*	eagle, legionary standard
	clades -is *f*	disaster
	tundo -ere	I strike
7	umbra -ae *f*	ghost
	Germanicus -i *m*	Germanicus (*nephew of Tiberius*)
	ultor -oris *m*	avenger
	os ossis *n*	bone
	membrum -i *n*	limb
11	sepelio -ire -ivi	I bury

Exercise 11.7

Tiberius

Tiberius succeeds Augustus as emperor, but has an uneasy reign.

Augustus, quod filium non habebat, diu nesciebat quis post mortem suam
imperator futurus esset. nonnullos <u>propinquos</u> in animo habebat; qui tamen
omnes <u>ante</u> Augustum ipsum mortui sunt. tandem igitur, ubi senex iam erat,
<u>Tiberium</u> <u>privignum</u> legere coactus est. Tiberius ipse iussus est <u>Germanicum</u>,
5 fratris filium, <u>heredem</u> suum facere. sic Augustus omnia parabat ut imperatores
se sequerentur; numquam tamen reges vocati sunt, quamquam imperium regis
paene habebant. ubi <u>Tacitus</u> <u>historicus</u> postea scripsit reges primo Romam
habuisse, omnes qui legebant intellexerunt reges nunc alio nomine rediisse.
Tiberius bonus miles, vir miser erat: sciebat enim Augustum alios maluisse. cives
10 Tiberium non amabant. Germanicus tamen iuvenis fortis et pulcher erat, ab
omnibus laudatus. ubi mortuus est, multi credebant Tiberium eum necari
iussisse. <u>Seianus</u>, <u>praefectus</u> custodum imperatoris, magnum imperium in urbe
habebat. Tiberius ei in omnibus rebus credebat. tandem <u>Capreas</u> abiit, nec postea
Romae visus est. ubi tamen audivit Seianum consilium cepisse ut ipse imperator
15 esset, eum quoque necari iussit.

	propinquus -i *m*	relative
	ante (+ *acc*)	before
	Tiberius -i *m*	Tiberius
	privignus -i *m*	step-son (*Tiberius was son of Augustus'*
4		*wife Livia by her first marriage*)
	Germanicus -i *m*	Germanicus (*nephew of Tiberius*)
	heres -edis *m*	heir
	Tacitus -i *m*	Tacitus (AD *56-about 120*)
	historicus -i *m*	historian
12	Seianus -i *m*	Sejanus
	praefectus -i *m*	prefect, officer in charge
	Capreae -arum *f pl*	Capri (*island in the Bay of Naples*)

Exercise 11.8

Caligula

Caligula acquires his name as a popular child, but as emperor proves to be insane.

Gaius, filius Germanici, duo vel tres annos natus semper cum patre in exercitu
erat. mater minima vestimenta militis ei fecit et caligulas; nomen igitur
'Caligulam' inter milites habebat, qui eum amabant. ubi Augustus mortuus est,
milites Germanici seditionem facere conabantur, quod eum imperatorem habere
5 malebant quam Tiberium. Germanicus igitur uxorem filiumque e periculo misit.
milites tamen, quod puerum sibi felicem esse credebant, rogaverunt ut Caligula
rediret; promiserunt se duci suo parituros esse; Caligula mox rediit.

postea, ubi Germanicus mortuus est, Tiberius Caligulam, qui puer adhuc erat,
heredem suum fecit, quamquam de eo dubitabat. nam dixit se aspidem populo
10 Romano, Phaethontem mundo dare. multis post annis, Tiberio ipso mortuo,
Caligula imperator factus est. Caligula tamen iam insanus erat. equum suum
consulem Romae facere conatus est. ubi expeditionem in Britanniam fecit, milites
testas in litore colligere iussit; deinde Romam regressi sunt. paucis post mensibus
a custodibus suis interfectus est.

	Gaius -i *m*	Gaius
	Germanicus -i *m*	Germanicus
	vel	or
	natus -a -um	old, aged (+ *acc for number of years*)
2	vestimenta -orum *n pl*	clothes
	caligula -ae *f*	little boot
	Caligula -ae *m*	Caligula
	seditio -onis *f*	mutiny, rebellion
	Tiberius -i *m*	Tiberius (*stepson and heir of Augustus*)
7	pareo -ere -ui -itus	I obey (+ *dat*)
	adhuc	still
	heres -edis *m*	heir
	dubito -are	I have doubts
	aspis -idis *f*	viper
10	Phaethon -ontis *m*	Phaethon (*in myth crashed the chariot of the sun, causing great destruction*)
	mundus -i *m*	world
	insanus -a -um	mad
	expeditio -onis *f*	expedition
12	Britannia -ae *f*	Britain
	testa -ae *f*	sea-shell
	litus -oris *n*	shore
	colligo -ere	I collect
	mensis -is *m*	month

Exercise 11.9

Claudius

Claudius, not an obvious choice as emperor, seeks to prove himself by invading Britain (AD 43).

custodes imperatoris, postquam <u>Caligula</u> occisus est, per <u>palatium</u> currentes
<u>Claudium</u> <u>patruum</u> eius post <u>aulaeum</u> se celantem invenerunt. Claudius, cum
<u>surdus</u> et <u>claudus</u> esset, Romae non clarus erat, quamquam multos libros
scripserat. nunc tamen imperator factus est. imperium Romanum statim <u>augere</u>
5 constituit. <u>Iulius Caesar</u> <u>Britanniam</u> vincere non potuerat, quamquam <u>bis</u>
conatus erat. nunc centum post annis Claudius maximo cum exercitu hanc
insulam <u>invasit</u>. ipse in Britannia breve tempus manebat. <u>Aulus Plautius</u> tamen
cum quattuor legionibus magnam partem insulae <u>provinciam</u> Romanam fecit. in
bello <u>Caractacus</u>, dux Britannorum qui Romanis resistebant, victus et captus est.
10 deinde Romam missus est ut captivus in <u>triumpho</u> ostentus necaretur. virtutem
tamen Romanorum, quamquam hostes erant, adeo laudavit ut Claudius ei
<u>parceret</u>.

	Caligula -ae *m*	Caligula
	palatium -i *n*	palace
	Claudius -i *m*	Claudius
	patruus -i *m*	uncle, father's brother
2	aulaeum -i *n*	curtain
	surdus -a -um	deaf
	claudus -a -um	lame
	augeo -ere	I extend
	Iulius -i Caesar -aris *m*	Julius Caesar
5	Britannia -ae *f*	Britain
	bis	twice
	invado -ere invasi	I invade
	Aulus -i Plautius -i *m*	Aulus Plautius (*a Roman commander*)
	provincia -ae *f*	province
9	Caractacus -i *m*	Caractacus
	triumphus -i *m*	triumphal procession
	parco -ere	I spare (+ *dat*)

Exercise 11.10

Nero and Agrippina

Nero becomes emperor (AD 54) but is dominated by his formidable mother Agrippina. This, and all the remaining passages in this chapter, are adapted from the account by the Roman historian Tacitus, who was writing about fifty years later.

> omnes credebant <u>Claudium</u> <u>veneno</u> interfectum esse. nam <u>Agrippina</u>, ut dicitur,
> imperatoris uxor <u>quarta</u>, <u>boletum</u> ei dedit in quo <u>venenum</u> posuerat. Claudius
> ipse filium iam habebat, <u>Britannicum</u> nomine. Agrippina tamen marito antea
> persuaserat ut <u>Neronem</u>, filium suum, <u>heredem</u> faceret. itaque Claudius
> 5 <u>privignum</u> legit. quod tamen Agrippina timebat ne animo <u>mutato</u> Britannicum
> mallet, maritum necare consituit. Nero igitur post mortem Claudii imperator
> factus est. milites eum salutaverunt; Nero tamen nolebat 'pater patriae' vocari
> quod iuvenis <u>adhuc</u> erat. Agrippina multa <u>officia</u> sibi cepit; Nero primo eam
> 'optimam matrem' vocavit, quod ipse <u>carmina</u> scribere et in <u>scaena</u> agere
> 10 malebat. mox tamen Agrippina imperium sibi cupere videbatur. ubi Nero <u>legatos</u>
> accepit, mater cum eo sedere volebat. Nero <u>Octaviam</u> <u>in matrimonium duxerat</u>,
> sed multas <u>amicas</u> habebat; ubi Agrippina eum <u>reprehensit</u>, iratus erat.

	Claudius -i *m*	Claudius
	venenum -i *n*	poison
	Agrippina -ae *f*	Agrippina
	quartus -a -um	fourth
2	boletus -i *m*	mushroom
	Britannicus -i *m*	Britannicus
	Nero -onis *m*	Nero
	heres -edis *m*	heir
	privignus -i *m*	step-son
5	muto -are -avi -atus	I change (something)
	adhuc	still
	officium -i *n*	duty, job
	carmen -inis *n*	verse, song
	scaena -ae *f*	stage
10	legatus -i *m*	ambassador
	Octavia -ae *f*	Octavia (*daughter of Claudius and step-sister of Nero*)
	in matrimonium duco -ere duxi	I marry
	amica -ae *f*	girl-friend
12	reprehendo -ere reprehensi	I criticise

- The proper names *Nero* and *Agrippina* will not be glossed again in this chapter.

Exercise 11.11

Matricide planned

Nero decides to murder his mother and considers possible methods (AD 59).

Nero de scelere diro cogitabat. amore enim <u>Poppaeae</u> incensus est; uxorem
<u>Octaviam</u> <u>dimittere</u> volebat. Poppaea <u>matrimonium</u> sibi cupiebat. hoc tamen
difficile esse videbatur quod Nero, quamquam ipse summum imperium tenebat,
imperium matris timebat. Agrippinam igitur interficere constituit. nesciebat
5 tamen quomodo mortem <u>efficere</u> posset. Agrippina a servis suis semper
custodiebatur. Nero igitur nec <u>venenum</u> in cibo ponere nec eam gladio
oppugnare poterat.

tandem libertus quidam <u>Anicetus</u> nomine, qui amicus Neronis olim fuerat, dixit
navem sic aedificari posse ut pars <u>solveretur</u> et in mare caderet; Agrippinam
10 ipsam sic in aquam casuram esse. 'magnum' inquit 'est periculum maris. multae
res ibi accidere possunt. si mater dum navigat morietur, quis eam scelere necatam
esse putabit? omnes credent <u>ventum</u> <u>undas</u>que Agrippinam forte delevisse. post
mortem eius templum aedificare poteris: sic amorem <u>dolorem</u>que ostendes.'

	Poppaea -ae *f*	Poppaea
	Octavia -ae *f*	Octavia
	dimitto -ere	I dismiss, I divorce
	matrimonium -i *n*	marriage
5	efficio -ere	I cause, I bring about
	venenum -i *n*	poison
	Anicetus -i *m*	Anicetus
	solvo -ere	I detach
	ventus -i *m*	wind
12	unda -ae *f*	wave
	dolor -oris *m*	grief

Exercise 11.12

Matricide averted

The plot to kill Agrippina in a sabotaged ship misfires.

Nero consilium laudavit. navis igitur parata est ad matrem necandam. imperator
matrem invitavit ad villam quae prope mare erat. cum Agrippina advenisset, a
filio libenter accepta est. Nero magnam cenam parari iusserat, ut scelus nocte
accideret. post cenam navem pulchram matri luce <u>astrorum</u> ostendit; illa ingressa
5   est. mare <u>placidum</u> erat: Nero igitur timebat ne homines non crederent navem
tempestate deletam esse. navis tamen navigare coepit. ancilla Agrippinae cum
domina de <u>benignitate</u> Neronis loquebatur. mox tamen, <u>signo</u> dato, <u>tectum</u> multo
<u>plumbo</u> <u>oneratum</u> cecidit.

unus amicus Agrippinae statim necatus est. illa tamen et ancilla altis <u>lateribus</u>
10 <u>lecti</u> <u>protectae sunt</u>; nec <u>dissolutio</u> navis secuta est. alii de consilio sciebant, alii
quid accideret nesciebant: omnes vehementer clamabant. alii navem <u>submergere</u>,
alii servare conabantur. multi qui in nave erant in mare <u>leniter</u> iacti sunt; inter
quos erant Agrippina ancillaque. ancilla infelix clamavit se Agrippinam esse,
ut auxilium celeriter acciperet; statim tamen <u>remis</u> oppugnata et confecta est.
15 Agrippina ipsa quod tacebat non conspecta est, sed omnia visa intellexit.
quamquam parvum vulnus acceperat, <u>nare</u> poterat; mox <u>lenunculo</u> servata ad
villam suam portata est.

	astra -orum *n pl*	stars
	placidus -a -um	calm
	benignitas -atis *f*	kindness
	signum -i *n*	sign, signal
7	tectum -i *n*	roof, canopy
	plumbum -i *n*	lead
	oneratus -a -um	weighed down
	latus -eris *n*	side
	lectus -i *m*	couch
10	protego -ere protexi protectus	I protect
	dissolutio -onis *f*	break-up
	submergo -ere	I sink (something)
	leniter	gently
	remus -i *m*	oar
16	no nare	I swim
	lenunculus -i *m*	small fishing-boat

Exercise 11.13

Nero thinks again

Nero is alarmed by Agrippina's survival but finds a volunteer assassin.

Agrippina consilium Neronis intellegere nunc poterat. nam sciebat se ad villam,
ad cenam, ad navem invitatam esse ut necaretur. nec ventus nec tempestas sed
filius scelestus navem delere conatus erat. de morte ancillae putans, Agrippina
sibi 'tutissima ero' inquit 'si nihil scire videbor.' nuntium igitur Neroni misit ut
5   diceret se auxilio deorum servatam esse; deinde vulnus suum curabat. Nero
interea, ubi matrem adhuc vivere audivit, perterritus erat. timebat enim ne
Agrippina totam rem senatoribus nuntiaret. amicos igitur vocatos rogavit quid
facere deberet. illi diu tacebant. tandem unus Neronem hortatus est ut auxilium
Aniceti iterum peteret. cum libertus se Agrippinam necaturum esse promisisset,
10   Nero dixit imperium illo die sibi dari; se dono liberti liberari.

tutus -a -um	safe
curo -are	I tend
adhuc	still
Anicetus -*i* *m*	Anicetus

Figure 11.2 *Statue of Agrippina, daughter of Germanicus and mother of the emperor
Nero.* (Photo by Hulton Archive/Getty Images)

Exercise 11.14

The murder of Agrippina

After Nero tries to frame her messenger, Agrippina is killed.

Nero alterum consilium nunc cepit. ubi nuntius Agrippinae advenit, gladium
inter pedes eius dum loquitur iaci iussit, <u>sicut</u> in <u>vestimentis</u> antea celatum.
deinde nuntium capi iussit, locutus eum ab Agrippina missum esse ut se necaret.
in animo enim habebat postea dicere matrem ipsam mortem petivisse, cum filium
5　necare frustra conata esset. interea magna turba ad villam Agrippinae convenit.
nam omnes eam e periculo servatam salutare volebant.

ubi tamen viros <u>armatos</u> appropinquantes conspexerunt, statim discesserunt.
nonnulli milites <u>Aniceto</u> duce ianuam villae <u>fregerunt</u>. servi etiam fugerunt.
Agrippina in <u>cubiculo</u> cum ancilla quadam erat. ubi ancilla abitura surrexit,
10　Agrippina rogavit 'tu quoque me relinquis?' deinde viris ingressis 'si salutaturi
venistis,' inquit 'dicite Neroni me bene agere; si necaturi, nihil malum de filio
credam.' milites circum <u>lectum</u> steterunt. Agrippina uni militi gladium <u>stringenti</u>
<u>uterum</u> obtulit. '<u>ventrem</u> <u>feri</u>' exclamavit 'unde venit ille scelestus', multisque
vulneribus confecta est.

	sicut		as if
	vestimenta -orum	*n pl*	clothes
	armatus -a -um		armed
	Anicetus *-i* *m*		Anicetus
8	frango -ere fregi		I break down
	cubiculum -i *n*		bedroom
	lectus -i *m*		couch
	stringo -ere		I draw
	uterus -i *m*		womb
13	venter -tris *m*		belly
	ferio -ire		I strike

Exercise 11.15

Boudicca's rebellion

The British tribal queen Boudicca leads a rebellion against Roman rule (AD 61).

Prasutagus Icenorum rex, clarus quod multam pecuniam habebat et multos annos
regebat, mortuus est. Caesarem heredem fecit cum duabus filiabus, ut regnum
villamque servaret. sed frustra, nam regnum a militibus vastatum est, villa a servis.
uxor Boudicca verberata est, filiae stupratae; multi propinquorum
5 servi facti sunt. Romani totam terram sicut donum ceperunt.

itaque principes Icenorum arma rapuerunt, aliasque gentes incitaverunt.
consilium ceperunt ut omnes liberarentur, Romanis ex insula discedere coactis.
maxime detestati sunt veteranos qui Camulodunum coloniam acceperant. illi
enim Britannos e villis expellebant, ex agris agebant; eos servos captivosque
10 vocabant. milites Romani veteranos hortabantur, quod ipsi talia facere volebant.
templum Divi Claudii signum aeternae dominationis esse videbatur, et Britanni
qui sacerdotes lecti sunt multam pecuniam expendere cogebantur. Britanni
putabant se coloniam facile delere posse. urbs enim muros non habebat, quod
duces Romani numquam timuerant ne oppugnaretur.

	Prasutagus -i *m*	Prasutagus
	Iceni -orum *m pl*	the Iceni (*a tribe in East Anglia*)
	Caesar -aris *m*	Caesar (*by now hereditary title*)
	heres -edis *m*	heir
3	vasto -are -avi -atus	I lay waste
	Boudicca -ae *f*	Boudicca
	verbero -ere -avi -atus	I beat
	stupro -are -avi -atus	I rape
	propinquus -i *m*	relative
5	sicut	as if, like
	incito -are -avi	I urge on, I rouse
	detestor -ari -atus sum	I hate intensely
	veterani -orum *m pl*	veterans, retired soldiers
	Camulodunum -i *n*	Camulodunum (*modern Colchester*)
8	colonia -ae *f*	colony (*settlement of veterans*)
	Britanni -orum *m pl*	Britons
	Divus -i Claudius -i *m*	Divine Claudius (*Roman emperors were worshipped as gods after their death*)
	signum -i *n*	sign, symbol
11	aeternus -a -um	eternal, everlasting
	dominatio -onis *f*	despotism, tyranny
	sacerdos -otis *m*	priest
	expendo -ere	I expend, I pay out

Exercise 11.16

Growing alarm

Amid bad omens the British rebellion spreads.

statua Victoriae quae in colonia erat forte ad terram cecidit; victa esse et ab
hostibus fugere videbatur. feminae nuntiaverunt voces diras auditas esse, speciem
coloniae deletae prope flumen Tamesam visam esse, mare colorem sanguinis
habere. quae omnia Britannis spem, timorem Romanis dederunt. veterani in
5   templum fugerunt; ibi a Britannis duos dies oppugnabantur; deinde victi sunt.

ubi Cerialis cum nona legione auxilium ferens advenit, etiam ipse victus est.
Suetonius, qui procul aberat cum Druidis pugnans, Londinium quam celerrime
festinavit. castra ibi ponere primo in animo habebat; cum tamen locum non
validum esse vidisset, maluit provinciam quam Londinium solum servare.
10 Britanni Verulamium quoque praedam petentes oppugnaverunt; plurimi cives
Romani occisi sunt. Suetonius igitur proelium facere paravit.

	statua -ae *f*		statue
	Victoria -ae *f*		Victory (*worshipped as a goddess*)
	colonia -ae *f*		colony
	species -ei *f*		vision
3	Tamesa -ae *f*		the Thames
	color -oris *m*		colour
	Britanni -orum	*m pl*	Britons
	veterani -orum	*m pl*	veterans
	Cerialis -is *m*		Cerialis (*a Roman officer*)
6	nonus -a -um		ninth
	Suetonius -i *m*		Suetonius (*governor of Britain*)
	procul		far away
	Druidae -arum	*m pl*	Druids
	Londinium -i *n*		Londinium (*modern London*)
9	provincia -ae *f*		province
	Verulamium -i *n*		Verulamium (*modern St Albans*)
	praeda -ae *f*		booty

Figure 11.3 *The London statue of Boudicca in her chariot.* Westminster Bridge monument, London, 1926–1927. From *Wonderful London, volume II*, edited by Arthur St John Adcock, published by Amalgamated Press (London, 1926–1927). (Photo by The Print Collector/Print Collector/Getty Images)

Exercise 11.17

The rebels defeated

Boudicca makes a proud speech but is defeated in battle.

Suetonius <u>quartam decimam</u> legionem ducens locum in <u>valle</u> legit et suos in
<u>ordine</u> posuit. <u>Britanni</u> nullo <u>ordine</u> <u>passim</u> currebant. quod tamen credebant se
victuros esse, uxores secum duxerant. illae in <u>plaustris</u> stabant, ut victoriam
spectarent. <u>Boudicca</u> ipsa in <u>curru</u> stans turbae locuta est: 'Britanni, femina duce,
5   saepe pugnaverunt. ego tamen pro regno <u>amisso</u>, pro corpore <u>verberato</u>,
pro filiabus raptis pugno. Romani omnia sibi capere cupiunt. dei tamen nos
custodient. una legio iam cecidit; ceterae in castris manere quam nobiscum
pugnare malunt. nec clamores nec arma nostra ferre poterunt. nisi servi esse
vultis, hodie vincere debemus.' Suetonius interea milites suos hortatus est: 'nolite
10 turbam clamoremque hostium timere. plures feminas quam viros videtis.' deinde
<u>signo</u> dato Romani in <u>ordine</u> hostes oppugnaverunt. Britanni celeriter fugerunt,
sed <u>plaustris</u> <u>impediti sunt</u>; plurimi occisi sunt. Boudicca vitam suam <u>veneno</u>
confecit.

	Suetonius -i *m*	Suetonius
	quartus -a -um decimus -a -um	fourteenth
	vallis -is *f*	valley
	ordo -inis *m*	order, rank
2	Britanni -orum *m pl*	Britons
	passim	in all directions
	plaustrum -i *n*	wagon
	Boudicca -ae *f*	Boudicca
	currus -us *m*	chariot
5	amitto -ere amisi amissus	I lose
	verbero -are -avi -atus	I beat
	signum -i *n*	signal
	impedio -ire -ivi -itus	I obstruct
	venenum -i *n*	poison

Exercise 11.18

Rome on fire

When a great fire devastates Rome, Nero's involvement and reaction are questionable
(AD 64).

<u>clades</u>, Nerone imperatore, urbem oppressit, gravior omnibus quae antea
acciderant. nam <u>incendium</u> ingens maiorem partem Romae delevit. nemo sciebat
<u>utrum</u> forte accidisset <u>an</u> scelere imperatoris. <u>initium</u> prope <u>Circum</u> erat, inter
tabernas ubi <u>mercimonium</u> vendebatur quo <u>flammae</u> <u>aluntur</u>. <u>incendium</u> vento
5   actum mox validum erat. <u>flammae</u> altissimae surrexerunt; muros et domuum et
templorum facile superaverunt. <u>incendium</u> per vias <u>angustas</u>, <u>pridem</u> aedificatas,
celeriter processit.

cives perterriti clamabant: senes, feminae, liberi lacrimabant. alii alios
<u>impediverunt</u>. si in proximam partem urbis fugerunt, <u>incendium</u> ibi quoque
10 invenerunt. nullus locus sine periculo esse videbatur. nonnulli qui ipsi effugere
poterant mortui sunt quod <u>propinquos</u> servare conabantur. nemo se contra
<u>incendium</u> defendere conabatur. erant in viis homines qui <u>flammas</u> <u>exstingui</u>
<u>vetuerunt</u>: se hoc facere iussos esse dixerunt. alii etiam <u>faces</u> iaciebant.

Nero ipse ubi <u>incendium</u> coepit Roma aberat. ubi rediit, <u>flammae</u> domui eius
15 quae in <u>Palatio</u> erat iam appropinquabant; quae mox deleta est. imperator
<u>Campum Martium</u>, templa, etiam hortos suos <u>patefecit</u> ut cives <u>refugium</u>
haberent; <u>pretium</u> cibi <u>minui</u> iussit. omnia fecit ut a civibus laudaretur; sed
frustra. <u>rumor</u> enim <u>pervasit</u> Neronem, cum urbs <u>ureretur</u>, <u>lyram</u> cepisse et in
<u>tecto</u> de <u>excidio</u> <u>Troiae</u> <u>cecinisse</u>, <u>incendium</u> Romae rebus <u>antiquis</u> <u>adsimulantem</u>.

	clades -is *f*	disaster
	incendium -i *n*	fire
	utrum . . . an	whether . . . or
	initium -i *n*	beginning
3	Circus -i *m*	the Circus Maximus (*chariot-racing stadium*)
	mercimonium -i *n*	merchandise, goods
	flamma -ae *f*	flame
	alo -ere	I feed
6	angustus -a -um	narrow
	pridem	long ago
	impedio -ire -ivi	I get in the way of
	propinquus -i *m*	relative
	exstinguo -ere	I extinguish
13	veto -are -ui	I forbid (+ *inf*)
	fax facis *f*	torch, firebrand
	Palatium -i *n*	the Palatine hill (*residence of emperors*)
	Campus -i Martius -i *m*	the Campus Martius (*military and religious meeting place*)
	patefacio -ere patefeci	I throw open
16	refugium -i *n*	place of refuge
	pretium -i *n*	price
	minuo -ere	I reduce
	rumor -oris *m*	rumour
	pervadeo -ere pervasi	I spread
18	uro -ere	I burn, I destroy by fire
	lyra -ae *f*	lyre (*stringed instrument*)
	tectum -i *n*	roof
	excidium -i *n*	destruction
	Troia -ae *f*	Troy
19	cano -ere cecini	I sing
	antiquus -a -um	ancient
	adsimulo -are	I compare

Exercise 11.19

Old Rome lost

The fire is finally put out, revealing the extent of damage to Rome's historic monuments.

    tandem <u>sexto</u> die <u>finis</u> <u>incendii</u> factus est, multis <u>aedificiis</u> <u>prorutis</u> ne progredi
posset. cives tamen <u>adhuc</u> perterriti erant. multi credebant Neronem mediam
urbem <u>vacuam</u> facere velle, ut domum ingentem sibi aedificaret; multi dicebant
eum etiam novam urbem <u>conditurum esse</u>, nomine suo vocatam. multae domus,
5 insulae, templa deorum <u>incendio</u> deleta sunt. <u>ara</u> ab <u>Evandro</u> olim <u>sacrata</u>,
templum a <u>Romulo</u> ipso aedificatum incensum est. <u>praeda</u> multarum victoriarum,
praemia artis <u>Graecae</u>, libri a <u>maioribus</u> traditi <u>amissi sunt</u>. nova urbs mox
surgebat; sed, quamquam pulchra erat, senes in animo tenebant omnia quae
numquam iterum visuri erant. erant ei qui dixerunt hoc <u>incendium</u> eodem die
10 coepisse quo <u>Galli</u> urbem captam olim incenderant.

	sextus -a -um	sixth
	finis -is *m*	end
	incendium -i *n*	fire
	aedificium -i *n*	building
1	proruo -ere -i -tus	I demolish
	adhuc	still
	vacuus -a -um	empty
	condo -ere -idi -itus	I found
	ara -ae *f*	altar
5	Evander -dri *m*	Evander (*king of early settlement on the site of Rome, visited by Aeneas*)
	sacro -are -avi -atus	I dedicate
	Romulus -i *m*	Romulus
	praeda -ae *f*	spoil, booty
7	Graecus -a -um	Greek
	maiores -um *m pl*	ancestors
	amitto -ere amisi amissus	I lose
	Galli -orum *m pl*	Gauls

Exercise 11.20

Christians blamed

Nero, accused of ordering the fire, finds the Christians in Rome a convenient target to blame. Tacitus comments in negative terms both on the new faith and on the city itself.

multi incendium ab imperatore iussum esse credebant. Nero igitur, ut rumorem
deleret, culpare constituit eos qui a turba Christiani vocati sunt. illi nomen
habebant a Christo qui, Tiberio imperatore, a Pontio Pilato supplicio punitus est.
dira superstitio, breve tempus oppressa, iterum erupit, non modo per Iudaeam
5 ubi coepit, sed etiam Romae quo omnia mala confluunt. ei qui fatebantur se
Christianos esse capti sunt; deinde multi alii inventi sunt. poenas pessimas dare
coacti sunt. a canibus laniati sunt; in crucibus positi, incensi sunt ut lucem nocte
darent. Nero hortos suos huic spectaculo obtulerat; ipse per turbam ambulabat,
aurigae vestimenta gerens. sed cives tandem Christianorum miserebantur, cum
10 non pro salute urbis sed pro gaudio imperatoris saevissimi punirentur.

	incendium -i *n*	fire
	rumor -oris *m*	rumour
	culpo -are	I blame
	Christiani -orum *m pl*	Christians
3	Christus -i *m*	Christ
	Tiberius -i *m*	Tiberius
	Pontius -i Pilatus -i *m*	Pontius Pilate (*governor of Judaea* AD 26–36)
	supplicium -i *n*	death penalty
4	superstitio -onis *f*	superstition
	erumpo -ere erupi	I break out
	modo	only
	Iudaea -ae *f*	Judaea
	confluo -ere	I flow together
5	fateor -eri	I confess
	canis -is *m*	dog
	lanio -are -avi -atus	I tear apart
	crux crucis *f*	cross
	spectaculum -i *n*	show, spectacle
9	auriga -ae *m*	charioteer
	vestimenta -orum *n pl*	clothes
	misereor -eri	I pity (+ *gen*)
	salus -utis *f*	safety

Chapter Twelve

This chapter consists of 400 revision sentences covering all constructions and grammar points, lists of the restricted vocabulary and grammar for GCSE English to Latin sentences, ten additional English to Latin exercises, and five complete practice GCSE Latin Language papers (following the layout and glossing conventions of OCR papers).

Exercise RS.1

Agreement of nouns and adjectives

Translate into English:

1. novus consul omnes amicos salutabat.
2. nauta bonus consilium audax habet.
3. servus miser in medio flumine stabat.
4. iter lentum totam noctem faciebamus.
5. parvus puer magnos pedes habebat.
6. templum ingens in foro Romano aedificatum est.
7. cives stulti equum infelicem in urbem suam traxerunt.
8. quot ianuas habet villa ingens?
9. senex clarus librum brevem olim scripsit.
10. liberi fortes ad summum montem advenerunt.

Exercise RS.2

Adverbs

Translate into English:

1. milites nostri fortiter pugnabant.
2. ancillam iterum dormientem inveni.
3. pueri laborem facile confecerunt.
4. servus pecuniam domini fideliter custodiebat.
5. ille senator irate surrexit.
6. nuntius regis forte advenit.
7. urbem hostium frustra oppugnavimus.
8. puella me laete salutavit.
9. muri postea deleti sunt.
10. senex mihi breviter respondit.

Exercise RS.3

Comparative and superlative adjectives

Translate into English:

1. uxor senatoris pulcherrima erat.
2. hic puer stultior est amico.
3. illud templum maximum omnium est.
4. milites Romani fortiores sunt quam ceteri.
5. cenam optimam mihi parate, servi!
6. peius vulnus numquam vidi.
7. murus meus altior est quam tuus.
8. iter facillimum esse videtur.
9. femina plus pecuniae habet quam maritus.
10. portam minimam tandem inveni.

Exercise RS.4

Comparative and superlative adverbs

Translate into English:

1. puella celerius cucurrit quam frater.
2. dominus servum saevissime punivit.
3. hic puer audacius respondit quam ceteri.
4. librum tuum quam celerrime invenire conabor.
5. nemo fortius pugnavit quam dux noster.
6. haec domus pessime aedificata est.
7. talia nunc saepius accidunt quam antea.
8. nonne puellam quam clarissime loqui iussisti?
9. servos meos laetius laudo quam punio.
10. ubi minime progredi videmur, saepe progredimur maxime.

Exercise RS.5

Personal pronouns and possessives

Translate into English:

1. ego vinum bibo, tu aquam.

2. amicus noster mox adveniet.

3. illa femina et maritum suum et pecuniam eius amabat.

4. quid tu in bello fecisti, pater?

5. regina 'ego et maritus' inquit 'vos salutamus'.

6. puer se in silva celavit.

7. fratrem tuum in foro conspexi.

8. pecuniam eis dare volo.

9. ubi villam vestram aedificabitis?

10. putavi me eam antea vidisse.

Exercise RS.6

This and *that*

Translate into English:

1. hic cibus pessimus est.

2. cur illam puellam salutavisti?

3. nuntius, postquam haec dixit, statim discessit.

4. servum capere conabar. ille tamen effugit.

5. senator his verbis nobis persuasit.

6. illud iterum audire nolo.

7. hi mortui sunt ut ceteri viverent.

8. hunc servum in horto laborantem conspexi.

9. pars huius itineris difficilis erit.

10. cenam illi seni paravi.

Exercise RS.7

Self and *same*

Translate into English:

1. rex ipse subito intravit.
2. eadem in foro semper audio.
3. eandem puellam heri iterum conspexi.
4. verba senatoris, non senatorem ipsum, laudare volo.
5. et Romani et hostes eodem die profecti sunt.
6. librumne ipsa scripsisti, domina?
7. omnes captivi eodem modo necati sunt.
8. filii eiusdem patris sumus.
9. nonne putas idem semper accidere?
10. nuntius dei ipsius adest.

Exercise RS.8

Relative pronoun and clause

Translate into English:

1. nuntius quem heri audivimus iterum adest.
2. ubi est puella cuius librum habeo?
3. amicum quaero qui semper fidelis erit.
4. ei qui festinant saepe cadunt.
5. captivus cui cibum dederam postea fugit.
6. hic est gladius quo rex necatus est.
7. milites a quibus servatus sum mox iterum videbo.
8. felices sunt servi quorum dominam amo.
9. omnes qui Romam venerunt redire volunt.
10. librum inveni sine quo nihil facere possum.

Exercise RS.9

Less common pronouns

Translate into English:

1. quis praemium accipere vult?
2. nauta captus nihil dixit.
3. hoc consilium stultum est, sed aliud non habeo.
4. nonne donum quoddam accepisti?
5. nomen pueri nemo scit.
6. intravit quidam donum ferens.
7. alter consul Romae semper aderat.
8. inveni quendam cenam meam consumentem.
9. cui hunc librum dabo?
10. unum equum quaero; ceteri iam adsunt.

Exercise RS.10

Prepositions (i)

Translate into English:

1. filia regis inter captivos inventa est.
2. vita nihil sine labore hominibus dat.
3. villam prope flumen aedificare nolo.
4. iuvenis cum fratre profectus est.
5. multas per terras iter fecimus.
6. senex pro ianua templi sedebat.
7. audesne trans mare hoc tempore navigare?
8. de monte descendere coacti sumus.
9. corpus circum muros urbis tractum est.
10. servus ex horto effugit.

Exercise RS.11

Prepositions (ii)

Translate into English:

1. ille contra amicos patriamque pugnavit.
2. amici in tabernam intraverunt.
3. quid in templo invenisti?
4. ab insula regis scelesti celeriter navigare volebam.
5. senex post cenam in horto sedere solebat.
6. multis post annis bellum cum eisdem hostibus gessimus.
7. cur ad forum festinatis, cives?
8. dei omnia vident quae sub caelo accidunt.
9. maritus sub terram iter fecit ut uxorem reduceret.
10. miles propter virtutem laudatus est.

Exercise RS.12

Prefixes and compound verbs

Translate into English:

1. imperator tandem redire constituit.
2. mox ad insulam adveniemus.
3. homines scelesti Roma expulsi sunt.
4. pueri libros abicere volebant.
5. in urbem captam ingressi sumus.
6. quando pecuniam meam reddes?
7. pater huius puellae diu aberat.
8. cives in forum exierunt.
9. flumen transire conabamur.
10. liberi in via convenerunt.

Exercise RS.13

Verb tenses

Translate into English:

1. nuntius nunc castris appropinquat.
2. amicos nostros cras videbimus.
3. servi in agro multas horas laborabant.
4. illum librum olim legi.
5. alii iam advenerunt, alii mox advenient.
6. equum inveni quem antea vendideram.
7. tres dies navigabamus; postridie terram conspeximus.
8. si hoc iterum facies, ego te puniam.
9. in ea villa diu habitabam.
10. urbs Roma manet semperque manebit.

Exercise RS.14

Irregular perfect and pluperfect tenses

Translate into English:

1. senator omnes e foro exire iussit.
2. puellam inveni quae epistulam miserat.
3. pater mihi pecuniam dedit.
4. nihil de hac re antea cognoveram.
5. consul locuturus surrexit.
6. cives qui Roma discesserant tandem redierunt.
7. nonne deus quidam caelum sustulit?
8. nemo equum aquam bibere coegerat.
9. multi pueri cucurrerunt; pauci ceciderunt.
10. quod alios libros non intellexeram, hunc scripsi.

Exercise RS.15

Very irregular verbs

Translate into English:

1. nemo arma in foro fert.
2. urbs quae valida fuerat nunc deleta est.
3. ego iter facere volo; tu domi manere mavis.
4. nemo laborem conficere potuerat.
5. cur vinum in hortum tulisti?
6. nuntius 'victoriam' inquit 'in proelio habemus.'
7. nova verba cognoscere coepi.
8. tale donum accipere nolumus.
9. pecunia mea ablata est.
10. senes in templum nunc eunt.

Exercise RS.16

Passive: agent and instrument

Translate into English:

1. puer fortis ab omnibus laudabatur.
2. imperator gladio necatus est.
3. haec femina a turba spectari vult.
4. servi scelesti a domino punientur.
5. urbs olim ab hostibus capta erat.
6. milites qui capti erant postea effugerunt.
7. vinum a senibus in taberna bibebatur.
8. multi libri ab amico meo scripti sunt.
9. hi muri tempore non delebuntur.
10. portae a militibus fortiter custodiebantur.

Exercise RS.17

Deponent and semi-deponent verbs

Translate into English:

1. omnes templa Romae mirati sunt.
2. prima luce proficisci constituimus.
3. ego celeriter ambulare soleo.
4. miles vulnus grave passus mox morietur.
5. verba nuntii intellegere conabar.
6. cives, ubi de victoria audiverunt, maxime gavisi sunt.
7. dux nos hortatus est ut regrederemur.
8. quis nobis respondere audebit?
9. hostes multas horas sequebamur.
10. hic senator scelestus est sed bene loquitur.

Exercise RS.18

Direct commands

Translate into English:

1. laborem tuum confice, ancilla!
2. nolite cibum nostrum auferre!
3. alteram epistulam quam celerrime scribe, serve!
4. novas copias statim parate!
5. da mihi plus vini!
6. si potestis, pecuniam celate!
7. arma fer! iter fac!
8. audite verba nuntii, cives!
9. noli contra amicos pugnare!
10. domi mane! noli timere!

Exercise RS.19

Direct questions

Translate into English:

1. quando domum redibis, pater?
2. tene in foro heri vidi?
3. ubi est gladius meus?
4. nonne haec verba intellegitis?
5. quis vinum meum bibit?
6. cur eundem librum semper legis?
7. quot captivi in castris inventi sunt?
8. num villam vendere vis?
9. quo festinas, amice, et quid petis?
10. quomodo senator tot civibus persuasit?

Exercise RS.20

Numerals and time expressions

Translate into English:

1. puer novem fratres habet.
2. mille milites decem annos pugnabant.
3. post cenam dormire solebam.
4. imperator duas legiones in magnum periculum duxit.
5. amicus meus quinque diebus Romam veniet.
6. multis post annis illum librum iterum legi.
7. per totam noctem navigabamus; prima luce ad insulam advenimus.
8. multa dira illo anno acciderunt.
9. centum equi in agris erant.
10. tres puellae a sene docebantur.

Exercise RS.21

Time clauses

Translate into English:

1. ubi clamores audivimus, auxilium statim tulimus.
2. cives, postquam urbs capta est, perterriti erant.
3. ubi de hac re plura audies, dic mihi!
4. puer dum domum ambulat clamorem in via audivit.
5. ubi Romam adveni, domum amici quaerere coepi.
6. femina, simulac epistulam accepit, statim respondere constituit.
7. postquam tantum cibum consumpsi, nihil aliud agere poteram.
8. multi, ubi pecuniam habent, putant se felices esse.
9. ubi hostes tandem superabimus, omnes gaudebimus.
10. servi postquam laborem confecerunt dormire cupiebant.

Exercise RS.22

Because, although and *if* clauses

Translate into English:

1. huic ancillae credo quod semper fidelis est.
2. si me iterum videre vis, da mihi plus pecuniae!
3. pueri laeti erant quamquam diligenter laborare debebant.
4. quod saevus est, dominus noster timetur.
5. quamquam saevus est, dominus noster amatur.
6. puer stultissimus erat si hoc fecit.
7. quod gladium non habeo, pugnare non possum.
8. si hanc epistulam accipies, statim responde!
9. illum servum vendidi quod vinum abstulerat.
10. ancillam emere nolo nisi bonam cenam parare potest.

Exercise RS.23

Conjunctions and connecting relative

Translate into English:

1. cibum atque vinum emere volumus.
2. femina quam olim amaveram rediit; quam iterum visam libenter salutavi.
3. tempestas heri fuit. itaque navigare non poteramus.
4. nuntius verba regis nuntiavit. quibus auditis, cives laetissimi erant.
5. hic puer nihil intellexit. stultus enim erat.
6. consilium habeo. quod ubi audies, miraberis.
7. in foro manere debetis. nam imperator mox adveniet.
8. servum de scelere rogavi. ille tamen nihil dixit.
9. milites nostri terra marique vicerunt. quod cum cognovissemus, gavisi sumus.
10. dominus iratus erat. ancilla igitur in horto se celavit.

Exercise RS.24

Paired words

Translate into English:

1. alter frater rex factus est, alter ex urbe discessit.
2. hic servus et malus et stultus est.
3. alii in taberna bibebant, alii domum redierunt.
4. alter consulum exercitum duxit, alter in urbe manebat.
5. verbis nuntii et credo et faveo.
6. puella nec laeta nec misera esse videtur.
7. aliae naves deletae sunt, aliae navigare possunt.
8. et fortis et fidelis esse volo.
9. alii alia de imperio Romano dicunt.
10. neque tempus neque artem habeo.

Exercise RS.25

Participles

Translate into English:

1. domum currens in via cecidi.
2. imperator urbem captam incendere constituit.
3. nuntius discessurus magnos clamores audivit.
4. pueri per viam ambulantes puellam salutaverunt.
5. femina epistulam lectam marito tradidit.
6. seni auxilium petenti pecuniam dedi.
7. navem Romam navigaturam conspeximus.
8. servus fugiens a domino captus est.
9. hanc ancillam lacrimantem inveni.
10. villam aedificaturus agrum emi.

Exercise RS.26

Ablative absolute

Translate into English:

1. rege adveniente, quidam clamare coepit.
2. consule de victoria locuturo, omnes tacuerunt.
3. his verbis dictis, senator e foro discessit.
4. ad tabernam cibo consumpto ire debeo.
5. te duce hostes vincemus.
6. omnibus rebus paratis, iter faciemus.
7. labore confecto, domum redibo.
8. num scelus civibus spectantibus accidit?
9. exercitu profecturo, nuntius appropinquans conspectus est.
10. epistulis scriptis, in viam egressus sum.

Exercise RS.27

Indirect statement (i)

Translate into English:

1. puer dixit servum in horto dormire.
2. miles hostes appropinquare nuntiat.
3. cives audiverunt navem principis advenisse.
4. sciebam hanc feminam ab omnibus laudari.
5. liberi laborem facilem esse mox cognoscent.
6. omnes credebant nuntium bene dixisse.
7. portam ab hostibus oppugnari videmus.
8. audivimus hunc locum optimum esse.
9. dominus servum fugisse intellexit.
10. scitisne bellum ibi geri?

Exercise RS.28

Indirect statement (ii)

Translate into English:

1. puella respondit se nihil in via vidisse.
2. urbem deletam esse audivimus.
3. spero matrem donum mihi missuram esse.
4. dux custodum captivos fugisse cognovit.
5. sentio quendam me sequi.
6. ancilla promisit se cenam optimam paraturam esse.
7. nuntius rettulit exercitum superatum esse.
8. putasne tempestatem silvam delevisse?
9. credimus hanc ancillam fidelissimam esse.
10. multi nesciebant templum incensum esse.

Exercise RS.29

Purpose clauses

Translate into English:

1. omnes ad forum festinaverunt ut verba imperatoris audirent.
2. ego in taberna manebam ne verba imperatoris audirem.
3. pater laborabat ut liberi cibum haberent.
4. currebam ut domum celerius advenirem.
5. servus in silva se celabat ne a domino inveniretur.
6. ancilla cibum emere debebat ut cenam pararet.
7. exercitus missus est ut auxilium civibus ferret.
8. Romam redire constitui ut amicos iterum viderem.
9. captivi a milite custodiebantur ne nocte effugerent.
10. puer prope portam manebat ut puellam salutaret.

Exercise RS.30

Other ways of expressing purpose; uses of *dum*

Translate into English:

1. puer prope portam manebat ad puellam salutandam.
2. dum per silvam ambulamus hominem mortuum invenimus.
3. femina domi manere constituit ad epistulas scribendas.
4. cives in foro exspectabant dum imperator adveniret.
5. ancilla tabernam intravit ad cibum emendum.
6. navis dum Romam navigat tempestate deleta est.
7. senator surrexit ad cives de periculo belli monendos.
8. matres ad portam manebant dum nuntius rediret.
9. agrum emi ad villam aedificandam.
10. puella librum legere constituit dum omnia verba intellegeret.

Exercise RS.31

Verbs of fearing

Translate into English:

1. servus timebat ne a domino videretur.
2. timebam ne custos me vocantem non audiret.
3. senex periculum itineris timebat.
4. omnes timebamus ne urbs ab hostibus oppugnaretur.
5. num times in illam silvam ire?
6. liberi timebant ne numquam adveniremus.
7. nihil de exercitu nostro audiveram, sed iterum rogare timebam.
8. puer timebat ne domi relinqueretur.
9. puella timuit ne clamor senem terreret.
10. femina olim timuerat ne spectaretur; postea timebat ne non spectaretur.

Exercise RS.32

Indirect commands

Translate into English:

1. dominus servo imperavit ut celerius laboraret.
2. senator turbam tacere iubebat.
3. pater filiam monuit ne huic puero crederet.
4. puella patri persuasit ut pecuniam sibi daret.
5. imperator suos hortabatur ut pro patria fortiter pugnarent.
6. rex servos liberari iussit.
7. domina ancillis imperavit ut cibum atque vinum pararent.
8. pueri domum ire iussi sunt?
9. senex omnes rogavit ne in templo loquerentur.
10. cives deos oraverunt ut auxilium urbi ferrent.

Exercise RS.33

Result clauses

Translate into English:

1. puella tam diligens erat ut omnia de hac re cognosceret.
2. captivus adeo clamabat ut a custode audiretur.
3. servus tam lente laborabat ut dominus eum puniret.
4. hortus villae tantus erat ut plures servos emere cogerer.
5. adeo timebamus ut dormire non possemus.
6. puer tam celeriter cucurrit ut praemium acciperet.
7. senex tot libros habebat ut maiorem domum quaereret.
8. tanta erat tempestas ut omnes naves delerentur.
9. senator ita locutus est ut cives ei crederent.
10. liber tam bene scriptus erat ut omnes intellegere possent.

Exercise RS.34

Cum clauses

Translate into English:

1. cum nox esset, nihil videre poteramus.
2. cum nihil audivissem, imperatorem de proelio iterum rogavi.
3. senex, cum epistulam uxoris accepisset, multo laetior erat.
4. cum domina irata esset, ancillae laborantes tacebant.
5. cives, cum nuntius victoriam narravisset, diu gaudebant.
6. cum montem ascenderem, exercitum appropinquantem vidi.
7. cum Romam advenissem, forum templaque spectare constitui.
8. cum dominus dormiret, servi ad tabernam iverunt.
9. liberi, cum nihil facere deberent, laeti erant.
10. cum domum rediissem, de itinere nostro saepe cogitabam.

Exercise RS.35

Indirect questions

Translate into English:

1. militem rogavi num de victoria audivisset.
2. dominus servum rogavit cur non laboraret.
3. liberos rogavi quo festinarent.
4. dux mox cognovit quot milites abessent.
5. puerumne rogavisti ubi pecuniam celavisset?
6. puellam rogavimus quid ibi faceret.
7. custos nesciebat quomodo omnes captivi effugissent.
8. senem rogabam num cibum haberet.
9. difficile erat cognoscere quis epistulam scripsisset.
10. ancilla rogata est num pecuniam abstulisset.

Exercise RS.36

Words easily confused (i)

Translate into English:

1. libertus novem novos libros liberis dedit.
2. in summo monte tandem sumus.
3. viam per totam vitam invenire conatus sum.
4. de verbis quae cognovistis cogitare cogemini, pueri.
5. senex nos monebat ne prope flumen maneremus.
6. dominus, quod domina donum rogaverat, novam domum aedificavit.
7. villam habeo, sed Romae habitare malo.
8. servus primo post ianuam iacebat; postea libros in flumen iaciebat.
9. miles fortis forte advenit et portam fortiter custodivit.
10. ubi regem conspexi, totam rem ei narrare constitui.

Exercise RS.37

Words easily confused (ii)

Translate into English:

1. imperator nunc abest, sed heri aderat: hic est locus ubi locutus est.
2. hostes subito de monte descenderunt et statim discesserunt.
3. tandem profecti sumus; lente tamen progressi sumus.
4. per silvam solus ambulare soleo.
5. hi milites, ubi verba imperatoris audiunt, omnia facere audent.
6. ancilla cibum emere vult ut cenam pararet.
7. alter mons altior, alter difficilior est.
8. ubi gladium capio, pugnare cupio.
9. senex uxorem hortatus est ut in horto sederet.
10. dux noster multos hostes vicit et multos annos vixit.

Exercise RS.38

Words easily confused (iii)

Translate into English:

1. iter ad insulam iterum facere volo.
2. imperator dicit se optimos milites ducere.
3. femina laeta est quod trans flumen lata est.
4. malo pecuniam bono servo quam malo liberto dare.
5. amicus a taberna ridens rediit et pecuniam mihi reddidit.
6. senator semper ita loquitur; itaque saepe a civibus laudatur.
7. arma quae portare potui pro porta posui.
8. simulac Romam advenimus, amicos simul discessisse cognovimus.
9. servos equum mortuum per agrum trahere et domino tradere iussimus.
10. hic miles, qui olim pugnare timebat, nunc omnes oppugnans terret.

Exercise RS.39

Words with more than one meaning (i)

Translate into English:

1. ubi est puella quam heri conspexi?
2. pueri per vias quam celerrime currebant.
3. quam longum est iter nostrum!
4. quam longum erat iter vestrum?
5. iter quod facere debemus longum est.
6. quod iter longum facimus, multum cibum portamus.
7. quando adveniemus ad locum ubi antea habitabamus?
8. exercitus ad insulam missus est ad hostes capiendos.
9. iuvenis cum fratre Romam advenit.
10. iuvenis, cum frater advenisset, Romae manere constituit.

Exercise RS.40

Words with more than one meaning (ii)

Translate into English:

1. servus celeriter laborabat ut laborem conficeret.
2. servo imperavi ut celeriter laboraret.
3. servus tam celeriter laborabat ut a domino laudaretur.
4. servus, ut antea dixi, celeriter laborabat.
5. servus celeriter laborabat ne a domino puniretur.
6. servo imperavi ne in agro dormiret.
7. servus, quamquam celeriter laborabat, timebat ne a domino puniretur.
8. laborasne, serve?
9. num in agro dormiebas, serve?
10. servum rogavi num in agro dormivisset.

RESTRICTED VOCABULARY AND GRAMMAR FOR GCSE ENGLISH TO LATIN SENTENCES

English to Latin sentences in the additional exercises below and in the practice papers use the following restricted vocabulary of 125 words (full details can be checked in the English to Latin and Latin to English vocabularies):

a/ab (+ *abl*)	cum (+ *abl*)	habeo	novus	scribo
ad (+ *acc*)	cur?	habito	nuntio	semper
advenio	curro	hora	nuntius	servo
aedifico	custodio	hortus	paro	servus
ager	dea	in (+ *acc*)	parvus	silva
ambulo	defendo	in (+ *abl*)	patria	statim
amicus	deus	intro	pecunia	subito
ancilla	dico	invenio	periculum	sum
annus	diu	invito	peto	supero
aqua	domina	ira	pono	taberna
arma	dominus	iratus	porta	taceo
audio	donum	laboro	porto	tandem
auxilium	dormio	laetus	possum	templum
bene	duco	libertus	puella	teneo
bibo	e/ex (+ *abl*)	longus	puer	terreo
bonus	epistula	magnus	quando?	timeo
cado	et	malus	-que	trado
capio	facio	maritus	regina	traho
cena	femina	mitto	regnum	venio
cibus	festino	multus	rego	via
clamo	filia	murus	relinquo	villa
consilium	filius	nauta	rogo	vinco
conspicio	forum	navigo	saepe	vinum
constituo	fugio	neco	saevus	vir
contra (+ *acc*)	gladius	non	saluto	voco

The sentences will test the following aspects of accidence and syntax:

Accidence

- The forms of regular verbs in the present, imperfect and perfect indicative active
- The present active infinitive of regular verbs
- The present and imperfect indicative of the verbs *sum* and *possum*
- The forms of regular nouns of the first and second declensions
- The forms of first and second declension adjectives of the *bonus/laetus* type (excluding their comparative and superlative forms)

Syntax

- Standard uses of the cases
- Use of the accusative case to express duration of time
- The cases taken by prepositions contained in the restricted vocabulary list
- Direct statements and direct questions

Each sentence is marked out of 3 or 4, as shown (one mark per word; a prepositional phrase, e.g. *in the garden*, can count as one mark).

ADDITIONAL GCSE ENGLISH
TO LATIN SENTENCES

Exercise EL.1

Translate into Latin:

   (a)   We have a good plan.   [3]

   (b)   The slaves were working in the garden.   [3]

   (c)   I immediately decided to seek help.   [4]

Exercise EL.2

Translate into Latin:

   (a)   I was afraid of the master's son.   [3]

   (b)   The men were guarding the walls.   [3]

   (c)   The gods and goddesses are silent.   [4]

Exercise EL.3

Translate into Latin:

   (a)   I sailed to my homeland at last.   [3]

   (b)   We hurried out of the wood.   [3]

   (c)   They were building the temple for many years.   [4]

Exercise EL.4

Translate into Latin:

   (a)   We often overcome danger.   [3]

   (b)   The girl sent a letter.   [3]

   (c)   Why do you not have a sword?   [4]

Exercise EL.5

Translate into Latin:

   (a)   They greeted the happy girl.   [3]

   (b)   I was not able to run.   [3]

   (c)   The woman's husband is a sailor.   [4]

Exercise EL.6

Translate into Latin:

    (a)   The boys were shouting in the street.   [3]

    (b)   The new slave-girl arrived.   [3]

    (c)   We always defend the kingdom with weapons.   [4]

Exercise EL.7

Translate into Latin:

    (a)   There is a gate in the wall.   [3]

    (b)   I suddenly fell into the water.   [3]

    (c)   The freedmen were drinking wine in the inn.   [4]

Exercise EL.8

Translate into Latin:

    (a)   We were walking for many hours.   [3]

    (b)   I caught sight of the messenger in the forum.   [3]

    (c)   The slave-girl is able to write well.   [4]

Exercise EL.9

Translate into Latin:

    (a)   They live in a big house.   [3]

    (b)   When did you find the money?   [3]

    (c)   I handed over the gift to the queen's daughter.   [4]

Exercise EL.10

Translate into Latin:

    (a)   I was sleeping in the field for a long time.   [3]

    (b)   He announced new plans.   [3]

    (c)   The angry master frightens the slaves.   [4]

GCSE PRACTICE PAPER 1

1 hour 30 minutes   Total mark 100

Answer **both** Section A **and** Section B

Section A

Read Passage 1 and answer the questions

Passage 1

The giant Atlas joins the wrong side in a war between Saturn and Jupiter, and is punished. Hercules later asks a favour.

Saturnus primus rex deorum erat. Iuppiter tamen, filius eius, patrem e caelo expulit. Saturnus igitur, ut regnum suum reciperet, auxilium ab amicis petivit; inter eos Atlas ad caelum ascendit. sed Iuppiter omnes vicit et Atlantem punire constituit: eum caelum in capite ferre coegit. Atlas in horto suo poma aurea habebat. Hercules a
5   Iunone iussus erat nonnulla horum pomorum ei ferre. Atlantem igitur rogavit ut tria poma sibi daret. Atlas 'hoc faciam' inquit 'si caelum unam horam tenebis.' caelo in capite Herculis posito, Atlas abiit ut poma quaereret. ubi tandem rediit, quod caelum iam tenere nolebat, promisit se ipsum poma deae traditurum esse.

Names

Saturnus, Saturni *m*	Saturn (*a god*)
Iuppiter, Iovis *m*	Jupiter (*a god*)
Atlas, Atlantis *m*	Atlas (*a giant*)
Hercules, Herculis *m*	Hercules (*a Greek hero*)
Iuno, Iunonis *f*	Juno (*queen of the gods*)

Vocabulary

expello, expellere, expuli, expulsus	I drive out
pomum, pomi *n*	apple
aureus, aurea, aureum	golden

1. *Saturnus primus rex deorum erat* (line 1): who was Saturn?   [1]

2. *Iuppiter tamen, filius eius, patrem e caelo expulit* (line 1): what did Jupiter do?   [2]

3. *Saturnus igitur, ut regnum suum reciperet, auxilium ab amicis petivit; inter eos Atlas ad caelum ascendit* (lines 2–3): why did Saturn seek the help of Atlas and other friends?   [2]

4. *sed Iuppiter omnes vicit et Atlantem punire constituit: eum caelum in capite ferre coegit* (lines 3–4): how did the victorious Jupiter punish Atlas?   [2]

5. *Atlas in horto suo poma aurea habebat. Hercules a Iunone iussus erat nonnulla horum pomorum ei ferre* (lines 4–5):

(a) where were the golden apples?   [1]

(b) what had Juno ordered Hercules to do?   [2]

6. *Atlantem igitur rogavit ut tria poma sibi daret. Atlas 'hoc faciam'*
    inquit 'si caelum unam horam tenebis' (lines 5–6): on what condition
    did Atlas say he would do what Hercules asked?   [3]

7. *caelo in capite Herculis posito, Atlas abiit ut poma quaereret*
    (lines 6–7): what did Atlas go away to do?   [1]

8. *ubi tandem rediit, quod caelum iam tenere nolebat, promisit se ipsum*
    poma deae traditurum esse (lines 7–8): why did Atlas promise that he
    himself would fulfil the order given to Hercules?   [2]

9. For each of the Latin words below, give one English word that has
    been derived from the Latin word and give the meaning of the English
    word. One has been done for you.

auxilium	auxiliary	giving help
capite		[2]
horto		[2]

Answer **either** Question 10 **or** Question 11

10. Answer the following questions based on part of the story you have
    already read.

    Saturnus igitur, ut regnum suum reciperet, auxilium ab amicis petivit; inter
    eos Atlas ad caelum ascendit. sed Iuppiter omnes vicit et Atlantem punire
    constituit: eum caelum in capite ferre coegit. Atlas in horto suo poma aurea
    habebat. Hercules a Iunone iussus erat nonnulla horum pomorum ei ferre.

    (a) Identify an example of the **accusative** case in line 1   [1]
    (b) *auxilium ab amicis petivit* (line 1): identify the **case** of *amicis* **and**
        explain why this case is used here.   [2]
    (c) Identify an example of the **perfect** tense in line 2.   [1]
    (d) *in capite ferre* (line 3): identify the **case** of *capite* **and** explain
        why this case is used here.   [2]
    (e) *caelum . . . ferre coegit* (line 3): identify the **form** of *ferre* **and**
        explain why it is used here.   [2]
    (f) *Atlas . . . poma aurea habebat* (lines 3–4): identify the **tense** of
        habebat.   [1]
    (g) Pick out a **pronoun** in line 4.   [1]

Do **not** answer Question 11 if you have already answered Question 10.

11. Translate the following sentences into Latin:
    (a) The boys are carrying the food.   [3]
    (b) The woman went into the house.   [3]
    (c) I was working in the forum for many hours.   [4]

Section B

Read Passage 2 and answer the questions.

Passage 2

Tiberius Gracchus introduces new laws to help the poor in Rome, but angers the senators.

eo tempore <u>Tiberius Gracchus</u>, iuvenis optimus atque patris clarissimi filius, <u>tribunus</u> factus est. <u>Gracchus</u>, qui miles fortis antea fuerat, multas virtutes habebat sed urbem Romam in periculum grave adduxit. nuntiavit enim se novas <u>leges</u> facturum esse ut agros civibus <u>pauperibus</u> daret. multi igitur ei favebant.

5 nam <u>pauperes</u> saepe nec terram nec cibum habebant; <u>Gracchus</u> eos defendebat contra <u>divites</u> qui multam terram plurimosque servos habebant. itaque multi cives novas <u>leges</u> vehementer laudaverunt. <u>Gracchus</u> tamen iram senatorum celeriter <u>incitavit</u>, quod consilium eorum non petiverat. nonnulli etiam timebant ne <u>Gracchus</u> se regem facere conaretur.

Name

Tiberius Gracchus, Tiberii Gracchi *m*	Tiberius Gracchus (*also called just* Gracchus)

Vocabulary

tribunus, tribuni *m*	tribune (*a type of Roman official*)
lex, legis *f*	law
pauper, pauperis	poor
dives, divitis	rich
incito, incitare, incitavi, incitatus	I provoke, I stir up

12. *eo tempore <u>Tiberius Gracchus</u>, iuvenis optimus atque patris clarissimi filius, <u>tribunus</u> factus est* (lines 1–2): what do we learn about Tiberius Gracchus here? Make three points.   [3]

13. *<u>Gracchus</u>, qui miles fortis antea fuerat, multas virtutes habebat sed urbem Romam in periculum grave adduxit* (lines 2–3): describe the contrast between different aspects of Gracchus' character and actions.   [4]

14. *nuntiavit enim se novas <u>leges</u> facturum esse ut agros civibus <u>pauperibus</u> daret* (lines 3–4): what was the purpose of the new laws?   [2]

15. *nam <u>pauperes</u> saepe nec terram nec cibum habebant; <u>Gracchus</u> eos defendebat contra <u>divites</u> qui multam terram plurimosque servos habebant* (lines 5–6):
    (a) what did the poor people often not have?   [2]
    (b) what did the rich people have?   [2]

16. *itaque multi cives novas <u>leges</u> vehementer laudaverunt* (lines 6–7): write down and translate the Latin phrase that tells us the way many citizens reacted to the new laws.   [2]

17. *Gracchus tamen iram senatorum celeriter <u>incitavit</u>, quod consilium eorum non petiverat* (lines 7–8): why were the senators angry?   [2]

18. *nonnulli etiam timebant ne <u>Gracchus</u> se regem facere conaretur* (lines 8–9): what did some senators fear Gracchus might try to do?   [3]

Passage 3

After Scipio persuades the senators to attack Gracchus and his supporters on the Capitol, Gracchus is killed.

senatores igitur, ubi cognoverunt <u>Gracchum</u> comitesque ad <u>Capitolium</u> convenisse, in foro cogitaverunt quid facere deberent. <u>Scipio</u>, qui consul tum erat, timebat ne <u>Gracchus</u> imperium senatorum delere vellet. itaque omnes hortatus est ut Romam ex hoc periculo servarent. quibus verbis auditis, senatores
5   statim ad <u>Capitolium</u> festinaverunt arma ferentes. ibi <u>Gracchus</u> amicique omnia parabant ut eis resisterent. senatores tamen eos tam ferociter oppugnaverunt ut plurimi perterriti fugerent. ceteri, qui <u>Gracchum</u> summa virtute defenderant, mox oppressi sunt. dum <u>Gracchus</u> ipse de <u>Capitolio</u> currit, ad terram forte cecidit. eum surgere conantem <u>Lucius Rufus</u> gladio vulneravit. hoc modo <u>Gracchus</u>,
10   vulnere gravissimo accepto, mortem crudelem passus est. eodem die corpus eius in flumen iactum est.

Names

Gracchus, Gracchi *m*	Gracchus
Capitolium, Capitolii *n*	the Capitol (*a hill in Rome*)
Scipio, Scipionis *m*	Scipio
Lucius Rufus, Lucii Rufi *m*	Lucius Rufus (*a senator*)

19. Translate Passage 3 into good English.   [50]

GCSE PRACTICE PAPER 2

1 hour 30 minutes   Total mark 100

Answer **both** Section A **and** Section B

Section A

Read Passage 1 and answer the questions

Passage 1

Proserpina is abducted by Pluto, causing her mother great grief.

Proserpina erat filia deae Cereris. olim cum comitibus per agros ambulabat. ubi
flores pulchros conspexit, 'puellae,' inquit 'nonne vultis hos flores carpere?' sed
tanto amore florum capta est ut procul a comitibus erraret. mox igitur ceterae
puellae, quod eam videre non poterant, Proserpinam saepe vocabant. illa tamen
5   comites audire non poterat. tum Pluto, rex mortuorum, puellam conspectam
rapuit et in regnum suum traxit. Proserpina magna voce matrem oravit ut
auxilium ferret. sed Ceres filiam perterritam non audivit. cum tamen cognovisset
Proserpinam abductam esse, tristissima erat. deinde iter multas per terras facere
constituit, ut filiam quaereret.

Names

Proserpina, Proserpinae *f*	Proserpina
Ceres, Cereris *f*	Ceres (*goddess of agriculture*)
Pluto, Plutonis *m*	Pluto (*god of the Underworld*)

Vocabulary

flos, floris *m*	flower
carpo, carpere, carpsi, carptus	I pick
procul	far away
erro, errare, erravi, erratus	I wander

1. *Proserpina erat filia deae Cereris* (line 1): who was Proserpina?   [1]

2. *olim cum comitibus per agros ambulabat. ubi flores pulchros conspexit,*
    'puellae,' inquit 'nonne vultis hos flores carpere ?' (lines 1–2):
    (a) what were Proserpina and her companions doing?   [1]
    (b) what did Proserpina ask her companions when she saw the flowers?   [2]

3. *sed tanto amore florum capta est ut procul a comitibus erraret*
    (lines 2–3): why did Proserpina wander off on her own?   [2]

4. *mox igitur ceterae puellae, quod eam videre non poterant, Proserpinam*
    saepe vocabant. illa tamen comites audire non poterat (lines 3–5):
    (a) what could the other girls not do?   [1]
    (b) how does the second sentence show that Proserpina had
        wandered a long way from her companions?   [2]

5. *tum* <u>Pluto</u>, *rex mortuorum, puellam conspectam rapuit et in regnum suum traxit* (lines 5–6):
   (a) who was Pluto?   [1]
   (b) what did he do when he caught sight of the girl?   [2]

6. <u>*Proserpina*</u> *magna voce matrem oravit ut auxilium ferret. sed* <u>*Ceres*</u> *filiam perterritam non audivit* (lines 6–7): why did Ceres not respond to her daughter's cry for help?   [1]

7. *cum tamen cognovisset* <u>*Proserpinam*</u> *abductam esse, tristissima erat* (lines 7–8): how did Ceres feel when she found out that Proserpina had been taken away?   [1]

8. *deinde iter multas per terras facere constituit, ut filiam quaereret* (lines 8–9): why did Ceres make a journey through many lands?   [2]

9. For each of the Latin words below, give one English word that has been derived from the Latin word and give the meaning of the English word. One has been done for you.
agros	agriculture	farming
audire		[2]
mortuorum		[2]

Answer **either** Question 10 **or** Question 11

10. Answer the following questions based on part of the story you have already read.

    tum <u>Pluto</u>, rex mortuorum, puellam conspectam rapuit et in regnum suum traxit. <u>Proserpina</u> magna voce matrem oravit ut auxilium ferret. sed <u>Ceres</u> filiam perterritam non audivit. cum tamen cognovisset <u>Proserpinam</u> abductam esse, tristissima erat. deinde iter multas per terras facere constituit, ut filiam quaereret.

    (a) Identify an example of the **nominative** case in line 1.   [1]
    (b) Pick out a **participle** in line 1.   [1]
    (c) *magna voce . . . oravit* (line 2): identify the **case** of *voce* **and** explain why this case is used here.   [2]
    (d) *oravit ut auxilium ferret* (line 2): explain why *ferret* is in the **subjunctive** mood.   [1]
    (e) Identify an example of the **perfect** tense in line 3.   [1]
    (f) Pick out a **superlative** adjective in line 4.   [1]
    (g) *iter . . . facere constituit* (line 4): identify the **form** of *facere* **and** explain why it is used here.   [2]
    (h) Identify the **case** of *filiam* (line 4).   [1]

Do **not** answer Question 11 if you have already answered Question 10.

11. Translate the following sentences into Latin:
    (a) Why are you holding a sword?   [3]
    (b) The girls entered the temple.   [3]
    (c) The slave was afraid of the savage master.   [4]

Section B

Read Passage 2 and answer the questions.

Passage 2

The retired general Publius Scipio receives some surprise visitors.

Publius Scipio dux Romanus olim erat qui multas gentes bello vicerat. clarissimus
inter cives propter magnas victorias erat; etiam hostes eum propter virtutem
mirabantur. cum senex iam esset, in villa sua prope mare habitabat. tam clarus
erat ut plurimi ad villam iter facerent, quod sperabant se tantum ducem
5 conspecturos esse. olim nonnulli piratae, qui antea contra Romanos pugnaverant,
ad villam navigaverunt ut eum viderent. Scipio tamen, ubi piratas in armis adesse
vidisset, timebat ne villam oppugnare et pecuniam auferre conarentur. itaque
servos villam defendere iussit. ipse interea cogitabat quomodo piratas repellere et
e periculo effugere posset.

Names
> Publius Scipio, Publii Scipionis *m*   Publius Scipio (*also called just* Scipio)

Vocabulary
> pirata, piratae *m*   pirate

12. *Publius Scipio dux Romanus olim erat qui multas gentes bello vicerat*
    (line 1): what does this sentence tell us about Scipio's success as a
    Roman general?   [2]

13. *clarissimus inter cives propter magnas victorias erat; etiam hostes eum
    propter virtutem mirabantur* (lines 1–3): what do we learn here about
    his reputation?   [4]

14. *cum senex iam esset, in villa sua prope mare habitabat* (line 3): how
    was Scipio spending his old age?   [3]

15. *tam clarus erat ut plurimi ad villam iter facerent, quod sperabant se
    tantum ducem conspecturos esse* (lines 3–5): why did so many people
    come to Scipio's villa?   [3]

16. *olim nonnulli piratae, qui antea contra Romanos pugnaverant, ad
    villam navigaverunt ut eum viderent* (lines 5–6): what was surprising
    about these particular visitors?   [3]

17. *Scipio tamen, ubi piratas in armis adesse vidisset, timebat ne villam
    oppugnare et pecuniam auferre conarentur* (lines 6–7): what was
    Scipio afraid the pirates would do?   [2]

18. *itaque servos villam defendere iussit. ipse interea cogitabat quomodo
    piratas repellere et e periculo effugere posset* (lines 7–9):
    (a) what did Scipio order his slaves to do?   [1]
    (b) write down and translate the Latin phrase that indicates what
        Scipio hoped to achieve by driving the pirates away.   [2]

Passage 3

When their intentions become clear, Scipio welcomes his visitors.

<u>piratae</u> igitur, ubi omnia sic parata esse viderunt, arma sua statim deposuerunt. ianuae villae lente appropinquaverunt. deinde magna voce nuntiaverunt se <u>Scipionem</u> non necaturos venisse, sed propter virtutem laudaturos. 'credemus nos' inquiunt 'donum a deis accepisse si te videre poterimus.' <u>piratae</u> sic orabant ut
5 <u>Scipio</u> nunc e villa exiret. postquam servi haec verba <u>Scipioni</u> rettulerunt, ipse ianuam <u>aperuit</u> atque <u>piratas</u> ad cenam invitavit. hoc modo salutati, <u>piratae</u> in villam sicut in templum intraverunt et <u>Scipioni</u> multa dona dederunt quae deis offerri solent. tandem <u>piratae</u> ad naves suas redierunt, maxime gaudentes quod a <u>Scipione</u> libenter accepti erant.

Names

Scipio, Scipionis *m*	Scipio

Vocabulary

pirata, piratae *m*	pirate
aperio, aperire, aperui	I open

19. Translate Passage 3 into good English. [50]

GCSE PRACTICE PAPER 3

1 hour 30 minutes   Total mark 100

Answer **both** Section A **and** Section B

Section A

Read Passage 1 and answer the questions

Passage 1

Jupiter is upset by the wickedness of human beings and tells the other gods what he intends to do about it.

Iuppiter iratus erat quod homines scelesti erant. iter igitur ad terram facere constituit ut ipse videret quid facerent. itaque formam viri cepit, ne homines scirent quis esset. deinde ad regem Lycaonem venit, quem crudelissimum esse audiverat. Lycaon tamen statim intellexit deum adesse, et consilium dirum cepit: deum salutatum invitavit
5   ut in villa sua maneret. nam in animo habebat eum ibi dormientem nocte necare. sed Iuppiter, cum cognovisset quid a rege pararetur, ad caelum rediit. omnes homines diluvio delere constituit. ubi ceteri dei rogaverunt 'si hoc facies, quis nobis dona dabit?', Iuppiter promisit se aliam gentem hominum postea facturum esse. deinde Neptunum vocatum imbres gravissimos in terram mittere iussit.

Names

Iuppiter, Iovis *m*	Jupiter (*king of the gods*)
Lycaon, Lycaonis *m*	Lycaon
Neptunus, Neptuni *m*	Neptune (*god of the sea*)

Vocabulary

forma, formae *f*	form, shape
diluvium, diluvii *n*	flood
imber, imbris *m*	shower of rain

1. *Iuppiter iratus erat quod homines scelesti erant* (line 1): why was
    Jupiter angry?   [1]

2. *iter igitur ad terram facere constituit ut ipse videret quid facerent*
    (lines 1–2): what did Jupiter decide to do, and why?   [2]

3. *itaque formam viri cepit, ne homines scirent quis esset. deinde ad regem*
    Lycaonem venit, quem crudelissimum esse audiverat (lines 2–3):
    (a) why did Jupiter take on human form?   [1]
    (b) why did he visit Lycaon?   [2]

4. *Lycaon tamen statim intellexit deum adesse, et consilium dirum cepit.*
    deum salutatum invitavit ut in villa sua maneret, nam in animo
    habebat eum ibi dormientem nocte necare (lines 3–5):
    (a) what did Lycaon invite his visitor to do?   [1]
    (b) what did he plan to do while his visitor was asleep?   [1]

5. *sed Iuppiter, cum cognovisset quid a rege pararetur, ad caelum rediit*
    (line 6): what did Jupiter do when he realised what Lycaon was
    planning?   [1]

6. *omnes homines diluvio delere constituit* (lines 6–7): what did Jupiter
    decide to do?   [1]

7. *ubi ceteri dei rogaverunt 'si hoc facies, quis nobis dona dabit?', Iuppiter*
    promisit se aliam gentem hominum postea facturum esse (lines 7–9):
    (a) what did the other gods ask?   [2]
    (b) what did Jupiter promise to create later?   [2]

8. *deinde Neptunum vocatum imbres gravissimos in terram mittere iussit*
    (line 9): after summoning Neptune, what did Jupiter order him
    to do?   [2]

9. For each of the Latin words below, give one English word that has been
    derived from the Latin word and give the meaning of the English word.
    One has been done for you.

    nocte   nocturnal   operates by night
    dona   [2]
    terram   [2]

Answer **either** Question 10 **or** Question 11

10. Answer the following questions based on part of the story you have already
     read.

     Lycaon tamen statim intellexit deum adesse, et consilium dirum cepit: deum
     salutatum invitavit ut in villa sua maneret. nam in animo habebat eum ibi
     dormientem nocte necare. sed Iuppiter, cum cognovisset quid a rege pararetur,
     ad caelum rediit. omnes homines diluvio delere constituit.

     (a) Identify an example of the **accusative** case in line 1.   [1]
     (b) *invitavit* (line 2): identify the **tense** of this verb.   [1]
     (c) *in villa sua* (line 2): identify the **case** of *villa* **and** explain why
         this case is used here.   [2]
     (d) Pick out a **pronoun** in line 2.   [1]
     (e) *cum cognovisset* (line 3): explain why *cognovisset* is in the
         subjunctive mood.   [1]
     (f) *ad caelum* (line 4): identify the case of *caelum* **and** explain why
         this case is used here.   [2]
     (g) *diluvio delere* (line 4): identify the **form** of *delere* **and** explain
         why it is used here.   [2]

Do **not** answer Question 11 if you have already answered Question 10.

11. Translate the following sentences into Latin:
     (a) The road was long.   [3]
     (b) We have good friends.   [3]
     (c) When did the slave kill the master?   [4]

Section B

Read Passage 2 and answer the questions.

Passage 2

An incident in battle shows Caesar's leadership qualities.

<u>Caesar</u> erat imperator audacissimus qui omnium ducum Romanorum virtutem maximam habebat. periculum enim numquam timebat; semper pugnare quam fugere malebat. in omnibus rebus celer erat: longissima enim itinera brevissimo tempore saepe faciebat. nec montes nec flumina exercitum eius <u>impediebant</u>. hoc
5 modo <u>Caesar</u> hostes et terrere et capere poterat. olim in proelio <u>Caesar</u> <u>aquiliferum</u> conspexit periculo perterritum atque fugere parantem. quem ubi vidit, manum suam ad hostes tendens, clamavit <u>Caesar</u> 'quo tu abis? <u>illic</u> sunt ei cum quibus pugnamus!' tum <u>aquiliferum</u> <u>iugulo</u> rapuit ut eum in proelium contra hostes remitteret. hoc modo, cum unum militem manibus verbisque monuisset,
10 toti exercitui spem victoriae reddidit.

Names

Caesar, Caesaris *m*	Caesar

Vocabulary

impedio, impedire, impedivi	I hinder, I get in the way of
aquilifer, aquiliferi *m*	standard-bearer (*soldier who carried a legion's standard into battle*)
illic	over there
iugulum, iuguli *n*	throat

12. *Caesar erat imperator audacissimus qui omnium ducum Romanorum virtutem maximam habebat* (lines 1–2): what do we learn here about Caesar's qualities as a general?   [3]

13. *periculum enim numquam timebat; semper pugnare quam fugere malebat* (lines 2–3): what made him such a great leader?   [2]

14. *in omnibus rebus celer erat: longissima enim itinera brevissimo tempore saepe faciebat. nec montes nec flumina exercitum eius impediebant* (lines 3–4):
    (a) what did Caesar's speed enable him to do?   [2]
    (b) what features of the landscape proved no obstacle to his army?   [2]

15. *hoc modo Caesar hostes et terrere et capere poterat* (lines 4–5): what was Caesar able to do?   [2]

16. *olim in proelio Caesar aquiliferum conspexit periculo perterritum atque fugere parantem* (lines 5–6): when Caesar saw the standard-bearer, what two things did he notice about him?   [2]

17. *quem ubi vidit, manum suam ad hostes tendens, clamavit Caesar 'quo tu abis? illic sunt ei cum quibus pugnamus!'* (lines 6–8): what did Caesar say to the standard-bearer?   [3]

18. *tum aquiliferum iugulo rapuit ut eum in proelium contra hostes remitteret* (lines 8–9): why did Caesar grab the standard-beaerer by the throat?   [2]

19. *hoc modo, cum unum militem manibus verbisque monuisset, toti exercitui spem victoriae reddidit* (lines 9–10): write down and translate the Latin phrase which expresses what Caesar's treatment of this one soldier restored to the whole army.   [2]

Passage 3

When his men are under attack, Caesar inspires them with his bravery.

illo tempore milites Romani virtutem Caesaris adeo mirabantur ut eum libenter sequerentur. olim, in bello quod contra Gallos a Caesare gerebatur, Galli copias Romanas ferocissime opprimebant. Caesar, cum conspexisset nonnullos centuriones occisos esse atque ceteros tam gravibus vulneribus confectos esse ut
5 armis hostium iam resistere non possent, ipse in primam aciem audacissime procedere ausus est. deinde centuriones nominatim vocatos vehementer hortatus est ut hostes fortiter repellerent. hoc viso, milites antea perterriti nunc fortius pugnare coeperunt. sic Caesar legiones vinci paratas vincere saepissime docuit. octo annos in Gallia pugnabat. tandem, ubi multas gentes ibi superavit, totam
10 Galliam vicit imperioque Romano addidit.

Names

Caesar, Caesaris *m*	Caesar
Galli, Gallorum *m pl*	the Gauls
Gallia, Galliae *f*	Gaul (*modern France and surrounding area*)

Vocabulary

centurio, centurionis *m*	centurion
acies, aciei *f*	line of battle
nominatim	by name
addo, addere, addidi, additus	I add

20. Translate Passage 3 into good English.   [50]

GCSE PRACTICE PAPER 4

1 hour 30 minutes   Total mark 100

Answer **both** Section A **and** Section B

Section A

Read Passage 1 and answer the questions

Passage 1

Apollo and Neptune offer to help Laomedon, king of Troy, but he cheats them. His city is punished, but Hercules comes to the rescue.

Laomedon erat rex Troiae. olim Apollo regem muros aedificare parantem conspexit. deus 'si nobis' inquit 'dona dabis, Neptunus muros aedificabit, et ego oves tuas custodiam.' Laomedon tamen, cum muri aedificati essent, deis dona promissa non tradidit. Neptunus igitur regem punire constituit: anguem ingentem Troiam misit ut

5 puellas consumeret. Laomedon perterritus ceteros deos rogavit quid facere deberet. dei monuerunt ut filiam eius angui daret. cum rex hoc facere nollet, Neptunus imbres ingentes in terram Troiae misit. agri deleti sunt; cives miserrimi erant quod nullum cibum habebant. tandem igitur rex filiam lacrimantem prope mare reliquit. Hercules tamen, qui forte aderat, puellam servavit.

Names

Laomedon, Laomedontis *m*	Laomedon
Troia, Troiae *f*	Troy (*a city*)
Apollo, Apollinis *m*	Apollo (*a god*)
Neptunus, Neptuni *m*	Neptune (*god of the sea*)
Hercules, Herculis *m*	Hercules

Vocabulary

ovis, ovis *f*	sheep
anguis, anguis *m*	snake
imber, imbris *m*	shower of rain

1. *Laomedon erat rex Troiae. olim Apollo regem muros aedificare parantem conspexit* (line 1):
    (a) who was Laomedon?   [1]
    (b) what did Apollo find him doing?   [2]

2. *deus 'si nobis' inquit 'dona dabis, Neptunus muros aedificabit, et ego oves tuas custodiam'* (lines 2–3): Apollo said that, in return for gifts, he would look after Laomedon's sheep. What would Neptune do?   [2]

3. *Laomedon tamen, cum muri aedificati essent, deis dona promissa non tradidit* (lines 3–4): how did Laomedon break his promise?   [3]

4. *Neptunus igitur regem punire constituit: anguem ingentem Troiam
   misit ut puellas consumeret* (lines 4–5): how did Neptune punish
   the king?   [3]

5. *Laomedon perterritus ceteros deos rogavit quid facere deberet. dei
   monuerunt ut filiam eius angui daret* (lines 5–6): when Laomedon
   asked the other gods for advice, what did they say he should do? [2]

6. *cum rex hoc facere nollet, Neptunus imbres ingentes in terram
   Troiae misit* (lines 6–7): what did Neptune do next to punish Troy? [2]

7. *agri deleti sunt; cives miserrimi erant quod nullum cibum habebant*
   (lines 7–8): why did the destruction of the fields make the citizens
   very miserable?   [1]

8. *tandem igitur rex filiam lacrimantem prope mare reliquit. Hercules
   tamen, qui forte aderat, puellam servavit* (lines 8–9):
   (a) what did the king do?   [3]
   (b) what lucky event led to the girl being saved?   [1]

9. For each of the Latin words below, give one English word that has been
   derived from the Latin word and give the meaning of the English word.
   One has been done for you.

   muros   mural   wall painting
   custodiam   [2]
   cives   [2]

Answer **either** Question 10 **or** Question 11

10. Answer the following questions based on part of the story you have already
    read.

    Laomedon tamen, cum muri aedificati essent, deis dona promissa non tradidit.
    Neptunus igitur regem punire constituit: anguem ingentem Troiam misit ut puellas
    consumeret. Laomedon perterritus ceteros deos rogavit quid facere deberet. dei
    monuerunt ut filiam eius angui daret. cum rex hoc facere nollet, Neptunus imbres
    ingentes in terram Troiae misit.

    (a) Identify an example of the **nominative** case in line 1.   [1]
    (b) *deis dona . . . non tradidit* (line 1): identify the case of *deis* **and**
        explain why this case is used here.   [2]
    (c) Identify an example of the **perfect** tense in line 2.   [1]
    (d) Pick out an **adjective** in line 2.   [1]
    (e) *rogavit quid facere deberet* (line 3): explain why *deberet* is in the
        subjunctive mood.   [1]
    (f) Pick out a **pronoun** in line 4.   [1]
    (g) *hoc facere nollet* (line 4): identify the **form** of *facere* and explain
        why it is used here.   [2]
    (h) Pick out a **preposition** in line 5.   [1]

Do **not** answer Question 11 if you have already answered Question 10.

11. Translate the following sentences into Latin:
     (a) I was not able to run away.   [3]
     (b) When did you hear the message?   [3]
     (c) The queen was ruling the kingdom well.   [4]

Section B

Read Passage 2 and answer the questions.

Passage 2

After Nero gets rid of his mother's favourite, Pallas, she turns against him and supports his rival for the throne, Britannicus. Nero attemps to kill Britannicus.

Pallas libertus erat cui Agrippina, mater imperatoris, in omnibus rebus favebat. Nero tamen Pallanti non credebat, quod magnum imperium multamque pecuniam habebat. ille igitur Roma discedere ab imperatore coactus est. postquam Nero Pallantem expulit, Agrippina iratissima erat. statim filium minari coepit.
5 'Britannicus,' inquit 'cuius pater erat imperator Claudius, iam adultus est. ille, non filius meus, imperator esse debet.' Nero, his verbis territus, Britannicum interficere constituit. hoc tamen aperte facere nolebat, quod cives Romani Britannicum maxime amabant; itaque militi cuidam imperavit ut venenum in cibum Britannici poneret. iuvenis tamen, consumpto veneno, non mortuus est. Nero igitur iterum
10 conari coactus est.

Names

Pallas, Pallantis *m*	Pallas
Agrippina, Agrippinae *f*	Agrippina
Nero, Neronis *m*	Nero
Britannicus, Britannici *m*	Britannicus
Claudius, Claudii *m*	Claudius

Vocabulary

minor, minari, minatus sum	I threaten
adultus, adulta, adultum	adult
aperte	openly
venenum, veneni *n*	poison

12. *Pallas libertus erat cui Agrippina, mater imperatoris, in omnibus rebus favebat* (line 1): what do we learn about Pallas here?   [3]

13. *Nero tamen Pallanti non credebat, quod magnum imperium multamque pecuniam habebat. ille igitur Roma discedere ab imperatore coactus est* (lines 1–3):
     (a) why did Nero not trust Pallas?   [2]
     (b) what was Pallas forced to do as a result?   [1]

14. *postquam Nero Pallantem expulit, Agrippina iratissima erat. statim filium minari coepit* (lines 3–4): how did Agrippina react to her son's treatment of Pallas?   [2]

15. *'Britannicus,'* inquit *'cuius pater erat imperator* <u>Claudius</u>, *iam* <u>adultus</u>
    est. ille, non filius meus, imperator esse debet' (lines 5–6): describe
    fully what Agrippina said about Britannicus.   [4]

16. <u>Nero</u>, *his verbis territus,* <u>Britannicum</u> *interficere constituit* (lines 6–7):
    what did Nero decide to do?   [1]

17. *hoc tamen* <u>aperte</u> *facere nolebat, quod cives Romani* <u>Britannicum</u>
    maxime amabant (lines 7–8): why was Nero unwilling to take
    action openly?   [2]

18. *itaque militi cuidam imperavit ut* <u>venenum</u> *in cibum* <u>Britannici</u>
    poneret. iuvenis tamen, consumpto <u>veneno</u>, *non mortuus est* (lines 8–9):
    (a) what did Nero order the soldier to do?   [2]
    (b) what was the result?   [2]

19. <u>Nero</u> *igitur iterum conari coactus est* (lines 9–10): what was Nero forced
    to do?   [1]

Passage 3

Nero makes a second and more successful attempt to dispose of Britannicus.

<u>Britannicus</u> cum <u>familia</u> et amicis sedebat ut cenam consumeret. quod semper
timebat ne inimicus quidam se interficere conaretur, unus e servis omnem cibum
vinumque <u>gustavit</u>, <u>priusquam</u> <u>Britannico</u> data sunt. ubi <u>poculum</u> vini <u>nimis</u>
<u>calidi</u>, in quod nullum <u>venenum</u> positum erat, ei datum est, <u>Britannicus</u> iussit
5 servum aquam <u>frigidam</u> vino <u>addere</u>. in hac aqua fuit <u>venenum</u>, validius quam
antea; quod per totum corpus tam celeriter <u>pervasit</u> ut vox et <u>spiritus</u> statim
raperentur. omnes <u>Neronem</u> spectabant: ille tamen dixit <u>Britannicum</u> talia saepe
pati, et mox iterum locuturum esse. ceteris ad cenam reversis, <u>Agrippina</u> sola,
quae filium suum bene cognoverat, intellexit <u>Britannicum</u> iam mori.

Names

Britannicus, Britannici *m*	Britannicus
Nero, Neronis *m*	Nero
Agrippina, Agrippinae *f*	Agrippina

Vocabulary

familia, familiae *f*	family
gusto, gustare, gustavi, gustatus	I taste
priusquam	before
poculum, poculi *n*	cup
nimis	too
calidus, calida, calidum	hot
venenum, veneni *n*	poison
frigidus, frigida, frigidum	cold
addo, addere, addidi, additus	I add
pervado, pervadere, pervasi	I spread
spiritus, spiritus *m*	breath

20. Translate Passage 3 into good English.   [50]

GCSE PRACTICE PAPER 5

1 hour 30 minutes   Total marks 100

Answer **both** Section A **and** Section B

Section A

Read Passage 1 and answer the questions

Passage 1

Hercules' master has ordered him to fetch some cows. On the return journey via Rome, he stops by a river. Cacus steals some of the cows, but his trickery is later exposed.

olim Hercules cum novem vaccis pulcherrimis Romam iter faciebat. Tiberi appropinquavit ut vaccae aquam biberent. Hercules ipse multum vinum bibit et mox dormiebat. deinde Cacus, pastor qui prope flumen habitabat, vaccas auferre constituit. 'Hercules tamen' sibi inquit 'vestigia earum facile videbit. quomodo
5   eum decipere possum?' tum consilium callidum cepit. tres vaccas in speluncam suam caudis retro traxit. Hercules, ubi postea surrexit, statim sensit has vaccas abesse: vestigia tamen a spelunca ducentia conspexit. perterritus igitur e tam diro loco discedere parabat. deinde tamen vaccae ablatae, quae ceteras vaccas discedere senserunt, mugire coeperunt. Hercules igitur, cum cognovisset ubi
10 vaccae essent, Caco necato omnes servavit.

Names

Hercules, Herculis *m*	Hercules
Tiberis, Tiberis *m*	the Tiber (*river which flows through Rome*)
Cacus, Caci *m*	Cacus

Vocabulary

vacca, vaccae *f*	cow
pastor, pastoris *m*	shepherd
vestigium, vestigii *n*	footprint, track
decipio, decipere, decepi, deceptus	I deceive, I cheat
callidus, callida, callidum	clever
spelunca, speluncae *f*	cave
cauda, caudae *f*	tail
retro	backwards
mugio, mugire, mugivi	I moo, I bellow

1. *olim Hercules cum novem vaccis pulcherrimis Romam iter faciebat* (line 1): what do we learn about the cows Hercules had with him on his journey to Rome? Make two points.   [2]

2. *Tiberi appropinquavit ut vaccae aquam biberent* (lines 1–2): why did
    he approach the river?   [2]

3. *Hercules ipse multum vinum bibit et mox dormiebat. deinde Cacus,*
    pastor qui prope flumen habitabat, vaccas auferre constituit
    (lines 2–4):
    (a) who was Cacus?   [1]
    (b) what did he decide to do while Hercules was asleep?   [1]

4. *'Hercules tamen' sibi inquit 'vestigia earum facile videbit. quomodo eum*
    decipere possum?' tum consilium callidum cepit. tres vaccas in speluncam
    suam caudis retro traxit (lines 4–6): Cacus realised that Hercules would
    easily see the cows' footprints. Explain how his plan got round this
    problem.   [3]

5. *Hercules, ubi postea surrexit, statim sensit has vaccas abesse: vestigia*
    tamen a spelunca ducentia conspexit (lines 6–7):
    (a) what did Hercules immediately realise when he got up?   [1]
    (b) what did he see?   [1]

6. *perterritus igitur e tam diro loco discedere parabat* (lines 7–8): Hercules
    was terrified. Write down and translate the Latin words that describe
    the place that he wanted to leave.   [2]

7. *deinde tamen vaccae ablatae, quae ceteras vaccas discedere senserunt,*
    mugire coeperunt (lines 8–9): how did the stolen cows react to the
    departure of the others?   [1]

8. *Hercules igitur, cum cognovisset ubi vaccae essent, Caco necato omnes*
    servavit (lines 9–10): what did Hercules do after finding out where the
    cows were? Make two points.   [2]

9. For each of the Latin words below, give one English word that has been
    derived from the Latin word and give the meaning of the English word.
    One has been done for you.

    aquam   aquatic   takes place in water
    dormiebat   [2]
    loco   [2]

Answer **either** Question 10 **or** Question 11

10. Answer the following questions based on part of the story you have already
    read.

    olim Hercules cum novem vaccis pulcherrimis Romam iter faciebat. Tiberi
    appropinquavit ut vaccae aquam biberent. Hercules ipse multum vinum bibit et
    mox dormiebat. deinde Cacus, pastor qui prope flumen habitabat, vaccas
    auferre constituit. 'Hercules tamen' sibi inquit 'vestigia earum facile videbit.
    quomodo eum decipere possum?'

    (a) Identify an example of the **accusative** case in line 1.   [1]
    (b) Pick out a **superlative adjective** in line 1.   [1]
    (c) *appropinquavit* (line 2): identify the **tense** of this verb.   [1]

(d) *ut . . . biberent* (line 2): explain why *biberent* is in the **subjunctive**
mood.   [1]
(e) Identify an example of the **imperfect** tense in line 3.   [1]
(f) *prope flumen* (line 3): identify the case of *flumen* **and** explain
why this case is used here.   [2]
(g) Identify an example of the **future** tense in line 4.   [1]
(h) Pick out a **pronoun** in line 4.   [1]
(i) Pick out an **adverb** in line 4.   [1]

Do **not** answer Question 11 if you have already answered Question 10.

11. Translate the following sentences into Latin:
    (a) I am writing a long letter.   [3]
    (b) The men were building walls.   [3]
    (c) Why did you not invite the girls?   [4]

Section B

Read Passage 2 and answer the questions.

Passage 2

The senators of Rome consider what to do after the death of Pedanius.

Pedanius plurimos servos habebat. antea promiserat se unum ex his servis
liberaturum esse; ille igitur, quod non liberatus est, tam iratus erat ut dominum
interficeret. eo tempore, Romani morem antiquum servabant: domino sic
mortuo, omnes servos qui in eadem domo habitabant morte punire solebant.
5 dum senatores de hac re cogitant, magna turba civium ad curiam festinavit
clamantium 'nolite tot servos innocentes occidere!' in curia, alii dicebant poenam
nimis crudelem esse, alii morem antiquum laudabant. sed vir quidam, Cassius
nomine, orationem validam inter senatores fecit in qua gravissimam poenam pro
scelere dirissimo petivit.

Names

Pedanius, Pedanii *m*	Pedanius
Cassius, Cassii *m*	Cassius

Vocabulary

mos, moris *m*	tradition, custom
antiquus, antiqua, antiquum	ancient
curia -ae *f*	senate-house
innocens, innocentis	innocent
nimis	too
oratio, orationis *f*	a speech

12. *Pedanius plurimos servos habebat* (line 1): what do we learn about
    Pedanius?   [1]

13. *antea promiserat se unum ex his servis liberaturum esse; ille igitur, quod non liberatus est, tam iratus erat ut dominum interficeret* (lines 1–3):
    (a) what had Pedanius promised to do? [2]
    (b) why was the slave angry, and what did he do as a result? [2]

14. *eo tempore, Romani morem antiquum servabant: domino sic mortuo, omnes servos qui in eadem domo habitabant morte punire solebant* (lines 3–4): what was the ancient tradition in Rome in a case like this involving the killing of a master? [4]

15. *dum senatores de hac re cogitant, magna turba civium ad curiam festinavit clamantium 'nolite tot servos innocentes occidere!'* (lines 5–6):
    (a) when the senators discussed the case, who came to the senate-house? [2]
    (b) what were they shouting? [3]

16. *in curia, alii dicebant poenam nimis crudelem esse, alii morem antiquum laudabant* (lines 6–7): what difference of opinion was there in the senate-house? [2]

17. *sed vir quidam, Cassius nomine, orationem validam inter senatores fecit in qua gravissimam poenam pro scelere dirissimo petivit* (lines 7–9): in his speech to the senators, what was the opinion of Cassius? [4]

Passage 3

Cassius successfully urges strong action against Pedanius' slaves.

Cassius 'senatores,' inquit 'non semper bonum est mores a maioribus traditos sequi. nunc tamen quid accidet si servi dominos sine poena necare possunt? num creditis hunc servum solum sine aliis consilia sua paravisse? nonne ceteri sciebant quid unus facere vellet?' his verbis Cassius senatoribus persuadere conabatur ut omnes servos
5 Pedanii, et scelestos et fideles, punirent. nonnulli timebant ne innocentes sic poenas iniustas darent. sed Cassius tam vehementer inter senatores locutus erat ut nemo contra sententiam eius loqui auderet. senatores igitur, paucis resistentibus, milites statim emiserunt ad omnes servos Pedanii occidendos. senator quidam etiam libertos Pedanii punire volebat; ceteri tamen hoc facere noluerunt. servi, inter quos erant et
10 senes et feminae, a militibus custoditi per vias ad mortem ducti sunt.

Names

Cassius, Cassii *m*	Cassius
Pedanius, Pedanii *m*	Pedanius

Vocabulary

mos, moris *m*	tradition, custom
maiores, maiorum *m pl*	ancestors
innocens, innocentis	innocent
iniustus, iniusta, iniustum	unfair
sententia, sententiae *f*	opinion

18. Translate Passage 3 into good English. [50]

REFERENCE GRAMMAR

NOUNS

First and second declensions

		first declension		second declension		
		girl		master	war	
		f	*endings*	*m*	*n*	*endings*
sg	nom	puella	-a	dominus*	bellum	-us (-um *if n*)
	acc	puellam	-am	dominum	bellum	-um
	gen	puellae	-ae	domini	belli	-i
	dat	puellae	-ae	domino	bello	-o
	abl	puella	-a (*long*)	domino	bello	-o
				(*voc domine)		
pl	nom	puellae	-ae	domini	bella	-i (-a *if n*)
	acc	puellas	-as	dominos	bella	-os (-a *if n*)
	gen	puellarum	-arum	dominorum	bellorum	-orum
	dat	puellis	-is	dominis	bellis	-is
	abl	puellis	-is	dominis	bellis	-is

- First declension nouns are nearly all feminine, but *nauta* (sailor) is masculine. There is no neuter version of first declension.
- *dea* (goddess) and *filia* (daughter) have dative and ablative plural *deabus*, *filiabus*, to distinguish from equivalent parts of *deus* (god) and *filius* (son); *filius* has vocative *fili*.
- Second declension nouns ending -*us* are the only ones with a vocative singular different from the nominative.
- Second declension masculine nouns with nominative singular ending in -*r* behave as if -*us* had disappeared. Hence *vir* (man), acc *virum*; *puer* (boy), acc *puerum*. Most others ending in -*er* drop the *e* in the other cases (reflecting pronunciation in practice): *ager* (field), acc *agrum*; *liber* (book), *librum*.

Third declension

		king	shout	ship	name	endings
		m	*m*	*f*	*n*	*endings*
sg	*nom*	rex	clamor	navis	nomen	-
	acc	regem	clamorem	navem	nomen	-em (*as nom if n*)
	gen	regis	clamoris	navis	nominis	-is
	dat	regi	clamori	navi	nomini	-i
	abl	rege	clamore	nave	nomine	-e
pl	*nom*	reges	clamores	naves	nomina	-es (-a *if n*)
	acc	reges	clamores	naves	nomina	-es (-a *if n*)
	gen	regum	clamorum	navium	nominum	-um *or* -ium
	dat	regibus	clamoribus	navibus	nominibus	-ibus
	abl	regibus	clamoribus	navibus	nominibus	-ibus

- There is a wide range of possibilities for the nominative singular, but other endings attach to the *genitive stem*. This and the gender need to be learned.
- The genitive plural is normally *-um*, but sometimes *-ium*. The genitive plural usually ends up one syllable longer than the nominative singular. If the noun 'increases' by a syllable from the nominative to the genitive singular (as most do), it does not increase again in the plural, so the genitive plural is *-um*. If (like *navis*) it does not increase in the singular, it does so in the plural, so the genitive plural is *-ium*. But there are exceptions:
  - (i) single-syllable nouns ending in two consonants increase twice: *urbs* (city), *urbis*, gen pl *urbium*; similarly *gens* (tribe), *mons* (mountain), *nox* (night) [*x* counts double]; but not *rex*.
  - (ii) a few nouns that would be expected to increase in the genitive plural do not do so: *frater* (brother), gen sg *fratris*, gen pl *fratrum*; similarly *iuvenis* (young man), *mater* (mother), *pater* (pater), *senex* (old man).
- Note that *mare* (sea) is slightly irregular, having abl *mari* (to avoid confusion with nom/acc) and nom/acc pl *maria*.

Fourth and fifth declensions

		fourth declension		*fifth declension*	
		hand, band		day	
		f	*endings*	*m*	*endings*
sg	*nom*	manus	-us	dies	-es
	acc	manum	-um	diem	-em
	gen	manus	-us	diei	-ei
	dat	manui	-ui	diei	-ei
	abl	manu	-u	die	-e
pl	*nom*	manus	-us	dies	-es
	acc	manus	-us	dies	-es
	gen	manuum	-uum	dierum	-erum
	dat	manibus	-ibus	diebus	-ebus
	abl	manibus	-ibus	diebus	-ebus

- The fourth declension can be thought of as a variant of the second, and the fifth as a variant of the third. Both are relatively uncommon.

- There are both masculine and feminine nouns in both fourth and fifth declensions: hence *exercitus* (army) goes like *manus* but is masculine; *spes* (hope) and *res* (thing) go like *dies* but are feminine. There a neuter version of fourth (though with no examples in GCSE), but not of fifth.

- Four different bits of a noun like *manus* (nominative and genitive singular, nominative and accusative plural) are spelled in the same way (the *u* in the nominative singular is short, the others long). Number and case have to be worked out from the context (NB: if the word is accusative, it must also be plural).

- *domus* (house, home *f*) has ablative singular *domo* (and usually accusative plural *domos*) as if second declension, and a locative form *domi* (at home); note also the accusative *domum* is used without a preposition for *home/homewards* (with verbs of motion).

ADJECTIVES

first and second declension (2-1-2, i.e. like dominus – puella – bellum)

happy

		m	*f*	*n*
sg	nom	laetus*	laeta	laetum
	acc	laetum	laetam	laetum
	gen	laeti	laetae	laeti
	dat	laeto	laetae	laeto
	abl	laeto	laeta	laeto
		(*voc laete)		
pl	nom	laeti	laetae	laeta
	acc	laetos	laetas	laeta
	gen	laetorum	laetarum	laetorum
	dat	laetis	laetis	laetis
	abl	laetis	laetis	laetis

- *miser* (miserable) keeps the *e* like *puer* does, hence m acc sg *miserum*, f nom sg *misera*;

  pulcher (beautiful) drops the *e* like *ager* does, hence m acc sg *pulchrum*, f nom sg *pulchra*.

- *alius* (another), *alter* (one . . . the other), *nullus* (no, not any), *solus* (alone), and *totus* (whole) are basically 2-1-2 adjectives, but have the distinctive gen sg *-ius* and dat sg *-i* across all three genders (as most pronouns also do).

third declension (3-3)

brave   huge

		m/f	*n*	*m/f*	*n*
sg	nom	fortis	forte	ingens	ingens
	acc	fortem	forte	ingentem	ingens
	gen	fortis	fortis	ingentis	ingentis
	dat	forti	forti	ingenti	ingenti
	abl	forti	forti	ingenti	ingenti
pl	nom	fortes	fortia	ingentes	ingentia
	acc	fortes	fortia	ingentes	ingentia
	gen	fortium	fortium	ingentium	ingentium
	dat	fortibus	fortibus	ingentibus	ingentibus
	abl	fortibus	fortibus	ingentibus	ingentibus

- Note that the ablative singular ending is *-i*, not *-e* as in third declension nouns.

- *celer* (swift) behaves as if it had started *celeris* (and does so in the feminine, here unusually different from the masculine):

		m	*f*	*n*
sg	nom	celer	celeris	celere
	acc	celerem	celerem	celere

Comparison of adjectives

Comparative adjective (*all third declension, i.e. 3-3*)

happier

		m/f	*n*
sg	nom	laetior	laetius
	acc	laetiorem	laetius
	gen	laetioris	laetioris
	dat	laetiori	laetiori
	abl	laetiore	laetiore
pl	nom	laetiores	laetiora
	acc	laetiores	laetiora
	gen	laetiorum	laetiorum
	dat	laetioribus	laetioribus
	abl	laetioribus	laetioribus

- The syllable *-ior* is added to the basic genitive singular stem, and the comparative is third declension (regardless of what declension the adjective was to start with). Note that the ablative singular ending is *-e* (like third declension nouns), not *-i* (like most third declension adjectives).

Superlative adjective (*all 2-1-2 declensions, like* laetus)

very happy, happiest

		m	*f*	*n*
sg	nom	laetissimus	laetissima	laetissimum
	acc	laetissimum	laetissimam	laetissimum
		etc	*etc*	*etc*

- The syllables *-issim-* are added to the basic genitive singular stem, and the superlative is regular 2-1-2 in form (regardless of what declension the adjective was to start with).

Irregular comparative and superlative adjectives

(1) Slight variations of the superlative form:
Adjectives with masculine nominative singular ending -*er* have the superlative ending
-*errimus* :

		comparative	*superlative*
miser	miserable	miserior	miserrimus
pulcher	beautiful	pulchrior	pulcherrimus

Some third declension adjectives with masculine/feminine nominative singular
ending -*ilis* have the superlative ending -*illimus*:

facilis	easy	facilior	facillimus
difficilis	difficult	difficilior	difficillimus

(2) Very irregular forms. Note that several of these are irregular in English too:

bonus	good	melior	optimus
malus	bad	peior	pessimus
magnus	big	maior	maximus
parvus	small	minor	minimus
multus	much	plus (+ *gen*)	plurimus
multi	many	plures	plurimi

- Irregular comparatives decline like *laetior*, except that *plus* behaves like a
  neuter noun (*gen* pluris) meaning *a greater amount*, followed by the genitive,
  e.g. *plus cibi* (more food).

ADVERBS

2-1-2 adjectives form their adverb by adding *-e* to the stem:

adjective	*adverb*	
laetus	laete	happily

Third declension adjectives normally add *-iter* to the stem:

brevis	breviter	briefly

The *-i-* in this ending is sometimes dropped to aid pronunciation:

audax	audacter	boldly

A few third declension adjectives ending *-is* instead use their neuter singular (*-e*) as adverb:

facilis	facile	easily

Comparative adverbs use the neuter form of the comparative adjective (the misleading ending *-ius*, which might be mistaken for second declension masculine):

laetior	laetius	more happily

Superlative adverbs are formed by adding *-e* in place of the superlative adjective endings (predictably, since these are 2-1-2 in declension):

laetissimus	laetissime	most happily

Note the following adverbs (corresponding to the irregular comparative and superlative adjectives):

		comparative	*superlative*
bene	well	melius	optime
male	badly	peius	pessime

NUMERALS

Arabic	Roman	
1	I	unus, una, unum
2	II	duo, duae, duo
3	III	tres, tria
4	IV (*or* IIII)	quattuor
5	V	quinque
6	VI	sex
7	VII	septem
8	VIII	octo
9	IX	novem
10	X	decem
100	C	centum
1000	M	mille, *pl* milia

The small numbers *unus*, *duo* and *tres* decline:

one

	m	*f*	*n*
nom	unus	una	unum
acc	unum	unam	unum
gen	unius	unius	unius
dat	uni	uni	uni
abl	uno	una	uno

- This is basically 2-1-2, but with the distinctive genitive *-ius* and dative *-i* across all three genders (like most pronouns).

two

	m	*f*	*n*
nom	duo	duae	duo
acc	duos (*or* duo)	duas	duo
gen	duorum	duarum	duorum
dat	duobus	duabus	duobus
abl	duobus	duabus	duobus

- This has a few parts in common with 2-1-2 pl.

three

	m and f	*n*
nom	tres	tria
acc	tres	tria
gen	trium	trium
dat	tribus	tribus
abl	tribus	tribus

- This is third declension plural.

- *milia* (plural of *mille* = 1000) declines like *tria*.

PRONOUNS

Summary of pronouns for basic recognition:

ego (*acc* me)	I (me)
nos	we
tu	you (*sg*)
vos	you (*pl*)
is, ea, id	he, she, it
se	himself/herself/itself (*reflexive*)
hic	this
ille	that
ipse	self
idem	the same
qui	who (*relative*)
quis?	who?
quid?	what?
quidam	a certain
alter	one of two, the other
ceteri	the rest
nemo	no-one

Personal pronouns

person:	first	second	third reflexive
	I, me, we, us	you	him/her/it(self), *pl* themselves

		first	second	third reflexive
sg	nom	ego	tu	-
	acc	me	te	se
	gen	mei	tui	sui
	dat	mihi	tibi	sibi
	abl	me	te	se
pl	nom	nos	vos	-
	acc	nos	vos	se
	gen	nostrum	vestrum	sui
	dat	nobis	vobis	sibi
	abl	nobis	vobis	se

- For the associated possessive adjectives *meus, noster, tuus, vester, suus* see pages 239–40.
- Note that *se* cannot be translated in isolation, but only in context: it refers back to the subject of the sentence.

third person

he, she, it, *pl* they, them (*can also be adj* that, those)

		m	*f*	*n*
sg	nom	is	ea	id
	acc	eum	eam	id
	gen	eius	eius	eius
	dat	ei	ei	ei
	abl	eo	ea	eo
pl	nom	ei	eae	ea
	acc	eos	eas	ea
	gen	eorum	earum	eorum
	dat	eis	eis	eis
	abl	eis	eis	eis

- Note the distinctive genitive and dative singular endings (*-ius* and *-i*), across all three genders, used also for other pronouns.

Possessives

A possessive indicates who something belongs to (e.g. *my, your, his*). Most of these are 2-1-2 adjectives, which agree in number/gender/case with the thing possessed (not the possessor).

first person
my

		m	*f*	*n*
sg	nom	meus*	mea	meum
	acc	meum	meam	meum
		etc	*etc*	*etc*
		(*voc* mi)		

our

		m	*f*	*n*
sg	nom	noster	nostra	nostrum
	acc	nostrum	nostram	nostrum
		etc	*etc*	*etc*

second person
your (belonging to you *sg*)

		m	*f*	*n*
sg	nom	tuus	tua	tuum
	acc	tuum	tuam	tuum
		etc	*etc*	*etc*

your (belonging to you *pl*)

		m	f	n
sg	*nom*	vester	vestra	vestrum
	acc	vestrum	vestram	vestrum
		etc	*etc*	*etc*

In the third person it is a bit more complicated.

(1) If the possessive refers back to the subject of the sentence or clause, the 2-1-2 adjective *suus* is used (like the associated reflexive pronoun *se*, *suus* cannot be translated in isolation but only in context):

third person reflexive

his/her/its/their (own) (*belonging to the subject of the sentence/clause*)

		m	f	n
sg	*nom*	suus	sua	suum
	acc	suum	suam	suum
		etc	*etc*	*etc*

- As with the first and second person possessive adjectives, the number and gender are those of the thing possessed, not the possessor. (Thus it is NOT the case that the masculine means *his*, the feminine *her*, and the plural *their*: any part of *suus* can mean any of these, depending on the number and gender of the subject.)

(2) If *his/her/its/their* refers to someone other than the subject of the sentence or clause, there is no adjective available and so the genitive of the pronoun *is*, *ea*, *id* is used instead: literally *of him, of her, of it, of them*. This time the number and gender are those of the possessor (not the thing possessed), though in the singular all three genders are the same anyway (*eius*).

- Note carefully that the ending of the possessive *eius* is the distinctive *-ius* genitive of a pronoun (not the masculine nominative singular of a 2-1-2 adjective, as it is with *suus*).

third person non-reflexive

his/her/its (*belonging to someone not the subject of the sentence/clause*)

	m	f	n
sg	eius	eius	eius

their (*belonging to people not the subject of the sentence/clause*)

	m	f	n
pl	eorum	earum	eorum

Demonstrative pronouns: *this* and *that*

this, *pl* these

		m	f	n
sg	nom	hic	haec	hoc
	acc	hunc	hanc	hoc
	gen	huius	huius	huius
	dat	huic	huic	huic
	abl	hoc	hac	hoc
pl	nom	hi	hae	haec
	acc	hos	has	haec
	gen	horum	harum	horum
	dat	his	his	his
	abl	his	his	his

- Again note the distinctive gen and dat sg endings, the dat here adding *-c* to the *-i* which most pronouns have. The pl is regular 2-1-2 apart from n nom and acc (and even this resembles regular 2-1-2 by being the same as f nom sg).

that, *pl* those

		m	f	n
sg	nom	ille	illa	illud
	acc	illum	illam	illud
	gen	illius	illius	illius
	dat	illi	illi	illi
	abl	illo	illa	illo
pl	nom	illi	illae	illa
	acc	illos	illas	illa
	gen	illorum	illarum	illorum
	dat	illis	illis	illis
	abl	illis	illis	illis

(regular 2-1-2 pl)

- Again note the distinctive gen and dat sg endings across all three genders.
- *ille* refers to something further away (that one there) than *hic* (this one here).
- *hic* and *ille* can be used on their own as pronouns, e.g. *hic* (this man), *illa* (those things); or with a noun, e.g. *hic servus* (this slave), *illa verba* (those words), where they are used as demonstrative *adjectives*. The pronoun *is, ea, id* can also be used in this way, with the same meaning as *ille*, e.g. *ea verba* (those words).
- If part of *ille* starts a new sentence, it changes the subject (to someone who was mentioned in the previous sentence, but was not the subject of it): e.g. *dominus servum vocavit. ille tamen aberat.* The master called the slave. He/that man however was away.

Self and *same*

self, *pl* selves

		m	*f*	*n*
sg	nom	ipse	ipsa	ipsum
	acc	ipsum	ipsam	ipsum
	gen	ipsius	ipsius	ipsius
	dat	ipsi	ipsi	ipsi
	abl	ipso	ipsa	ipso
pl	nom	ipsi	ipsae	ipsa
	acc	ipsos	ipsas	ipsa
	gen	ipsorum	ipsarum	ipsorum
	dat	ipsis	ipsis	ipsis
	abl	ipsis	ipsis	ipsis

(regular 2-1-2 pl)

- Again note the distinctive gen and dat sg endings across all three genders.

the same

		m	*f*	*n*
sg	nom	idem	eadem	idem
	acc	eundem	eandem	idem
	gen	eiusdem	eiusdem	eiusdem
	dat	eidem	eidem	eidem
	abl	eodem	eadem	eodem
pl	nom	eidem	eaedem	eadem
	acc	eosdem	easdem	eadem
	gen	eorundem	earundem	eorundem
	dat	eisdem	eisdem	eisdem
	abl	eisdem	eisdem	eisdem

- This is the pronoun *is, ea, id* with *-dem* stuck on the end, and minor adjustments of spelling to ease pronunciation (*-m* changes to *-n* before *-dem* is added). Again note the distinctive gen and dat sg endings (with *-dem* added).

Relative pronoun: *who, which*

who, which

		m	*f*	*n*
sg	nom	qui	quae	quod
	acc	quem	quam	quod
	gen	cuius	cuius	cuius
	dat	cui	cui	cui
	abl	quo	qua	quo

pl	nom	qui	quae	quae
	acc	quos	quas	quae
	gen	quorum	quarum	quorum
	dat	quibus	quibus	quibus
	abl	quibus	quibus	quibus

- This is used in relative clauses (*servus quem heri vidi* = the slave whom I saw yesterday).

Interrogative pronoun: *who? what?*

		who?		what?
		m	*f*	*n*
sg	nom	quis	quis	quid
	acc	quem	quam	quid

(other parts the same as the relative pronoun *qui, quae, quod*)

- This is used in direct questions (where it comes first word in the sentence), and in indirect questions.

Other pronouns

(1) *quidam* a, a certain, *pl* some

		m	*f*	*n*
sg	nom	quidam	quaedam	quoddam
	acc	quendam	quandam	quoddam
	gen	cuiusdam	cuiusdam	cuiusdam
	dat	cuidam	cuidam	cuidam
	abl	quodam	quadam	quodam
pl	nom	quidam	quaedam	quaedam
	acc	quosdam	quasdam	quaedam
	gen	quorundam	quarundam	quorundam
	dat	quibusdam	quibusdam	quibusdam
	abl	quibusdam	quibusdam	quibusdam

- This is *qui, quae, quod* with -*dam* stuck on the end. (Compare how *idem* is the pronoun *is, ea, id* with -*dem* stuck on the end.) In parts of *quidam* too, any part of the original pronoun ending -*m* changes it to -*n* before -*dam* is added, to ease pronunciation.

(2) *alter*   one . . . the other (*of two*), another, a/the second

		m	*f*	*n*
sg	*nom*	alter	altera	alterum
	acc	alterum	alteram	alterum
	gen	alterius	alterius	alterius
	dat	alteri	alteri	alteri
	abl	altero	altera	altero
pl	*nom*	alteri	alterae	altera
	acc	alteros	alteras	altera
		etc	*etc*	*etc*

(regular 2-1-2 plural)

- Again note the distinctive gen and dat sg forms.
- *alter* is often used in a pair, requiring a different translation each time (*one . . . the other*).
- The use of *alter . . . alter* implies that just two are involved. If there are more than two, *alius . . . alius* is used. In the singular this is translated *one . . . another*, but it is more often found in the plural as *some . . . others*.
- If forms of *alius* different from each other in gender and/or case are paired, a double statement is made (abbreviated in Latin, as it can be in English), e.g. *alii alia dicunt* (short for *alii alia, alii alia . . .*) lit *Some people say some things, others say other things*, i.e. *Different people say different things*.

(3) *ceteri*   the rest, the others (*pl only*)

		m	*f*	*n*
pl	*nom*	ceteri	ceterae	cetera
	acc	ceteros	ceteras	cetera
		etc	*etc*	*etc*

(regular 2-1-2 plural)

(4)   no-one   nothing

		m/f	*n*
sg	*nom*	nemo	nihil (*indeclinable*)
	acc	neminem	
	gen	nullius	
	dat	nemini	
	abl	nullo	

- This is formed like a third declension noun (stem *nemin-*), but its genitive and ablative are borrowed from the adjective *nullus* (no . . ., not any).

PREPOSITIONS

Prepositions are followed by either the accusative or the ablative. They often focus more closely a meaning the case already has. Prepositions with the accusative mostly indicate *motion towards* or *through*, whilst those with the ablative mostly indicate either *a position of rest in* a place or *going away from* it.

(1)   Prepositions with the accusative:

ad	to, towards, at
circum	around
contra	against
in	into, onto
inter	among, between
per	through, along
post	after, behind
prope	near
propter	on account of, because of
sub	(going) under, beneath
trans	across

(2)   Prepositions with the ablative:

a/ab*	from, away from, by
cum	with
de	from, down from, about
e/ex*	from, out of
in	in, on
pro	in front of, for, in return for
sine	without
sub	under, beneath

* the forms *ab* and *ex* are used if the next word begins with a vowel or *h*

- Note that *in* and *sub* can be used with either accusative or ablative according to meaning.

- For the idiom *multis post annis* (after many years, *lit* afterwards by many years) see p. 105.

- With the names of towns and cities, no preposition is used, but the case is what it would have been if the preposition had been there: hence *Romam* (acc) = to Rome, *Roma* (abl) = from Rome. The accusative of *domus* is used similarly (e.g. *domum festinavi* = I hurried home). This idiom must be distinguished from the use of the *locative*, meaning *in/at* a place, e.g. *Romae* (in Rome), *domi* (at home).

- Many prepositions are also used as prefixes to form compounds verbs: *a/ab-, ad-, e/ex-, in-, trans-*. Note also a prefix that is not found as a preposition: *re-* (back), e.g. *revenimus* = we came back.

VERBS

- The present tense describes something that is happening now or is currently true.

- The future tense describes something that will happen in the future.

- The imperfect and perfect tenses both describe something that happened in the past. The imperfect typically denotes an incomplete, repeated or long-lasting action (*X was happening/used to happen*). The perfect is either a simple past tense describing a completed action (*X happened*); or a 'true perfect' (*X has happened*, implying that the effects continue).

- The pluperfect describes something that *had* already happened by some point in the past.

- Regular verbs of all conjugations use the imperfect endings *-bam, -bas, -bat* etc, but there are two different ways of forming the future: first and second use *-bo, -bis, -bit* etc (hence *portabo, monebo*); third and fourth use *-am, -es, -et* etc (hence *traham, audiam*).

- The characteristic vowel(s) that precede *-bam* in the imperfect tense for each conjugation (first *a*, second *e*, third *e*, fourth *ie*) are also used to form the present participle (*portans, monens, trahens, audiens*) and the gerundive (*portandus, monendus, trahendus, audiendus*).

- The perfect and pluperfect of all verbs use the perfect stem (the third principal part minus *-i*) with perfect endings *-i, -isti, -it, -imus, -istis, -erunt*, and pluperfect *-eram, -eras, -erat, -eramus, -eratis, -erant*.

- Verbs of 'mixed' third/fourth conjugation (e.g. *capio*, sometimes called 'three and a half'), count as third because of their infinitive (*-ere*), and often also have perfect stems, which look like third (e.g. *cep-*), but form their present (3 pl *capiunt*), future (*capiam, capies* etc) and imperfect (*capiebam*) like fourth.

- Most present, future and imperfect active forms can be changed to their passive equivalents by a simple formula: the basic person endings *-o/m, -s, -t, -mus, -tis, -nt* change to *-r* (added to *o*/replacing *m*), *-ris, -tur, -mur, -mini, -ntur*. The vowel(s) in front of these person endings normally stay the same, except that in the second person singular the present tense of third and mixed third/fourth conjugations, and the future of first and second, have *-eris/-beris* instead of the expected *-iris/-biris*.

- The perfect and pluperfect passives of all verbs are made from the perfect passive participle (the fourth principal part) with an auxiliary verb (part of *to be*). The participle is always nominative, but agrees in number and gender with the subject.

- In the active, the imperfect subjunctive is formed from the present infinitive (the second principal part), and the pluperfect subjunctive from the perfect infinitive (perfect stem plus *-isse*), in each case with basic person endings *-m, -s, -t, -mus, -tis, -nt*. This works for both regular and irregular verbs: hence *porto* has imperfect subjunctive *portarem*, pluperfect subjunctive *portavissem*; *sum* has imperfect subjunctive *essem*, pluperfect subjunctive *fuissem*. In the passive, a similar principle works for the imperfect (hence *portarer*, with passive endings as above), but the pluperfect is *portatus essem* (subjunctive version of *portatus eram*).

- Deponent verbs in all tenses use the passive forms with an active meaning. Their perfect and pluperfect use the perfect active participle (which only these verbs have) with an auxiliary verb (part of *to be*). Because the third principal part includes this participle (e.g. *conatus sum* = I tried), it does not need to be given again as a fourth. Semi-deponent verbs use ordinary active forms for the present, future and imperfect tenses, but passive ones for the perfect and pluperfect. Deponent and semi-deponent verbs have normal present and future active participles.

Verb tenses: active

conjugation:		*1st*	*2nd*	*3rd*	*4th*	*mixed 3rd/4th*
present		I carry	I warn	I drag	I hear	I take
sg	*1*	porto	moneo	traho	audio	capio
	2	portas	mones	trahis	audis	capis
	3	portat	monet	trahit	audit	capit
pl	*1*	portamus	monemus	trahimus	audimus	capimus
	2	portatis	monetis	trahitis	auditis	capitis
	3	portant	monent	trahunt	audiunt	capiunt
future		I shall carry	I shall warn	I shall drag	I shall hear	I shall take
sg	*1*	portabo	monebo	traham	audiam	capiam
	2	portabis	monebis	trahes	audies	capies
	3	portabit	monebit	trahet	audiet	capiet
pl	*1*	portabimus	monebimus	trahemus	audiemus	capiemus
	2	portabitis	monebitis	trahetis	audietis	capietis
	3	portabunt	monebunt	trahent	audient	capient
imperfect		I was carrying	I was warning	I was dragging	I was hearing	I was taking
sg	*1*	portabam	monebam	trahebam	audiebam	capiebam
	2	portabas	monebas	trahebas	audiebas	capiebas
	3	portabat	monebat	trahebat	audiebat	capiebat
pl	*1*	portabamus	monebamus	trahebamus	audiebamus	capiebamus
	2	portabatis	monebatis	trahebatis	audiebatis	capiebatis
	3	portabant	monebant	trahebant	audiebant	capiebant
perfect		I (have) carried	I (have) warned	I (have) dragged	I (have) heard	I took, I have taken
sg	*1*	portavi	monui	traxi	audivi	cepi
	2	portavisti	monuisiti	traxisti	audivisti	cepisti
	3	portavit	monuit	traxit	audivit	cepit
pl	*1*	portavimus	monuimus	traximus	audivimus	cepimus
	2	portavistis	monuistis	traxistis	audivistis	cepistis
	3	portaverunt	monuerunt	traxerunt	audiverunt	ceperunt
conjugation:		*1st*	*2nd*	*3rd*	*4th*	*mixed 3rd/4th*
pluperfect		I had carried	I had warned	I had dragged	I had heard	I had taken
sg	*1*	portaveram	monueram	traxeram	audiveram	ceperam
	2	portaveras	monueras	traxeras	audiveras	ceperas
	3	portaverat	monuerat	traxerat	audiverat	ceperat
pl	*1*	portaveramus	monueramus	traxeramus	audiveramus	ceperamus
	2	portaveratis	monueratis	traxeratis	audiveratis	ceperatis
	3	portaverant	monuerant	traxerant	audiverant	ceperant

Verb tenses: passive

conjugation:			1st	2nd	3rd	4th	mixed 3rd/4th
present			I am carried	I am warned	I am dragged	I am heard	I am taken
sg	1		portor	moneor	trahor	audior	capior
	2		portaris	moneris	traheris	audiris	caperis
	3		portatur	monetur	trahitur	auditur	capitur
pl	1		portamur	monemur	trahimur	audimur	capimur
	2		portamini	monemini	trahimini	audimini	capimini
	3		portantur	monentur	trahuntur	audiuntur	capiuntur
future			I shall be carried	I shall be warned	I shall be dragged	I shall be heard	I shall be taken
sg	1		portabor	monebor	trahar	audiar	capiar
	2		portaberis	moneberis	traheris	audieris	capieris
	3		portabitur	monebitur	trahetur	audietur	capietur
pl	1		portabimur	monebimur	trahemur	audiemur	capiemur
	2		portabimini	monebimini	trahemini	audiemini	capiemini
	3		portabuntur	monebuntur	trahentur	audientur	capientur
imperfect			I was being carried	I was being warned	I was being dragged	I was being heard	I was being taken
sg	1		portabar	monebar	trahebar	audiebar	capiebar
	2		portabaris	monebaris	trahebaris	audiebaris	capiebaris
	3		portabatur	monebatur	trahebatur	audiebatur	capiebatur
pl	1		portabamur	monebamur	trahebamur	audiebamur	capiebamur
	2		portabamini	monebamini	trahebamini	audiebamini	capiebamini
	3		portabantur	monebantur	trahebantur	audiebantur	capiebantur
perfect			I was/have been carried	I was/have been warned	I was/have been dragged	I was/have been heard	I was/have been taken
sg	1		portatus sum	monitus sum	tractus sum	auditus sum	captus sum
	2		portatus es	monitus es	tractus es	auditus es	captus es
	3		portatus est	monitus est	tractus est	auditus est	captus est
pl	1		portati sumus	moniti sumus	tracti sumus	auditi sumus	capti sumus
	2		portati estis	moniti estis	tracti estis	auditi estis	capti estis
	3		portavi sunt	moniti sunt	tracti sunt	auditi sunt	capti sunt
pluperfect			I had been carried	I had been warned	I had been dragged	I had been heard	I had been taken
sg	1		portatus eram	monitus eram	tractus eram	auditus eram	captus eram
	2		portatus eras	monitus eras	tractus eras	auditus eras	captus eras
	3		portatus erat	monitus erat	tractus erat	auditus erat	captus erat
pl	1		portati eramus	moniti eramus	tracti eramus	auditi eramus	capti eramus
	2		portati eratis	moniti eratis	tracti eratis	auditi eratis	capti eratis
	3		portati erant	moniti erant	tracti erant	auditi errant	capti errant

Subjunctive forms: active

conjugation:			1st	2nd	3rd	4th	mixed 3rd/4th
imperfect							
sg		1	portarem	monerem	traherem	audirem	caperem
		2	portares	moneres	traheres	audires	caperes
		3	portaret	moneret	traheret	audiret	caperet
pl		1	portaremus	moneremus	traheremus	audiremus	caperemus
		2	portaretis	moneretis	traheretis	audiretis	caperetis
		3	portarent	monerent	traherent	audirent	caperent
pluperfect							
sg		1	portavissem	monuissem	traxissem	audivissem	cepissem
		2	portavisses	monuisses	traxisses	audivisses	cepisses
		3	portavisset	monuisset	traxisset	audivisset	cepisset
pl		1	portavissemus	monuissemus	traxissemus	audivissemus	cepissemus
		2	portavissetis	monuissetis	traxissetis	audivissetis	cepissetis
		3	portavissent	monuissent	traxissent	audivissent	cepissent

Subjunctive forms: passive

			1st	2nd	3rd	4th	mixed 3rd/4th
imperfect							
sg		1	portarer	monerer	traherer	audirer	caperer
		2	portareris	monereris	trahereris	audireris	capereris
		3	portaretur	moneretur	traheretur	audiretur	caperetur
pl		1	portaremur	moneremur	traheremur	audiremur	caperemur
		2	portaremini	moneremini	traheremini	audiremini	caperemini
		3	portarentur	monerentur	traherentur	audirentur	caperentur
pluperfect							
sg		1	portatus essem	monitus essem	tractus essem	auditus essem	captus essem
		2	portatus esses	monitus esses	tractus esses	auditus esses	captus esses
		3	portatus esset	monitus esset	tractus esset	auditus esset	captus esset
pl		1	portati essemus	moniti essemus	tracti essemus	auditi essemus	capti essemus
		2	portati essetis	moniti essetis	tracti essetis	auditi essetis	capti essetis
		3	portati essent	moniti essent	tracti essent	auditi essent	capti essent

Imperatives, infinitives and participles

Imperatives

conjugation	1st	2nd	3rd	4th	mixed 3rd/4th
	carry!	warn!	drag!	hear!	take!
sg	porta	mone	trahe	audi	cape
pl	portate	monete	trahite	audite	capite

- Note that a negative command is expressed by the imperative of *nolo* (sg *noli*, pl *nolite*) with an infinitive (*lit* be unwilling to do X!), hence e.g. *noli currere* (do not run!).
- Note the irregular singular imperatives *dic* (say!), *duc* (lead!), *fer* (carry!), *fac* (do!), which lose the final vowel – *fer* has plural *ferte*; also sg *i*, pl *ite* (go!) from *eo*.

Infinitives

conjugation	1st	2nd	3rd	4th	mixed 3rd/4th
present active	to carry	to warn	to drag	to hear	to take
	portare	monere	trahere	audire	capere
present passive	to be carried	to be warned	to be dragged	to be heard	to be taken
	portari	moneri	trahi	audiri	capi

- The active infinitives of second and third conjugations look the same, but note that the first *e* is long in second conjugation, short in third.
- Note that the passive infinitives of third and mixed third/fourth conjugations are *trahi, capi* (not the expected *traheri, caperi*; the short *er* has disappeared in pronunciation), which can give a misleading appearance, e.g. *regi* (to be ruled) looks like the dative singular of *rex*.

perfect active	to have carried	to have warned	to have dragged	to have heard	to have taken
	portavisse	monuisse	traxisse	audivisse	cepisse
perfect passive	to have been carried	to have been warned	to have been dragged	to have been heard	to have been taken
	portatus esse	monitus esse	tractus esse	auditus esse	captus esse

- The perfect active infinitive adds *-isse* to the perfect stem.
- The perfect passive infinitive uses the perfect passive participle plus *esse*. The participle changes number and gender as required, to agree with the subject of the infinitive. It is most commonly accusative (in accusative and infinitive for indirect statement), but can be nominative (in indirect statement where the introductory verb is passive, e.g. *urbs dicitur capta esse* = the city is said to have been captured). The participle cannot be in any other case when it forms part of an infinitive.

future active	to be about to carry	to be about to warn	to be about to drag	to be about to hear	to be about to take
	portaturus esse	moniturus esse	tracturus esse	auditurus esse	capturus esse

- The future active infinitive uses the future active participle plus *esse*. This participle changes exactly as described above for the perfect passive one when part of an infinitive.

Participles

conjugation	1st	2nd	3rd	4th	mixed 3rd/4th
present active	taking	warning	dragging	hearing	taking
	portans -antis	monens -entis	trahens -entis	audiens -ientis	capiens -ientis
perfect passive	having been carried	having been warned	having been dragged	having been heard	having been taken
	portatus	monitus	tractus	auditus	captus
future active	about to take	about to warn	about to drag	about to hear	about to take
	portaturus	moniturus	tracturus	auditurus	capturus

- The present active participle is third declension. It is shown here with its genitive, for the stem. It uses the characteristic vowel(s) of its conjugation, and declines like *ingens* (but abl sg is usually *-e*).
- The perfect passive and future active participles are 2-1-2 in declension (*-us -a -um*).
- The future participle is *formed from* the perfect passive one (with the extra syllable *-ur-*) but is not itself passive.

Irregular verbs

		sum = I am (*the verb* to be)	*possum* = I am able	*eo* = I go
present				
sg	*1*	sum	possum	eo
	2	es	potes	is
	3	est	potest	it
pl	*1*	sumus	possumus	imus
	2	estis	potestis	itis
	3	sunt	possunt	eunt
infinitive		esse	posse	ire
future				
sg	*1*	ero	potero	ibo
	2	eris	poteris	ibis
	3	erit	poterit	ibit

pl	1	erimus		poterimus		ibimus	
	2	eritis		poteritis		ibitis	
	3	erunt		poterunt		ibunt	

imperfect			*subjunctive*		*subjunctive*		*subjunctive*
sg	1	eram	essem	poteram	possem	ibam	irem
	2	eras	esses	poteras	posses	ibas	ires
	3	erat	esset	poterat	posset	ibat	iret

pl	1	eramus	essemus	poteramus	possemus	ibamus	iremus
	2	eratis	essetis	poteratis	possetis	ibatis	iretis
	3	erant	essent	poterant	possent	ibant	irent

perfect							
sg	1	fui		potui		i(v)i	
	2	fuisti		potuisti		i(vi)sti	
	etc			*etc*		*etc*	

pluperfect			*subjunctive*		*subjunctive*		*subjunctive*
sg	1	fueram	fuissem	potueram	potuissem	i(v)eram	i(vi)ssem
	2	fueras	fuisses	potueras	potuisses	i(v)eras	i(vi)sses
	etc	*etc*		*etc*	*etc*	*etc*	*etc*

- NB: *sum* has future participle *futurus*.
- *possum* is a compound of *sum*, using as prefix an original adjective *potis* (able), abbreviated to *pot-*, which changes to *pos-* before another *s*; the perfect and pluperfect of both verbs are regular (*possum* has perfect *potui*, abbreviated from original *potfui*).

		volo = I want		*nolo* = I do not want		*malo* = I prefer	
present							
sg	1	volo		nolo		malo	
	2	vis		non vis		mavis	
	3	vult		non vult		mavult	
pl	1	volumus		nolumus		malumus	
	2	vultis		non vultis		mavultis	
	3	volunt		nolunt		malunt	
infinitive		velle		nolle		malle	
future							
sg	1	volam		nolam		malam	
	2	voles		noles		males	
	etc			*etc*		*etc*	

imperfect			*subjunctive*		*subjunctive*		*subjunctive*
sg	1	volebam	vellem	nolebam	nollem	malebam	mallem
	2	volebas	velles	nolebas	nolles	malebas	malles
	etc	*etc*		*etc*	*etc*	*etc*	*etc*

perfect							
sg	1	volui		nolui		malui	
	2	voluisti		noluisti		maluisti	
	etc			*etc*		*etc*	

pluperfect			*subjunctive*		*subjunctive*		*subjunctive*
sg	1	volueram	voluissem	nolueram	noluissem	malueram	maluissem
	2	volueras	voluisses	nolueras	noluisses	malueras	maluisses
		etc	*etc*	*etc*	*etc*	*etc*	*etc*

- *nolo* and *malo* are abbreviated compounds of *volo*: *nolo* is *non volo* (three bits of the present indicative remain separated), and *malo* is *magis* (= more) *volo*.
- The future tenses are formed as if third conjugation. The imperfect subjunctives are formed regularly from the infinitives.
- Perfect tenses are *volui, nolui, malui*. Pluperfects (*volueram, nolueram, malueram*) and pluperfect subjunctives (*voluissem, noluissem, maluissem*) are formed regularly from them.

Note that *fero* (I carry) is basically third conjugation but loses some vowels from its endings and has unusual principal parts (*fero, ferre, tuli, latus*):

present			*active*	*passive*
sg		1	fero	feror
		2	fers	ferris
		3	fert	fertur
pl		1	ferimus	ferimur
		2	fertis	ferimini
		3	ferunt	feruntur

imperative	fer, *pl* ferte	*infinitive*	ferre

The following verbs are compounds of fero, with similar principal parts:

aufero, auferre, abstuli, ablatus	I take away, I steal
offero, offerre, obtuli, oblatus	I offer
refero, referre, rettuli, relatus	I bring/carry back, I report/tell

Note also the similar last two parts in:

tollo, tollere, sustuli, sublatus	I raise, I lift up

(formed as if it had started *subfero*, which would have the same meaning)

Deponent and semi-deponent verbs

present	infinitive	perfect	
1st conjugation			
conor	conari	conatus sum	I try
hortor	hortari	hortatus sum	I encourage, I urge
miror	mirari	miratus sum	I am amazed (at)

present	infinitive	perfect	
2nd conjugation			
videor	videri	visus sum	I seem
3rd conjugation			
loquor	loqui	locutus sum	I speak
proficiscor	proficisci	profectus sum	I set out
sequor	sequi	secutus sum	I follow
mixed 3rd/4th conjugation			
-gredior compounds			
egredior	egredi	egressus sum	I go out
ingredior	ingredi	ingressus sum	I enter
progredior	progredi	progressus sum	I advance
regredior	regredi	regressus sum	I go back
morior	mori	mortuus sum	I die
patior	pati	passus sum	I suffer
semi-deponent (second conjugation)			
audeo	audere	ausus sum	I dare
gaudeo	gaudere	gavisus sum	I rejoice
soleo	solere	solitus sum	I am accustomed

- Deponent verbs are passive in form but active in meaning. They are formed like the passive tenses of the appropriate conjugation. The third principal part shows the (very useful) perfect participle, which here always has an active meaning (e.g. *locutus* = having spoken); deponent verbs also have normal present and future active participles (e.g. *loquens* = speaking, *locuturus* = about to speak).

- Semi-deponent verbs use passive forms for the perfect and pluperfect tenses: their other tenses are formed like the actives of normal verbs.

Important irregular principal parts

accipio	accipere	accepi	acceptus	I accept, I receive
ago	agere	egi	actus	I do, I drive
ascendo	ascendere	ascendi	ascensus	I climb
cado	cadere	cecidi	casus	I fall
capio	capere	cepi	captus	I take, I capture
cognosco	cognoscere	cognovi	cognitus	I get to know
cogo	cogere	coegi	coactus	I force
conspicio	conspicere	conspexi	conspectus	I catch sight of
constituo	constituere	constitui	constitutus	I decide
credo	credere	credidi	creditus	I believe, I trust (+ *dat*)
curro	currere	cucurri	cursus	I run
defendo	defendere	defendi	defensus	I defend
deleo	delere	delevi	deletus	I destroy
dico	dicere	dixi	dictus	I say
discedo	discedere	discessi	-	I depart, I leave
do	dare	dedi	datus	I give
duco	ducere	duxi	ductus	I lead
emo	emere	emi	emptus	I buy
eo	ire	i(v)i	-	I go
facio	facere	feci	factus	I make, I do
fero	ferre	tuli	latus	I carry
fugio	fugere	fugi	-	I run away
gero	gerere	gessi	gestus	I wage, I wear
iacio	iacere	ieci	iactus	I throw
intellego	intellegere	intellexi	intellectus	I understand
iubeo	iubere	iussi	iussus	I order
lego	legere	legi	lectus	I read, I choose
maneo	manere	mansi	-	I remain, I stay
mitto	mittere	misi	missus	I send
moveo	movere	movi	motus	I move
pello	pellere	pepuli	pulsus	I drive
persuadeo	persuadere	persuasi	-	I persuade (+ *dat*)
peto	petere	petivi	petitus	I seek
pono	ponere	posui	positus	I place
possum	posse	potui	-	I am able
promitto	promittere	promisi	promissus	I promise
quaero	quaerere	quaesivi	quaesitus	I search for, I ask
rapio	rapere	rapui	raptus	I seize
rego	regere	rexi	rectus	I rule
relinquo	relinquere	reliqui	relictus	I leave
respondeo	respondere	respondi	responsus	I reply
rideo	ridere	risi	-	I laugh, I smile
scio	scire	scivi	scitus	I know
scribo	scribere	scripsi	scriptus	I write
sedeo	sedere	sedi	-	I sit
sentio	sentire	sensi	sensus	I feel, I notice
sto	stare	steti	-	I stand
sum	esse	fui	-	I am
surgo	surgere	surrexi	-	I get up, I rise
tollo	tollere	sustuli	sublatus	I raise, I remove
trado	tradere	tradidi	traditus	I hand over
traho	trahere	traxi	tractus	I drag
venio	venire	veni	-	I come
video	videre	vidi	visus	I see
vinco	vincere	vici	victus	I conquer
vivo	vivere	vixi	-	I live

APPENDIX 1: USE OF CASES

The *case* of a noun/pronoun/adjective shows its job in the sentence. It is named from *casus* (falling): the other cases are imagined as falling away at increasing angles from the upright purity of the nominative. This also explains *decline* and *declension*: listing the cases, you trace the pattern by which they fall away from the vertical.

NOMINATIVE

- The nominative case is used for the subject of a sentence or clause. Its name comes from *nomen -inis* (name): the nominative *names* the person or thing the sentence is about. With an active verb, it refers to the person who does the action:

  puer librum legit.   The boy reads the book.

- With a passive verb, the subject is the person or thing on the receiving end of the action:

  liber a puero legitur.   The book is read by the boy.

- The nominative is also used for a *complement* (another noun referring to the subject):

  puer est filius meus.   The boy is my son.

- A subordinate part of a sentence can only introduce a new nominative if it has its own finite verb (i.e. with person ending): the infinitive (as its name implies) does not qualify, so the subject of an indirect statement is *accusative*.

VOCATIVE

- The vocative case is used to address or speak directly to someone (less often to an inanimate object). Its name comes from *voco* (I call). It has the same form as the nominative for all plurals and for singulars apart from second declension nouns ending *-us* (e.g. *dominus*, voc *domine*; *filius*, voc *fili*). It is often found with an imperative (which if singular and second/third conjugation coincidentally also has the ending *-e*):

  discede, domine!   Depart, master!

- The vocative is preceded by *o* as a dignified form of address, e.g. in prayers to gods.

ACCUSATIVE

- The accusative case gets its name from *accuso* (I accuse). This captures by one example the idea of *homing in on a target*, which underlies several of the jobs it does.

  1. Direct object in a sentence or clause:

     puella pecuniam celavit.   The girl hid the money.

  2. Motion towards or through, the destination being thought of as a target just as the direct object is. It follows many prepositions expressing this idea:

     ad insulam navigabamus.   We were sailing towards the island.

     - Names of towns and cities use the accusative alone (also *domum* = home[wards]):

       Romam festinabo.   I shall hurry to Rome.

  3. Expressions of *time how long*:

     tres horas manebam.   I was waiting for three hours.

  4. Subject of the infinitive in indirect statement:

     senex dixit pueros fugisse.   The old man said that the boys had run away.

GENITIVE

- The genitive case is named from the adjective form of the Latin *genitus* (birth/origin); compare *Genesis*. The underlying idea is the source from which something comes, but in practice it expresses *possession* (things *belonging to* people being imagined as *originating from* them), and is usually translated *of* (or represented by an apostrophe). More generally it is a case of *definition* or *description*, often found in a phrase with another noun.

  1. Possession:

     librum fratris inveni.   I found my brother's book.

  2. Partitive (i.e. part or some *of*):

     da mihi plus cibi.   Give me more food (*lit* more *of* food)!

     - An extension of this is the use with a superlative:

       hic est optimus servorum. This is the best of the slaves.

  3. Descriptive, expressing a quality someone has:

     miles magnae virtutis   a very brave soldier (*lit* a soldier of great courage)

DATIVE

- The dative case is named from *do* (I give), perfect passive participle *datus*. Its basic idea is of giving: literally handing over something to someone, or doing something for their advantage (or disadvantage). It is often translated *to* or *for*.

    1. Indirect object:

    vir uxori donum dedit.   The man gave his wife a gift (*or* gave a gift to his wife).

    - Note that in English *to* is missed out if the indirect object comes before the direct, but put in if the indirect object comes second. (Contrast *gave his wife to a slave-dealer*.)

    2. Advantage (or disadvantage):

    femina cenam marito paravit.   The woman prepared dinner for her husband.

    3. After certain verbs, because of their meaning:

appropinquo	I approach	(come near *to* something)
credo	I believe, I trust	(give trust *to* someone)
faveo	I favour	(give favour *to* someone)
impero	I order	(give an order *to* someone)
persuadeo	I persuade	(apply persuasion *to* someone)
resisto	I resist	(put up resistance *to* someone)

ABLATIVE

- The ablative case is named from *ablatus*, the perfect passive participle of *aufero* (I carry away). This captures one important idea the ablative expresses: separation or going away. The ablative is in fact a bit of a ragbag (it can also express *staying put*), but many of its meanings are covered by the translations *by*, *with* or *from*.

    1. With prepositions meaning *going away from*, and also with ones meaning *staying in* a place (names of cities use the ablative alone to mean *from*):

    cives qui e templo festinaverunt nunc in foro sunt.
    The citizens who hurried out of the temple are now in the forum.

    2. Agent and instrument with a passive verb: the *agent* (the person by whom an action is done) uses *a/ab* and the ablative; the *instrument* (the thing with which an action is done) uses the ablative alone:

    imperator gladio necatus est a custode suo.
    The emperor was killed by his own guard with a sword.

3. Time: the ablative is used both for *time when* (*point* of time) and *time within which*:

   prima luce discessi, sed tribus diebus reveniam.
   I left at first light, but I shall come back within three days.

4. Comparison: the second item in a simple comparison can use the ablative without *quam*:

   hic puer fratre stultior est.   This boy is more stupid than his brother.

5. Description: the ablative (rather than the genitive) is used for *physical description*:

   servus ingentibus pedibus   a slave with huge feet

6. Ablative absolute: a noun and participle phrase grammatically unconnected with the rest of the sentence:

   hostibus victis, omnes gavisi sumus.
   When the enemy had been defeated, we all rejoiced.

APPENDIX 2: CONSTRUCTIONS

DIRECT QUESTIONS

- A question to which the answer will be *yes* or *no* uses *-ne* (open), *nonne* (expecting *yes*) or *num* (expecting *no*):

audivistine?*	Do you hear?
nonne audivisti?	Surely you heard?
num audivisti?	Surely you didn't hear?

* *-ne* is attached to the end of the first word, usually the verb.

- A question asking for specific information uses one of a range of question words (see list on page 71), many of them beginning *qu-*:

  quando adveniemus?   When shall we arrive?

DIRECT COMMANDS

- A direct command uses the imperative, often together with a vocative:

  festina, serve!   Hurry, slave!

- A negative direct command uses *noli* (pl *nolite*) with the infinitive:

  noli audire!   Don't listen!

ABLATIVE ABSOLUTE

- An ablative absolute is a phrase usually made up of noun and participle, grammatically unconnected with the rest of the sentence:

  urbe capta, cives perterriti erant.
  After (*or* Because) the city had been captured, the citizens were terrified.

RELATIVE CLAUSES

- The relative pronoun *qui, quae, quod* agrees with its antecedent (the noun it refers back to) in number and gender, but takes its case from the job it does in its own clause (which has an indicative verb):

    servus quem heri vidi iterum adest.
    The slave whom I saw yesterday is here again.

TIME, CAUSAL AND CONCESSIVE CLAUSES

- A clause indicating when something happened is introduced by *ubi* (when) or *postquam* (after) followed by a perfect indicative:

    ubi Romam adveni, amicos salutavi.
    When I arrived in Rome, I greeted my friends.

- A time clause referring to the future uses *ubi* with a 'hidden future' (a future tense translated as present):

    ubi Romam adveniam, laetus ero.
    When I arrive in Rome, I shall be happy.

- *dum* (while) is followed by a present indicative (translated like an imperfect) if it refers to an action or process during which something else occurred:

    dum in foro manemus, senator occisus est.
    While we were waiting in the forum, the senator was killed.

- A clause indicating a factual reason is introduced by *quod* and has an indicative verb:

    senex punitus est quod servum necaverat.
    The old man was punished because he had killed a slave.

- A *cum* (when/since) clause with the imperfect or pluperfect subjunctive (translated just like the equivalent indicative tense) expresses a likely reason (*when* with a suggestion of *because*):

    puella, cum praemium accepisset, laetissima erat.
    Since the girl had received the prize, she was very happy.

- *dum* with the imperfect subjunctive (translated *until*) has a suggestion of purpose:

    militem ad portam manere iussi dum nuntius rediret.
    I ordered the soldier to remain at the gate until the messenger returned.

- A concessive clause (giving a reason why what happens might have been expected not to) uses *quamquam* (although) with an indicative verb:

    quamquam crudelis est, dominus a servis amatur.
    Although he is cruel, the master is loved by his slaves.

CONDITIONALS

- Conditional sentences have the shape *if X, (then) Y*. The word for *if* is *si*, negative *nisi* (if . . . not *or* unless). Simple conditionals have ordinary indicative verbs and translate naturally:

  > si multos amicos habes, felix es.
  > If you have many friends, you are fortunate.

- Note the 'hidden future', where Latin uses the future tense but it is translated as present:

  > si audies, omnia intelleges.
  > If you listen, you will understand everything.

INDIRECT STATEMENT

- English normally expresses an indirect or reported statement by a *that* clause (*she said that it was true*), but can also use an infinitive (*she declared it to be true*). Latin uses only the infinitive method. The introductory verb need not be one of speaking, but can be e.g. *see, hear, learn, know, think*. There is no separate Latin word for *that* (it can also be missed out in English). The subject of the infinitive is accusative (if it is the same as that of the introductory verb, a reflexive pronoun is used). The tense of the infinitive is that of the original direct statement (what was said or thought at the time). If the introductory verb is past, English moves back a tense in translating the infinitive:

He declared X to be happening	*becomes*	He said that it was . . .
. . . to have happened		He said that it had . . .
. . . to be going to happen		He said that it would/ was going to . . .

  > nuntius dixit hostes appropinquare.
  > The messenger said that the enemy were approaching.

  > puella putavit se clamorem audivisse.
  > The girl thought she had heard a shout.

PURPOSE CLAUSES

- A purpose clause (expressing the aim or intention with which something was done) uses *ut* followed by an imperfect subjunctive verb:

  cives Romam festinaverunt ut novum imperatorem viderent.
  The citizens hurried to Rome (in order) to see the new emperor.

- The translation *to* often works if the subject of the purpose clause is the same as that of the main clause; if it is different, a fuller translation such as *in order that* is needed:

  hi mortui sunt ut nos viveremus.
  These men died in order that we might live.

- A negative purpose clause (expressing what someone was trying to avoid) uses *ne* instead of *ut*:

  servus fugit ne a domino puniretur.
  The slave ran away in order not to be punished by his master.

- Purpose can also be expressed by *ad* with a gerundive:

  senex tabernam intravit ad cibum emendum.
  The old man entered the shop to buy food.

- Latin does not use the infinitive to express purpose as English does.

INDIRECT COMMANDS

- *iubeo* (I order) is followed by an infinitive, as in English (but it cannot be used for a negative command):

  dux milites in castris manere iussit.
  The leader ordered the soldiers to stay in the camp.

- Other verbs use an *ut* clause, exactly like a purpose clause (imperfect subjunctive verb, negative *ne* instead of *ut*). It is usually translated simply . . . *to do X*:

  domina servis imperavit ut celerius laborarent.
  The mistress ordered the slaves to work more quickly.

- A 'command' in the grammatical sense need be no more than a request: indirect commands are often introduced by words such as *moneo* (I advise), *rogo* (I ask), *hortor* (I encourage), *persuadeo* (I persuade) or *oro* (I beg).

- Note that *impero* and *persuadeo* are followed by the dative of the person who is ordered or persuaded.

VERBS OF FEARING

- A verb expressing what someone feared would happen is expressed by *ne* with an imperfect subjunctive verb, but *ne* is not a negative here and should be translated *that*:

    cives timebant ne urbs caperetur.
    The citizens were afraid that the city would be captured.

- A fear that something would *not* happen uses *ne non*.

RESULT CLAUSES

- A result clause focuses on the *outcome* (rather than the intention, as a purpose clause does). There is normally a signpost word in the main clause, e.g. *tam* (see list on page 132). The result clause itself starts with *ut*, and has an imperfect subjunctive verb:

    pueri portam tam fortiter custodiverunt ut praemia acciperent.
    The boys guarded the gate so bravely that they received prizes.

- A negative result clauses uses *ut . . . non* (i.e. *non* as well as *ut*, in contrast to the use of *ne* instead of *ut* in purpose clauses and indirect commands):

    tempestas tanta erat ut clamorem non audirem.
    The storm was so great that I did not hear the shout.

INDIRECT QUESTIONS

- An indirect or reported question asking for specific information is introduced by one of the normal question words (see above on direct questions):

    puellam rogavi quid faceret.
    I asked the girl what she was doing.

- An indirect question to which the answer will be *yes* or *no* is introduced by *num* (which here means *whether*; an indirect question cannot be slanted to expect one answer or the other):

    senex uxorem rogavit num epistulam accepisset.
    The old man asked his wife whether she had received the letter.

- The verb in the indirect question is imperfect or pluperfect subjunctive. The subjunctive here (just as in a *cum* clause) is translated like the equivalent indicative tense. It translates naturally ('tense by sense') because Latin behaves like English in moving one tense back from the original direct question if the introductory verb is past:

    | What is happening? | *becomes* | She asked what was happening. |
    | What happened? | | She asked what had happened. |

APPENDIX 3: NEGATIVES

- The normal negative is *non* and its usual position is just in front of the verb:

    aquam non amo.
    I do not like water.

- If *non* is put elsewhere in the sentence, it negatives the word it is just in front of:

    non aquam sed vinum amo.
    I like not water but wine.

- Note that *et* (and) is never followed by *non* or any other negative; instead words or clauses must be joined by *nec* or *neque* (and not):

    miles profectus est nec umquam rediit.
    The soldier set off and did not ever return (*i.e.* never returned).

- Note the paired negatives *nec . . . nec* or *neque . . . neque* (neither . . . nor):

    nec aquam nec vinum amo.
    I like neither water nor wine.
    or   I do not like either water or wine.

- The negative for a possibility rather than a fact is *ne*. This is used (instead of *ut*) for a negative purpose clause:

    servus e villa cucurrit ne a domino videretur.
    The slave ran out of the house in order not to be seen by his master.

- Exactly the same construction is used for a negative indirect command:

    senex pueris imperavit ne in templo clamarent.
    The old man ordered the boys not to shout in the temple.

- Note that *ne* after a verb of fearing is translated *that* and is not really a negative:

    cives timebant ne urbs caperetur.
    The citizens were afraid that the city would be captured.

- Other subjunctive constructions, i.e. result clause, *cum* clause, and indirect question, use the normal negative *non*.

- The use of *ne* (long *e*) with a subjunctive must not be confused with *-ne* (short *e*, and not a negative) added to the first word of a direct question:

  > servumne vidisti?
  > Did you see the slave?

- A negative direct command uses *noli* (imperative of *nolo*, plural *nolite*) with the infinitive:

  > noli festinare.
  > Do not hurry!

- A negative conditional uses *nisi* (if not *or* unless):

  > nisi cibum accipiam, domum redibo.
  > Unless I receive food, I shall return home.

- *No* as the opposite of *yes* is *minime* (adverb of *minimus*, also used in its literal sense *very little, least*). *No* as an adjective meaning *not any* is *nullus*:

  > nullam pecuniam habeo.
  > I have no money.

- Note also:

  the pronouns *nemo* (no-one) and *nihil* (nothing)
  numquam (never), the negative of *umquam* (ever)
  the plural adjective *nonnulli -ae -a* (some, several), literally a double negative
  (not no)

APPENDIX 4: USES OF THE SUBJUNCTIVE

Expect to see an *imperfect* subjunctive in the following constructions (it is translated differently in each):

- *purpose clause:*

    Romam festinavimus ut imperatorem videremus.
    We hurried to Rome to see the emperor.

- *indirect command:*

    dominus servis imperavit ut celerius laborarent.
    The master ordered the slaves to work more quickly.

- *result clause:*

    puer tam stultus erat ut nihil intellegeret.
    The boy was so stupid that he understood nothing.

- *clause after verb of fearing:*

    cives timebant ne urbs oppugnaretur.
    The citizens were afraid that the city would be attacked

- *time clause also expressing purpose:*

    in foro manebam dum amici advenirent.
    I was waiting in the forum for my friends to arrive.

- cum *clause:*

    cum nullam pecuniam haberemus, miserrimi eramus.
    Since we had no money, we were very miserable.

- *indirect question:*

    senem rogavi quid consumeret.
    I asked the old man what he was eating.

Expect to see a *pluperfect* subjunctive in the following constructions:

- cum *clause:*

    cum nihil audivissem, domi manebam.
    Since I had heard nothing, I stayed at home.

- *indirect question:*

> puellam rogavi quid fecisset.
> I asked the girl what she had done.

Note that in a *cum* clause or indirect question the subjunctive (whether imperfect or pluperfect) is translated just like the equivalent indicative tense.

APPENDIX 5: WORDS EASILY CONFUSED

absum	I am away
adsum	I am here
alter	one (of two)/the other
altus	high, deep
audeo	I dare
audio	I hear
capio	I take
cupio	I want
cena	dinner
cibus	food
cogito	I think
cognosco	I get to know
cogo	I force
descendo	I go down
discedo	I depart
dico	I say
duco	I lead
domina	mistress
dominus	master
domus	house
forte	by chance
fortis	brave, strong
fortiter	bravely, strongly
habeo	I have
habito	I live
hortor	I encourage
hortus	garden
iaceo	I lie (down)
iacio	I throw

ita	in this way, so
itaque	and so, therefore
iter	journey
iterum	again
laetus	happy
latus	having been carried
liber	book
liberi	children
libero	I set free
libertus	freedman, ex-slave
locus	place
locutus	having spoken
malo	I prefer
malus	bad
maneo	I remain
moneo	I warn
novem	nine
novus	new
oppugno	I attack
pugno	I fight
porta	gate
porto	I carry
post	after (*prep + acc*)
postea	afterwards
postquam	after (*X happened, . . .*)
posui	I placed
potui	I was/have been able
poteram	I was able
potueram	I had been able

proficiscor	I set out	stat	he stands
progredior	I advance	statim	at once, immediately
		subito	suddenly
reddo	I give back		
redeo	I go back	summus	top (of)
rideo	I laugh	sumus	we are
res	thing (*acc* rem)	tamen	however
rex	king (*acc* regem)	tandem	at last
saepe	often	terreo	I frighten
semper	always	timeo	I fear
simul	at the same time	trado	I hand over
simulac	as soon as	traho	I drag
soleo	I am accustomed	via	road, way
solus	alone	vita	life
		vici	I conquered
		vixi	I lived

APPENDIX 6: WORDS WITH MORE THAN ONE MEANING

Some of these are alternative meanings of the same word, others are homonyms (unrelated words coincidentally spelled in the same way).

ad	(1)	to, towards, at	preposition with the accusative
	(2)	in order to	followed by gerundive
cum	(1)	with	preposition with the ablative
	(2)	when, since	introducing clause with subjunctive verb
ne	(1)	not, not to	negative in purpose clause or indirect command
	(2)	that	after verb of fearing
(-ne)	(3)	(e.g.) is it?	signals an open question, attached to the end of its first word
num	(1)	surely not?	in direct question
	(2)	whether	in indirect question
quam	(1)	how	in direct question or exclamation
	(2)	than	in comparison
	(3)	as . . . as possible	with superlative adverb
	(4)	whom, which	feminine accusative singular of relative pronoun
quod	(1)	because	introducing clause giving reason
	(2)	which	neuter nominative or accusative singular of relative pronoun
ubi	(1)	when	introducing a time clause
	(2)	where	introducing a question or a clause explaining location

Note: *ubi* as a question must be *where*; if not a question, it can be *when* or *where* (*when* in a question is *quando*).

ut	(1)	in order that, to	introducing a purpose clause
	(2)	to	introducing an indirect command
	(3)	that	introducing a result clause
	(4)	as, when	with indicative verb, or no verb

GLOSSARY OF GRAMMAR TERMS

ablative case expressing *by, with, from*; used with prepositions expressing motion away from, or being in a place.

ablative absolute phrase (usually made up of noun and participle) in the ablative, grammatically unconnected with the rest of the sentence, describing the circumstances in which the action described in the main clause took place (e.g *his verbis dictis* = when these words had been said).

accusative case of direct object; used with prepositions expressing motion towards; used for subject of infinitive in indirect statement.

active form of verb where the grammatical subject is the doer of the action (as distinct from passive).

adjective word describing a noun (with which in Latin it agrees in number, gender and case).

adverb word describing a verb (or an adjective, or another adverb).

agent person by whom the action of a passive verb is done, expressed by *a/ab* and the ablative.

agree have the same number (agreement of subject and verb); have the same number, gender and case (agreement of noun and adjective).

ambiguous can mean more than one thing.

antecedent noun or pronoun in main clause to which relative pronoun refers back.

auxiliary a verb (usually part of *to be*) used with a participle to form a tense of another verb (e.g. perfect passive *portati sumus* = we have been carried).

case form of a noun, pronoun or adjective that shows the job it does in the sentence (e.g. accusative for direct object); cases are arranged in the order

nominative, (vocative), accusative, genitive, dative, ablative.

causal clause subordinate clause stating why something happened, introduced by *quod* (= because).

clause part of a sentence with its own subject and verb.

comparative form of an adjective or adverb meaning *more, -er* (e.g. *longior* = longer).

complement another nominative word or phrase describing the subject, usually with the verb *to be*.

compound verb with prefix (e.g. *exire* = to go out).

concessive clause subordinate clause stating why something might have been expected not to happen (but nevertheless did), introduced by *quamquam* (= although).

conditional clause beginning *if* or *unless* (*si* or *nisi* in Latin).

conjugate go through the different parts of a verb (e.g. *porto, portas, portat* etc).

conjugation one of the four main patterns by which verbs change their endings.

conjunction word joining clauses, phrases or words together (e.g. *and, but, therefore*).

consonant letter representing a sound that can only be used together with a vowel.

construction pattern according to which a particular type of sentence or clause is formed (e.g. accusative and infinitive for indirect statement).

dative case of indirect object, often translated *to* or *for*.

declension one of the patterns (three main ones, also used for adjectives, and two less common) by which nouns change their endings.

decline go through the different parts of a noun, pronoun or adjective in case order.

deponent verb which is passive in form but active in meaning.

defective verb verb of which only a few parts exist.

direct object noun or pronoun on the receiving end of action of verb.

direct speech actual words of a speaker, usually enclosed by inverted commas.

ending last part of a word, added to the stem to give more information and show its job in the sentence.

feminine one of the three genders, for females or things imagined as female.

finite form of a verb with tense and person ending (as distinct from infinitive or participle).

future tense of verb referring to something that will happen in the future.

gender one of three categories (masculine, feminine, neuter) into which nouns and pronouns are put according to their actual or imagined sex or lack of it.

genitive case expressing possession or definition, often translated *of*.

gerundive adjective formed from verb, expressing the idea *needing to be done*; used with *ad* to express purpose.

homonym word coincidentally spelled in the same way as another unrelated word.

idiom common expression whose meaning differs from that of the separate words (e.g. *consilium capio* = I make a plan, *poenas do* = I pay the penalty).

imperative form of verb used for direct command.

imperfect tense of verb referring to incomplete, extended or repeated action in the past.

indeclinable does not change its endings.

indicative form of verb expressing a fact (usually as distinct from subjunctive).

indirect indirect statement, command or question is the reported form of it (as distinct from quotation of the speaker's actual words); indirect object is person or thing in the dative indirectly affected by object of verb, e.g. *I gave the money* (direct object) *to the old man* (indirect object).

infinitive form of verb introduced by *to*, expressing the basic meaning (e.g. *currere* = to run).

instrument thing with which the action of a passive verb is done, expressed by the ablative without a preposition.

intransitive verb that does not have a direct object (e.g. *festino* = I hurry).

irregular word that does not follow one of the standard declensions or conjugations.

literally translated in a way corresponding closely to the Latin words, but which needs to be modified to produce natural English.

locative special case ending of some nouns (usually names of cities) expressing *at* or *in*.

main clause clause which makes sense on its own, and expresses the main point of a sentence (as distinct from subordinate clause).

masculine one of the three genders, for males or things imagined as male.

negative expressing that something is not the case or should not happen.

neuter one of the three genders, for things imagined as neither male nor female.

nominative case used for subject of sentence.

noun word naming a person, place or thing (e.g. *urbs* = city; a *proper* noun with a capital letter gives its actual name e.g. *Roma* = Rome).

number singular or plural.

numerals numbers.

object noun or pronoun acted upon by a verb.

part of speech category of word (noun, adjective, pronoun, verb, adverb, preposition, conjunction).

participle adjective formed from a verb (e.g. *portans* = carrying, *portatus* = having been carried), which has the qualities of both a verb and an adjective.

passive form of verb where the subject does not do the action but is on the receiving end of it (e.g. *capior* = I am captured).

perfect tense of verb referring to a completed action in the past.

person term for the subject of verb: first person = *I*, *we*; second person = *you*, third person = *he*, *she*, *it*, *they* (or a noun replacing one of these).

phrase group of words not containing a finite verb (as distinct from clause).

pluperfect tense of verb referring to something that had already happened by a particular point in the past.

plural more than one.

possessive adjective or pronoun expressing who or what something belongs to.

prefix word or syllable added to the beginning of another word.

preposition word used with a noun or pronoun in the accusative or ablative to focus more closely the meaning of the case (e.g. *into*).

present tense of a verb referring to something that is happening now (or, in the case of a present participle, at the same time as the action described by main verb of the sentence).

principal parts set of (usually four) parts of a verb from which you can work out all necessary information about it: present tense (first person singular), infinitive, perfect tense (first person singular), perfect passive participle (if the verb has one).

pronoun word that stands instead of a noun (e.g. *he*, *she*, *they*), avoiding the need to repeat it.

purpose clause subordinate clause stating the aim with which something was done, usually expressed by *ut* (= in order to) with the imperfect subjunctive; a negative version uses *ne* instead of *ut*.

reflexive word referring back to the subject of the verb.

relative clause subordinate clause describing or giving further information about a person or thing just mentioned in the main clause, introduced by the relative pronoun *qui, quae, quod*.

result clause subordinate clause stating the outcome of an action, expressed (after a signpost *so . . .* in the main clause) by *ut* (= that) with the imperfect subjunctive; a negative version uses *ut . . . non*.

sentence group of words with subject and verb (and often other elements), which can stand on its own (as distinct from phrase or subordinate clause).

singular just one (as distinct from plural).

stem the part of a word which stays the same: different endings are added to give more information and show the job it does in the sentence.

subject noun or pronoun in the nominative case, expressing who or what does the action (with active verb) or is on the receiving end of it (with passive verb).

subjunctive form of verb referring not to a fact but to an idea or possibility (as distinct from indicative), used in several types of subordinate clause in Latin.

subordinate of secondary importance to something else; a subordinate clause cannot stand alone but only makes sense in relation to the main clause.

superlative form of adjective or adverb meaning *very*, *most*, *-est* (e.g. *altissimus* = very high, highest).

supply provide in translation a word which is not separately represented in Latin but worked out from the grammar and context (e.g. *multa dixit* = he said many *things*).

syllable part of a word forming a spoken unit, usually consisting of vowel with consonants before or after or both.

tense form of a verb showing when the action takes place (in the past, present or future).

transitive verb that has a direct object.

verb word expressing an action (e.g. *curro* = I run).

vocative case used for addressing someone or something.

vowel letter representing a sound that can be spoken by itself: *a, e, i, o, u, y* (but *y* is rare in Latin).

ENGLISH TO LATIN VOCABULARY

For further information about a word, check it in the Latin to English vocabulary.

able, be	possum, posse, potui
about	de (+ *abl*)
absent, be	absum, abesse, afui
accept	accipio, accipere, accepi, acceptus
account of, on	propter (+ *acc*)
accustomed, be	soleo, solere, solitus sum
across	trans (+ *acc*)
act	ago, agere, egi, actus
admire	miror, mirari, miratus sum
advance	progredior, progredi, progressus sum
advice	consilium -i *n* 2
advise	moneo, monere, monui, monitus
afraid (of), be	timeo, timere, timui
after (*prep*)	post (+ *acc*); *but as adv in e.g.* multis post annis (after many years)
after (*conj*)	postquam
afterwards (*adv*)	postea
again	iterum
against	contra (+ *acc*)
all	omnis -e
almost	paene
alone	solus -a -um
along	per (+ *acc*)
already	iam
also	quoque
although	quamquam
always	semper
amazed (at), be	miror, mirari, miratus sum
among	inter (+ *acc*)
and	et; ac/atque; -que (*attached to the second word*)
and . . . not	nec/neque
and so	itaque; igitur (*not first word*)
anger	ira -ae *f* 1
angry	iratus -a -um
announce	nuntio, nuntiare, nuntiavi, nuntiatus
another	alius -a -ud; alter -era -erum
answer (reply)	respondeo, respondere, respondi, responsus
appear	videor, videri, visus sum
approach	appropinquo, appropinquare, appropinquavi (+ *dat*)

arms, armour	arma -orum *n 2 pl*
army	exercitus -us *m 4*
around	circum (+ *acc*)
arrive	advenio, advenire, adveni
art	ars, artis *f 3*
as	ut
as . . . as possible	quam + *sup adv*, *e.g.* quam celerrime (as quickly as possible)
as soon as	simulac/simulatque
ask (question/request)	rogo, rogare, rogavi, rogatus
ask for	rogo, rogare, rogavi, rogatus; peto, petere, petivi, petitus
at	ad (+ *acc*)
at first	primo
at last	tandem
at once	statim
attack	oppugno, oppugnare, oppugnavi, oppugnatus
away, be	absum, abesse, afui
away from	a/ab (+ *abl*)
back (*prefix*)	re-, *e.g.* revenio (come back)
bad	malus -a -um
battle	proelium -i *n 2*
be	sum, esse, fui
be absent/away	absum, abesse, afui
be here/present	adsum, adesse, adfui
bear	fero, ferre, tuli, latus
beautiful	pulcher -chra -chrum
because	quod
because of	propter (+ *acc*)
before (*adv*)	antea
beg	oro, orare, oravi, oratus
began	coepi, coepisse
behind	post (+ *acc*)
believe	credo, credere, credidi, creditus (+ *dat*)
beneath	sub (+ *acc* [*motion*] or *abl* [*rest*])
best	optimus -a -um
better	melior -us
between	inter (+ *acc*)
big	magnus -a -um
bigger	maior -us
biggest	maximus -a -um
block of flats	insula -ae *f 1*
blood	sanguis -inis *m 3*
body	corpus -oris *n 3*
bold	audax *gen* -acis
book	liber -bri *m 2*
both . . . and	et . . . et
boy	puer -eri *m 2*
brave	fortis -e

bravely	fortiter
brief	brevis -e
bring	fero, ferre, tuli, latus
bring back	refero, referre, rettuli, relatus
brother	frater -tris *m 3*
build	aedifico, aedificare, aedificavi, aedificatus
burn (something)	incendo, incendere, incendi, incensus
but	sed
buy	emo, emere, emi, emptus
by	a/ab (+ *abl*)
call	voco, vocare, vocavi, vocatus
camp	castra -orum *n 2 pl*
can (be able)	possum, posse, potui
captive	captivus -i *m 2*
capture	capio, capere, cepi, captus
care	cura -ae *f 1*
careful	diligens *gen* -entis
carefully	diligenter
carry	porto, portare, portavi, portatus; fero, ferre, tuli, latus
carry off	aufero, auferre, abstuli, ablatus
catch	capio, capere, cepi, captus
catch sight of	conspicio, conspicere, conspexi, conspectus
certain, a	quidam, quaedam, quoddam
chance, by	forte
chief, chieftain	princeps -ipis *m 3*
children	liberi -orum *m 2 pl*
choose	lego, legere, legi, lectus
citizen	civis -is *m/f 3*
city	urbs, urbis *f 3*
clear	clarus -a -um
climb	ascendo, ascendere, ascendi, ascensus
come	venio, venire, veni
come down	descendo, descendere, descendi, descensus
come near to	appropinquo, appropinquare, appropinquavi (+ *dat*)
come together	convenio, convenire, conveni
command (*verb*)	impero, imperare, imperavi, imperatus (+ *dat*)
command (*noun*)	imperium -i *n 2*
companion	comes -itis *m/f 3*
compel	cogo, cogere, coegi, coactus
comrade	comes -itis *m/f 3*
conquer	vinco, vincere, vici, victus
consul	consul -ulis *m 3*
country (native land)	patria -ae *f 1*
courage	virtus -utis *f 3*
crime	scelus -eris *n 3*
crowd	turba -ae *f 1*
cruel	crudelis -e; saevus -a -um
crush	opprimo, opprimere, oppressi, oppressus
cry	lacrimo, lacrimare, lacrimavi

danger	periculum -i *n* 2
dare	audeo, audere, ausus sum
daring	audax *gen* -acis
daughter	filia -ae (*dat/abl pl* filiabus) *f* 1
day	dies -ei *m* 5
daylight	lux, lucis *f* 3
death	mors, mortis *f* 3
decide	constituo, constituere, constitui, constitutus
deep	altus -a -um
defeat	vinco, vincere, vici, victus
defend	defendo, defendere, defendi, defensus
depart (from)	discedo, discedere, discessi (+ *prep* + *abl*)
descend	descendo, descendere, descendi, descensus
desire	cupio, cupere, cupivi, cupitus
destroy	deleo, delere, delevi, deletus
die	morior, mori, mortuus sum; pereo, perire, perii
difficult	difficilis -e
dinner	cena -ae *f* 1
discover	invenio, invenire, inveni, inventus
distant (from), be	absum, abesse, afui (+ *abl*)
do	ago, agere, egi, actus; facio, facere, feci, factus
do not . . . !	noli, *pl* nolite (+ *inf*)
door	ianua -ae *f* 1
down from	de (+ *abl*)
drag	traho, trahere, traxi, tractus
dreadful	dirus -a -um
drink	bibo, bibere, bibi
drive	ago, agere, egi, actus; pello, pellere, pepuli, pulsus
drive back	repello, repellere, reppuli, repulsus
drive out	expello, expellere, expuli, expulsus
earth	terra -ae *f* 1
easily	facile
easy	facilis -e
eat	consumo, consumere, consumpsi, consumptus
eight	octo
emperor	imperator -oris *m* 3; princeps -cipis *m* 3
empire	imperium -i *n* 2
encourage	hortor, hortari, hortatus sum
endure	patior, pati, passus sum
enemy (in war)	hostis -is *m* 3 (*usu pl*)
enemy (personal)	inimicus -i *m* 2
enter	intro, intrare, intravi, intratus; ingredior, ingredi, ingressus sum
escape	effugio, effugere, effugi
even	etiam
ever	umquam
every	omnis -e
everyone (all the people)	omnes -ium *pl*
everything (all things)	omnia -ium *pl*
evil	malus -a -um

excellent	optimus -a -um
except	nisi
expect	exspecto, exspectare, exspectavi, exspectatus
ex-slave	libertus -i *m 2*
extent, to such an	adeo (*often with verb introducing result clause*)
faithful	fidelis -e
fall	cado, cadere, cecidi, casus
family	gens, gentis *f 3*
famous	clarus -a -um
fast	celer -eris -ere
father	pater -tris *m 3*
favour	faveo, favere, favi (+ *dat*)
fear	timeo, timere, timui
feel	sentio, sentire, sensi, sensus
ferocious	ferox *gen* -ocis
few, a few	pauci -ae -a
field	ager, agri *m 2*
fierce	ferox *gen* -ocis
fight	pugno, pugnare, pugnavi
finally	tandem
find	invenio, invenire, inveni, inventus
find out	cognosco, cognoscere, cognovi, cognitus
finish	conficio, conficere, confeci, confectus
first (*adj*)	primus -a -um
first, at first (*adv*)	primo
five	quinque
flee	fugio, fugere, fugi
follow	sequor, sequi, secutus sum
food	cibus -i *m 2*
foolish	stultus -a -um
foot	pes, pedis *m 3*
for (*giving explanation*)	enim (*not first word*); nam
for (*length of time*)	*use acc*
for (on behalf of)	pro (+ *abl*)
for (the benefit of)	*use dat*
force	cogo, cogere, coegi, coactus
forces	copiae -arum *f 1 pl*
fortunate	felix *gen* -icis
forum	forum -i *n 2*
four	quattuor
freedman	libertus -i *m 2*
friend	amicus -i *m 2*
frighten	terreo, terrere, terrui, territus
frightened, very	perterritus -a -um
from	a/ab (+ *abl*); de (+ *abl*); e/ex (+ *abl*)
garden	hortus -i *m 2*
gate	porta -ae *f 1*
gather (meet, assemble)	convenio, convenire, conveni
general	imperator -oris *m*

get to know	cognosco, cognoscere, cognovi, cognitus
get up	surgo, surgere, surrexi
gift	donum -i *n 2*
girl	puella -ae *f 1*
give	do, dare, dedi, datus
give back	reddo, reddere, reddidi, redditus
gladly	libenter
go	eo, ire, i(v)i
go back	redeo, redire, redii; regredior, regredi, regressus sum
go down	descendo, descendere, descendi, descensus
go out	exeo, exire, exii; egredior, egredi, egressus sum
god	deus -i *m 2*
goddess	dea -ae (*dat/abl pl* deabus) *f 1*
good	bonus -a -um
great	magnus -a -um
greater	maior -us
greatest	maximus -a -um
greet	saluto, salutare, salutavi, salutatus
ground	terra -ae *f 1*
group of people	manus -us *f 4*
guard (*verb*)	custodio, custodire, custodivi, custoditus
guard (*noun*)	custos -odis *m/f 3*
hand	manus -us *f 4*
hand over	trado, tradere, tradidi, traditus
handsome	pulcher -chra -chrum
happen	accido, accidere, accidi
happy	laetus -a -um; felix *gen* -icis
have	habeo, habere, habui, habitus
he	is, *gen* eius; ille, *gen* illius
head	caput -itis *n 3*
hear	audio, audire, audivi, auditus
heaven	caelum -i *n 2*
heavy	gravis -e
help	auxilium -i *n 2*
her, her own (*refl*)	suus -a -um
herself (*refl*)	se
here, be	adsum, adesse, adfui
hide (something)	celo, celare, celavi, celatus
high	altus -a -um
highest (part of)	summus -a -um
himself (*refl*)	se
his, his own (*refl*)	suus -a -um
hold	teneo, tenere, tenui, tentus; habeo, habere, habui, habitus
home	domus -us *f 4*
home, at	domi (*loc of* domus)
home (homewards)	domum (*acc without prep after verb of motion*)
homeland	patria -ae *f 1*
hope (to/that) (*verb*)	spero, sperare, speravi, speratus (*usu + acc + fut inf*)
hope (*noun*)	spes, spei *f 5*

horse	equus -i *m 2*
hour	hora -ae *f 1*
house	domus -us *f 4*; (country villa) villa -ae *f 1*
how (in what way)?	quomodo
how . . . ?/!	quam (+ *adj/adv in question or exclamation*)
how big?	quantus -a -um
how many?	quot (*indecl*)
how much?	quantus -a -um
however	tamen (*not first word*)
huge	ingens *gen* -entis
human being	homo -inis *m/f 3*
hundred	centum
hurry	festino, festinare, festinavi
husband	maritus -i *m 2*
I	ego, *gen* mei
idea	consilium -i *n 2*
if	si
if . . . not	nisi
immediately	statim
in	in (+ *abl*)
in front of	pro (+ *abl*)
in order that/to	ut (+ *subj*)
in order that . . . not	ne (+ *subj*)
in return for	pro (+ *abl*)
in this way	ita
in vain	frustra
inn	taberna -ae *f 1*
into	in (+ *acc*)
invite	invito, invitare, invitavi, invitatus
is it (the case that)?	-ne (*attached to first word of question*)
island	insula -ae *f 1*
it	id, *gen* eius
journey	iter -ineris *n 3*
joy	gaudium -i *n 2*
keep	servo, servare, servavi, servatus
kill	neco, necare, necavi, necatus; interficio, interficere, interfeci, interfectus; occido, occidere, occidi, occisus
king	rex, regis *m 3*
kingdom	regnum -i *n 2*
know	scio, scire, scivi, scitus
land	terra -ae *f 1*
large	magnus -a -um
laugh	rideo, ridere, risi
lead	duco, ducere, duxi, ductus
leader	dux, ducis *m 3*; imperator -oris *m 3*
le~~~ ~~~d)	~~~~nquo, relinquere, reliqui, relictus
	~~o, discedere, discessi (+ *prep* + *abl*)

legion	legio -onis *f 3*
letter	epistula -ae *f 1*
lie (be lying down)	iaceo, iacere, iacui
life	vita -ae *f 1*
lift up	tollo, tollere, sustuli, sublatus
light	lux, lucis *f 3*
like	amo, amare, amavi, amatus
listen (to)	audio, audire, audivi, auditus
little	parvus -a -um
live (be alive)	vivo, vivere, vixi
live (dwell)	habito, habitare, habitavi, habitatus
long	longus -a -um
long time, for a	diu (*comp* diutius, *sup* diutissime)
look!	ecce
look at	specto, spectare, spectavi, spectatus
look for	quaero, quaerere, quaesivi, quaesitus
loudly	vehementer
love (*verb*)	amo, amare, amavi, amatus
love (*noun*)	amor -oris *m 3*
loyal	fidelis -e
make	facio, facere, feci, factus
make for	peto, petere, petivi, petitus
man (human being)	homo, hominis *m 3*
man (male)	vir, viri *m 2*
manner	modus -i *m 2*
many	multi -ae -a
market-place	forum -i *n 2*
master	dominus -i *m 2*
matter (thing, event)	res, rei *f 5*
meal	cena -ae *f 1*
meanwhile	interea
meet	convenio, convenire, conveni
message	nuntius -i *m 2*
messenger	nuntius -i *m 2*
middle (mid part of, *adj*)	medius -a -um
mind	animus -i *m 2*
miserable	miser -era -erum
mistress	domina -ae *f 1*
money	pecunia -ae *f 1*
more (larger amount)	plus *as n noun* + *gen, e.g.* plus pecuniae (more money)
more (greater number)	plures -a
most (very many, the majority)	plurimi -ae -a
mother	mater -tris *f 3*
mountain	mons, montis *m 3*
move (something)	moveo, movere, movi, motus
much (*adj*)	multus -a -um; *or as n noun* + *gen, e.g.* multum pecuniae (much money)
much, by much (*adv with comp*)	multo
must	debeo, debere, debui, debitus

my	meus -a -um
name	nomen -inis *n 3*
near	prope (+ *acc*)
nearest	proximus -a -um
nearly	paene
neither . . . nor	nec/neque . . . nec/neque
never	numquam
new	novus -a -um
next (then, after that)	deinde
next (to)	proximus -a -um
next day, on the	postridie
night	nox, noctis *f 3*
nine	novem
no (*opposite of* yes)	minime
no (not any)	nullus -a -um
nobody, no-one	nemo, *gen* nullius
noise	clamor -oris *m 3*
nor	nec/neque
not (*with facts*)	non
not (*with possibilities*)	ne
not know	nescio, nescire, nescivi
not want	nolo, nolle, nolui
nothing	nihil
notice	conspicio, conspicere, conspexi, conspectus
now	nunc; (by now, already) iam
offer	offero, offerre, obtuli, oblatus
often	saepe
old man	senex -is *m 3*
on	in (+ *abl*)
on account of	propter (+ *acc*)
once (some time ago)	olim
once, at	statim
one	unus -a -um
one (of two)	alter -era -erum
only	solus -a -um
onto	in (+ *acc*)
order (to do something)	iubeo, iubere, iussi, iussus (+ *acc* + *inf*); impero, imperare, imperavi, imperatus (+ *dat* + ut + *subj*)
other	alius -a -ud
other (of two), the	alter -era -erum
others, the (the rest)	ceteri -ae -a
ought	debeo, debere, debui, debitus
our	noster -tra -trum
out of	e/ex (+ *abl*)
overcome, overpower	supero, superare, superavi, superatus
owe	debeo, debere, debui, debitus
part	pars, partis *f 3*
peace	pax, pacis *f 3*
penalty, pay the	poenas do

people (tribe, race)	gens, gentis *f 3*
perish	pereo, perire, perii
persuade	persuadeo, persuadere, persuasi (+ *dat*)
place (*verb*)	pono, ponere, posui, positus
place (*noun*)	locus -i *m 2, with n 2 pl* loca
plan	consilium -i *n 2*
pleased, be	gaudeo, gaudere, gavisus sum
pleasure	gaudium -i *n 2*
power	imperium -i *n 2*
praise	laudo, laudare, laudavi, laudatus
prefer	malo, malle, malui
prepare	paro, parare, paravi, paratus
present (gift)	donum -i *n 2*
present, be	adsum, adesse, adfui
previously	antea
prisoner	captivus -i *m 2*
prize	praemium -i *n 2*
proceed	procedo, procedere, processi
promise (to/that)	promitto, promittere, promisi, promissus (*usu* + *acc* + *fut inf*)
protect	servo, servare, servavi, servatus
provide	paro, parare, paravi, paratus
punish	punio, punire, punivi, punitus
punished, be	poenas do; *or use passive of* punio
punishment	poena -ae *f 1*
put	pono, ponere, posui, positus
queen	regina -ae *f 1*
quick	celer -eris -ere
quickly	celeriter
quiet, be	taceo, tacere, tacui, tacitus
race (people, tribe)	gens, gentis *f 3*
raise	tollo, tollere, sustuli, sublatus
read	lego, legere, legi, lectus
realise	intellego, intellegere, intellexi, intellectus
receive	accipio, accipere, accepi, acceptus
refuse	nolo, nolle, nolui
rejoice	gaudeo, gaudere, gavisus sum
relate (tell story)	narro, narrare, narravi, narratus
remain	maneo, manere, mansi
reply	respondeo, respondere, respondi, responsus
report	refero, referre, rettuli, relatus; nuntio, nuntiare, nuntiavi, nuntiatus
resist	resisto, resistere, restiti (+ *dat*)
rest, the (the others)	ceteri -ae -a
return (go back)	redeo, redire, redii; regredior, regredi, regressus sum
reward	praemium -i *n 2*
river	flumen -inis *n 3*
road	via -ae *f 1*
Roman	Romanus -a -um

Romans	Romani -orum *m 2 pl*
Rome	Roma -ae *loc* Romae (in/at Rome) *f 1*
rule (be king)	rego, regere, rexi, rectus
run	curro, currere, cucurri, cursus
run away	fugio, fugere, fugi
sacred	sacer -cra -crum
sad	tristis -e; miser -era -erum
sail	navigo, navigare, navigavi
sailor	nauta -ae *m 1*
same, the	idem, eadem, idem
same time, at the	simul
savage	saevus -a -um
save	servo, servare, servavi, servatus
say	dico, dicere, dixi, dictus
says/said, he/she	inquit, *pl* inquiunt (*interrupting quoted speech*)
sea	mare, maris *n 3*
search for	quaero, quaerere, quaesivi, quaesitus
second (of two), the	alter -era -erum
see	video, videre, vidi, visus
see!	ecce
seek	peto, petere, petivi, petitus
seem	videor, videri, visus sum
seize	rapio, rapere, rapui, raptus
self	ipse, ipsa, ipsum
sell	vendo, vendere, vendidi, venditus
senator	senator -oris *m 3*
send	mitto, mittere, misi, missus
serious	gravis -e
set free	libero, liberare, liberavi, liberatus
set on fire	incendo, incendere, incendi, incensus
set out	proficiscor, proficisci, profectus sum
set up	pono, ponere, posui, positus
seven	septem
several	nonnulli -ae -a
she	ea, *gen* eius; illa, *gen* illius
ship	navis -is *f 3*
shop	taberna -ae *f 1*
short	brevis -e
should	debeo, debere, debui, debitus
shout (*verb*)	clamo, clamare, clamavi, clamatus
shout, shouting (*noun*)	clamor -oris *m 3*
show	ostendo, ostendere, ostendi, ostentus
silent, be	taceo, tacere, tacui, tacitus
since	cum (+ *subj*)
sit	sedeo, sedere, sedi
six	sex
skill	ars, artis *f 3*
sky	caelum -i *n 2*
slave	servus -i *m 2*
slave-girl, slave-woman	ancilla -ae *f 1*

sleep	dormio, dormire, dormivi
slow	lentus -a -um
small	parvus -a -um
smaller	minor -us
smallest	minimus -a -um
smile	rideo, ridere, risi
so	tam (*with adj/adv introducing result clause*); ita
so great	tantus -a -um
so many	tot (*indecl*)
so much (to such an extent)	adeo (*with verb introducing result clause*)
so that (in order that)	ut (*introducing purpose clause*)
soldier	miles -itis *m 3*
some	nonnulli -ae -a
some . . . others	alii . . . alii
some time ago	olim
son	filius -i *m 2*
soon	mox
soon as, as	simulac/simulatque
soul	animus -i *m 2*
speak	dico, dicere, dixi, dictus; loquor, loqui, locutus sum
spirit	animus -i *m 2*
stand	sto, stare, steti
stand up	surgo, surgere, surrexi
stay	maneo, manere, mansi
steal	aufero, auferre, abstuli, ablatus
storm	tempestas -atis *f 3*
street	via -ae *f 1*
strong	fortis -e; validus -a -um
stupid	stultus -a -um
such (of such a kind)	talis -e
suddenly	subito
suffer	patior, pati, passus sum
support (favour, side with)	faveo, favere, favi (+ *dat*)
surely?	nonne
surely . . . not?	num
sword	gladius -i *m 2*
talk	loquor, loqui, locutus sum
take	capio, capere, cepi, captus
take (someone somewhere)	duco, ducere, duxi, ductus
take away	aufero, auferre, abstuli, ablatus
tell (inform)	dico, dicere, dixi, dictus (+ *dat*)
tell (order)	iubeo, iubere, iussi, iussus *(+ acc + inf)*; impero, imperare, imperavi, imperatus (+ *dat* + ut + *subj*)
tell (relate)	narro, narrare, narravi, narratus; refero, referre, rettuli, relatus
temple	templum -i *n 2*
ten	decem
terrified	perterritus -a -um
than	quam

that (that one there)	ille, illa, illud; is, ea, id
. . . that (*result clause*)	ut (+ *subj*)
. . . that (*indirect statement*)	*use acc and inf*
. . . that (*after verb of fearing*)	ne (+ *subj*)
their, their own (*refl*)	suus -a -um
themselves (*refl*)	se
then (at that time)	tum
then (next)	deinde
there (in that place)	ibi
therefore	igitur (*not first word*)
thing	res, rei *f 5*
think	puto, putare, putavi, putatus
this	hic, haec, hoc
thousand	mille, *pl* milia
three	tres, tria
through	per (+ *acc*)
throw	iacio, iacere, ieci, iactus
thus	sic
time	tempus -oris *n 3*
to	ad (+ *acc*)
to such an extent	adeo; ita
today	hodie
tomorrow	cras
too	quoque
top (part of, *adj*)	summus -a -um
towards	ad (+ *acc*)
tribe	gens, gentis *f 3*
troops	copiae -arum *f 1 pl*
trust	credo, credere, credidi, creditus (+ *dat*)
try	conor, conari, conatus sum
turn (something)	verto, vertere, verti, versus
two	duo, duae, duo
under	sub (+ *acc* [*motion*] or *abl* [*position*])
understand	intellego, intellegere, intellexi, intellectus
unhappy	infelix *gen* -icis
unless	nisi
unlucky	infelix *gen* -icis
until	dum (+ *subj*)
unwilling, I am	nolo, nolle, nolui
urge	hortor, hortari, hortatus sum
used to	*use imperfect tense*
vain, in	frustra
very good	optimus -a -um
very greatly	maxime
very little (*adv*)	minime
victorious, be	vinco, vincere, vici, victus
victory	victoria -ae *f 1*
villa	villa -ae *f 1*
violently	vehementer

virtue	virtus -utis *f 3*
voice	vox, vocis *f 3*
wage (war)	(bellum) gero, gerere, gessi, gestus
wait	maneo, manere, mansi
wait for	exspecto, exspectare, exspectavi, exspectatus
walk	ambulo, ambulare, ambulavi
wall	murus -i *m 2*
want	volo, velle, volui; cupio, cupere, cupivi, cupitus
war	bellum -i *n 2*
warn	moneo, monere, monui, monitus
watch	specto, spectare, spectavi, spectatus
water	aqua -ae *f 1*
way (route)	via -ae *f 1*
way (manner, method)	modus -i *m 2*
we	nos, *gen* nostrum
weapons	arma -orum *n 2 pl*
wear out, exhaust	conficio, conficere, confeci, confectus
weep	lacrimo, lacrimare, lacrimavi
well	bene
what?	quid
what sort of?	qualis -e
when?	quando
when (at the time when)	ubi
when (after)	postquam
when (*suggesting also* because)	cum (+ *subj*)
where (at)?, (in the place) where	ubi
where from?, from where	unde
where to?	quo
whether (*ind qu*)	num
which (the one which)	qui, quae, quod
while	dum (+ *present indicative*)
who?	quis
who (the one who)	qui, quae, quod
whole	totus -a -um
why?	cur
wicked	scelestus -a -um
wife	uxor -oris *f 3*
willingly	libenter
win (be victorious)	vinco, vincere, vici, victus
wine	vinum -i *n 2*
wish	volo, velle, volui
with (accompanied by)	cum (+ *abl*)
with (using, by means of)	*use abl, without prep*
within (a length of time)	*use abl, without prep*
without	sine (+ *abl*)
woman	femina -ae *f 1*
wonder at	miror, mirari, miratus sum
wood (forest)	silva -ae *f 1*
word	verbum -i *n 2*
work (*verb*)	laboro, laborare, laboravi

work (*noun*)	labor -oris *m 3*
worry	cura -ae *f 1*
worse	peior -us
worst	pessimus -a -um
wound (*verb*)	vulnero, vulnerare, vulneravi, vulneratus
wound (*noun*)	vulnus -eris *n 3*
write	scribo, scribere, scripsi, scriptus
year	annus -i *m 2*
yesterday	heri
you (*sg*)	tu, *gen* tui
you (*pl*)	vos, *gen* vestrum
young man	iuvenis -is *m 3*
your (of you *sg*)	tuus -a -um
your (of you *pl*)	vester -tra -trum

LATIN TO ENGLISH VOCABULARY

The second column has further information about each word:

- Verbs are shown with principal parts: present tense (first person singular) in the first column, then infinitive (showing conjugation, e.g. 3rd), perfect tense (first person singular), and perfect passive participle. Note that 3rd* = mixed 3rd/4th conjugation: these verbs count as 3rd because of infinitive -*ere*, but form their present, imperfect and future tenses like 4th.

- Nouns are shown with genitive singular, gender, and declension (e.g. 3).

- Adjectives are given with feminine and neuter. If only one other form is given, it is the neuter (and the feminine is the same as the masculine). Third declension adjectives of the *ingens* type are shown instead with the genitive singular (for the stem), signalled by *gen*.

- Common irregular forms are cross-referenced.

- The chapter in which the word forms part of the learning vocabulary is shown in square brackets.

- For explanation of abbreviations, see the list on p. x.

a/ab	+ *abl, or as prefix*	*prep*	from, away from, by (*as prefix* = away)	[2]
abstuli		(*perfect of* aufero)		
absum	abesse, afui	*verb irreg*	be absent, be away, be distant from	[6]
ac/atque	*indecl*	*conj*	and	[9]
accepi		(*perfect of* accipio)		
accido	accidere, accidi	*verb 3rd*	happen	[9]
accipio	accipere, accepi, acceptus	*verb 3rd**	accept, take in, receive	[6]
actus	acta, actum	(*perfect passive participle of* ago)		
ad	+ *acc, or as prefix*	*prep*	to, towards, at	[1]
adeo	*indecl*	*adv*	so much, so greatly, to such an extent	[10]
adsum	adesse, adfui	*verb irreg*	be here, be present	[6]
advenio	advenire, adveni	*verb 4th*	arrive	[3]
aedifico	aedificare, aedificavi, aedificatus	*verb 1st*	build	[3]
ager	agri	*noun m 2*	field	[2]

ago	agere, egi, actus	*verb 3rd*	do, act, drive	[9]
alius	alia, aliud	*adj/pron*	other, another, else	[9]
alii . . . alii			some . . . others	[8]
alter	altera, alterum	*adj/pron*	the other, another, one (of two), the second (of two)	[9]
alter . . . alter			one . . . the other	[9]
altus	alta, altum	*adj*	high; deep	[8]
ambulo	ambulare, ambulavi	*verb 1st*	walk	[1]
amicus	amici	*noun m 2*	friend	[1]
amo	amare, amavi, amatus	*verb 1st*	love, like	[1]
amor	amoris	*noun m 3*	love	[4]
ancilla	ancillae	*noun f 1*	slave-girl, slave-woman	[1]
animus	animi	*noun m 2*	mind, spirit, soul	[7]
annus	anni	*noun m 2*	year	[2]
antea	*indecl*	*adv*	before, previously	[9]
appropinquo	appropinquare, appropinquavi	*verb 1st*	approach, come near to (*usu + dat*)	[6]
aqua	aquae	*noun f 1*	water	[2]
arma	armorum	*noun n 2 pl*	arms, weapons	[2]
ars	artis	*noun f 3*	art, skill	[8]
ascendo	ascendere, ascendi, ascensus	*verb 3rd*	climb	[5]
audax	*gen* audacis	*adj*	bold, daring	[7]
audeo	audere, ausus sum	*verb 2nd s-dep*	dare	[9]
audio	audire, audivi, auditus	*verb 4th*	hear, listen to	[2]
aufero	auferre, abstuli, ablatus	*verb irreg*	take away, carry off, steal	[8]
auxilium	auxilii	*noun n 2*	help	[2]
bellum	belli	*noun n 2*	war	[2]
bellum gero			wage war, campaign	[7]
bene	*indecl*	*adv*	well	[5]
bibo	bibere, bibi	*verb 3rd*	drink	[2]
bonus	bona, bonum	*adj*	good	[3]
brevis	breve	*adj*	short, brief	[10]
cado	cadere, cecidi, casus	*verb 3rd*	fall	[3]
caelum	caeli	*noun n 2*	sky, heaven	[4]
capio	capere, cepi, captus	*verb 3rd**	take, catch, capture	[4]
captivus	captivi	*noun m 2*	captive, prisoner	[7]
captus	capta, captum	(*perfect passive participle of* capio)		
caput	capitis	*noun n 3*	head	[4]
castra	castrorum	*noun n 2 pl*	camp	[7]
cecidi		(*perfect of* cado) ·		
celer	celeris, celere	*adj*	quick, fast	[5]
celo	celare, celavi, celatus	*verb 1st*	hide (something)	[7]
cena	cenae	*noun f 1*	dinner, meal	[3]
centum	*indecl*	*num*	100	[6]
cepi		(*perfect of* capio)		

ceteri	ceterae, cetera	*adj/pron*	the rest, the others	[8]
cibus	cibi	*noun m 2*	food	[1]
circum	+ *acc*	*prep*	around	[1]
civis	civis	*noun m/f 3*	citizen	[5]
clamo	clamare, clamavi, clamatus	*verb 1st*	shout	[1]
clamor	clamoris	*noun m 3*	shout, shouting, noise	[4]
clarus	clara, clarum	*adj*	famous, clear	[7]
coactus	coacta, coactum	(*perfect passive participle of* cogo)		
coegi		(*perfect of* cogo)		
coepi	coepisse	*verb irreg*	began, have begun	[8]
cogito	cogitare, cogitavi, cogitatus	*verb 1st*	think, consider	[10]
cognosco	cognoscere, cognovi, cognitus	*verb 3rd*	get to know, find out	[9]
cogo	cogere, coegi, coactus	*verb 3rd*	force, compel	[8]
comes	comitis	*noun m/f 3*	companion, comrade	[7]
conficio	conficere, confeci, confectus	*verb 3rd**	finish, wear out	[8]
conor	conari, conatus sum	*verb 1st dep*	try	[9]
consilium	consilii	*noun n 2*	plan, idea, advice	[3]
conspectus	conspecta, conspectum	(*perfect passive participle of* conspicio)		
conspexi		(*perfect of* conspicio)		
conspicio	conspicere, conspexi, conspectus	*verb 3rd**	catch sight of, notice	[6]
constituo	constituere, constitui, constitutus	*verb 3rd*	decide	[6]
consul	consulis	*noun m 3*	consul	[7]
consumo	consumere, consumpsi, consumptus	*verb 3rd*	eat	[3]
contra	+ *acc*	*prep*	against	[1]
convenio	convenire, conveni	*verb 4th*	come together, gather, meet	[6]
copiae	copiarum	*noun f 1 pl*	forces, troops	[9]
corpus	corporis	*noun n 3*	body	[7]
cras	*indecl*	*adv*	tomorrow	[5]
credo	credere, credidi, creditus	*verb 3rd*	believe, trust (+ *dat*)	[5]
crudelis	crudele	*adj*	cruel	[7]
cucurri		(*perfect of* curro)		
cum	+ *abl*	*prep*	with	[2]
cum	*indecl*	*conj*	when, since (+ *subj*)	[10]
cupio	cupere, cupivi, cupitus	*verb 3rd**	want, desire	[6]
cur?	*indecl*	*adv*	why?	[4]
cura	curae	*noun f 1*	care, worry	[10]
curro	currere, cucurri, cursus	*verb 3rd*	run	[3]
custodio	custodire, custodivi, custoditus	*verb 4th*	guard	[2]
custos	custodis	*noun m/f 3*	guard	[7]

datus	data, datum	*(perfect passive participle of* do)		
de	+ *abl*	*prep*	from, down from, about	[2]
dea	deae	*noun f 1*	goddess	[1]
debeo	debere, debui, debitus	*verb 2nd*	ought, should, must; owe	[3]
decem	*indecl*	*num*	ten	[2]
dedi		*(perfect of* do)		
defendo	defendere, defendi, defensus	*verb 3rd*	defend	[5]
deinde	*indecl*	*adv*	then, next	[3]
deleo	delere, delevi, deletus	*verb 2nd*	destroy	[3]
descendo	descendere, descendi, descensus	*verb 3rd*	go down, come down	[6]
deus	dei	*noun m 2*	god	[1]
dico	dicere, dixi, dictus	*verb 3rd*	say, speak, tell	[6]
dies	diei	*noun m 5*	day	[10]
difficilis	difficile	*adj*	difficult	[5]
diligens	*gen* diligentis	*adj*	careful	[10]
dirus	dira, dirum	*adj*	dreadful	[10]
discedo	discedere, discessi	*verb 3rd*	depart, leave	[3]
diu	*indecl*	*adv*	for a long time	[3]
dixi		*(perfect of* dico)		
do	dare, dedi, datus	*verb 1st*	give	[2]
poenas do			pay the penalty, be punished	[10]
doceo	docere, docui, doctus	*verb 2nd*	teach	[8]
domina	dominae	*noun f 1*	mistress	[3]
dominus	domini	*noun m 2*	master	[1]
domus	domus (domi = at home)	*noun f 4*	house, home	[10]
donum	doni	*noun n 2*	gift, present	[2]
dormio	dormire, dormivi	*verb 4th*	sleep	[2]
duco	ducere, duxi, ductus	*verb 3rd*	lead, take	[2]
dum	*indecl*	*conj*	while (+ *present translated as imperfect*); until (+ *subj*)	[10]
duo	duae, duo	*num*	two	[6]
dux	ducis	*noun m 3*	leader	[4]
duxi		*(perfect of* duco)		
e/ex	+ *abl, or as prefix*	*prep*	from, out of, out	[2]
ecce!	*indecl*	*interjection*	look! see!	[5]
effugio	effugere, effugi	*verb 3rd**	escape	[6]
egi		*(perfect of* ago)		
ego	mei	*pron*	I, me	[4]
egredior	egredi, egressus sum	*verb 3rd* dep*	go out	[9]
emo	emere, emi, emptus	*verb 3rd*	buy	[6]
enim	*indecl*	*conj*	for	[5]
eo	ire, i(v)i	*verb irreg*	go	[6]
epistula	epistulae	*noun f 1*	letter	[1]

equus	equi	*noun m 2*	horse	[1]
et	*indecl*	*conj*	and, even	[1]
et . . . et			both . . . and	[7]
etiam	*indecl*	*adv*	also, even	[9]
eunt-		*(stem of present participle of* eo)		
exercitus	exercitus	*noun m 4*	army	[10]
exspecto	exspectare, exspectavi, exspectatus	*verb 1st*	wait for, expect	[6]
facilis	facile	*adj*	easy	[5]
facio	facere, feci, factus	*verb 3rd**	make, do	[4]
faveo	favere, favi, fautus	*verb 2nd*	favour, support (+ *dat*)	[10]
feci		*(perfect of* facio)		
felix	*gen* felicis	*adj*	fortunate, happy	[10]
femina	feminae	*noun f 1*	woman	[1]
fero	ferre, tuli, latus	*verb irreg*	bring, carry, bear	[8]
ferox	*gen* ferocis	*adj*	fierce, ferocious	[5]
festino	festinare, festinavi	*verb 1st*	hurry	[3]
fidelis	fidele	*adj*	faithful, loyal	[9]
filia	filiae	*noun f 1*	daughter	[5]
filius	filii	*noun m 2*	son	[5]
flumen	fluminis	*noun n 3*	river	[7]
forte	*indecl*	*adv*	by chance	[5]
fortis	forte	*adj*	brave	[5]
forum	fori	*noun n 2*	forum, marketplace	[3]
frater	fratris	*noun m 3*	brother	[4]
frustra	*indecl*	*adv*	in vain	[8]
fugio	fugere, fugi	*verb 3rd**	run away, flee	[4]
fui		*(perfect of* sum)		
futurus	futura, futurum	*(future participle of* sum)		
gaudeo	gaudere, gavisus sum	*verb 2nd s-dep*	rejoice, be pleased	[9]
gaudium	gaudii	*noun n 2*	joy, pleasure	[10]
gens	gentis	*noun f 3*	family, tribe, race, people	[9]
gero	gerere, gessi, gestus	*verb 3rd*	wage (war); wear (clothes)	[7]
gladius	gladii	*noun m 2*	sword	[1]
gravis	grave	*adj*	heavy, serious	[5]
habeo	habere, habui, habitus	*verb 2nd*	have, hold	[2]
habito	habitare, habitavi, habitatus	*verb 1st*	live, dwell	[3]
heri	*indecl*	*adv*	yesterday	[5]
hic	haec, hoc	*pron/adj*	this; he, she, it	[7]
hodie	*indecl*	*adv*	today	[5]
homo	hominis	*noun m 3*	man, human being	[8]
hora	horae	*noun f 1*	hour	[2]
hortor	hortari, hortatus sum	*verb 1st dep*	encourage, urge	[9]
hortus	horti	*noun m 2*	garden	[1]

hostis	hostis	*noun m 3*	enemy (*usu pl*)	[6]
iaceo	iacere, iacui	*verb 2nd*	lie, be lying down	[10]
iacio	iacere, ieci, iactus	*verb 3rd**	throw	[6]
	(*in compounds* -icio, e.g. eicio [throw out], inicio [throw in])			
iactus	iacta, iactum	(*perfect passive participle of* iacio)		
iam	*indecl*	*adv*	now, already	[7]
ianua	ianuae	*noun f 1*	door	[10]
ibi	*indecl*	*adv*	there	[7]
idem	eadem, idem	*pron/adj*	the same	[8]
ieci		(*perfect of* iacio)		
iens	*gen* euntis	(*present participle of* eo)		
igitur	*indecl*	*conj*	therefore, and so	[5]
ii		(= ivi, *perfect of* eo)		
ille	illa, illud	*pron/adj*	that; he, she, it	[7]
imperator	imperatoris	*noun m 3*	general, leader; emperor	[7]
imperium	imperii	*noun n 2*	empire, power, command	[8]
impero	imperare, imperavi, imperatus	*verb 1st*	order, command (+ *dat*)	[10]
in	+ *acc/abl, or as prefix*	*prep*	(+ *acc*) into, onto; (+ *abl*) in, on	[1] [2]
incendo	incendere, incendi, incensus	*verb 3rd*	set on fire, burn (something)	[7]
infelix	*gen* infelicis	*adj*	unlucky, unhappy	[10]
ingens	*gen* ingentis	*adj*	huge	[5]
ingredior	ingredi, ingressus sum	*verb 3rd* dep*	enter	[9]
inimicus	inimici	*noun m 2*	(personal) enemy	[8]
inquit	*pl* inquiunt	*verb irreg*	(s/he) says, (s/he) said	[2]
insula	insulae	*noun f 1*	island; block of flats	[1]
intellego	intellegere, intellexi, intellectus	*verb 3rd*	understand, realise	[6]
inter	+ *acc*	*prep*	among, between	[3]
interea	*indecl*	*adv*	meanwhile	[9]
interficio	interficere, interfeci, interfectus	*verb 3rd**	kill	[6]
intro	intrare, intravi, intratus	*verb 1st*	enter	[6]
invenio	invenire, inveni, inventus	*verb 4th*	find	[2]
invito	invitare, invitavi, invitatus	*verb 1st*	invite	[3]
ipse	ipsa, ipsum	*pron*	self (*any person*), himself, herself, itself, *pl* selves, themselves	[8]
ira	irae	*noun f 1*	anger	[6]
iratus	irata, iratum	*adj*	angry	[3]
is	ea, id	*pron*	he, she, it, *pl* they; that, *pl* those	[5]
ita	*indecl*	*adv*	so, in this way, in such a way, to such an extent	[10]

itaque	*indecl*	*conj*	and so, therefore	[10]
iter	itineris	*noun n 3*	journey	[4]
iterum	*indecl*	*adv*	again	[9]
iubeo	iubere, iussi, iussus	*verb 2nd*	order	[2]
iussi		*(perfect of* iubeo*)*		
iussus	iussa, iussum	*(perfect passive participle of* iubeo*)*		
iuvenis	iuvenis	*noun m 3*	young man	[4]
ivi		*(perfect of* eo*)*		
labor	laboris	*noun m 3*	work, toil	[8]
laboro	laborare, laboravi	*verb 1st*	work, toil	[1]
lacrimo	lacrimare, lacrimavi	*verb 1st*	weep, cry	[3]
laetus	laeta, laetum	*adj*	happy	[3]
latus	lata, latum	*(perfect passive participle of* fero*)*		
laudo	laudare, laudavi, laudatus	*verb 1st*	praise	[7]
lectus	lecta, lectum	*(perfect passive participle of* lego*)*		
legio	legionis	*noun f 3*	legion	[10]
lego	legere, legi, lectus	*verb 3rd*	read; choose	[2]
lentus	lenta, lentum	*adj*	slow	[9]
libenter	*indecl*	*adv*	willingly, gladly	[9]
liber	libri	*noun m 2*	book	[2]
liberi	liberorum	*noun m 2 pl*	children	[9]
libero	liberare, liberavi, liberatus	*verb 1st*	set free	[6]
libertus	liberti	*noun m 2*	freedman, ex-slave	[3]
locus	loci *(pl is n:* loca*)*	*noun m/n 2*	place	[5]
locutus sum		*(perfect of* loquor*)*		
longus	longa, longum	*adj*	long	[4]
loquor	loqui, locutus sum	*verb 3rd dep*	speak, talk	[9]
lux	lucis	*noun f 3*	light, daylight	[10]
magnus	magna, magnum	*adj*	big, large, great	[3]
maior	maius	*adj*	bigger, greater	[7]
malo	malle, malui	*verb irreg*	prefer	[8]
malus	mala, malum	*adj*	bad, evil	[3]
maneo	manere, mansi	*verb 2nd*	remain, stay	[3]
mansi		*(perfect of* maneo*)*		
manus	manus	*noun f 4*	hand; group of people	[10]
mare	maris	*noun n 3*	sea	[4]
maritus	mariti	*noun m 2*	husband	[4]
mater	matris	*noun f 3*	mother	[4]
maxime	*indecl*	*adv*	very greatly	[7]
maximus	maxima, maximum	*adj*	biggest, greatest, very big/great	[7]
medius	media, medium	*adj*	middle (of)	[4]
melior	melius	*adj*	better	[7]
meus	mea, meum	*adj*	my	[4]
miles	militis	*noun m 3*	soldier	[4]
mille	*pl* milia	*num*	1000	[6]
minime	*indecl*	*adv*	no; least, very little	[7]

minimus	minima, minimum	*adj*	very little, smallest	[7]
minor	minus	*adj*	smaller, less	[7]
miror	mirari, miratus sum	*verb 1st dep*	wonder at, admire	[9]
miser	misera, miserum	*adj*	miserable, wretched, sad	[3]
misi		(*perfect of* mitto)		
missus	missa, missum	(*perfect passive participle of* mitto)		
mitto	mittere, misi, missus	*verb 3rd*	send	[2]
modus	modi	*noun m 2*	manner, way, kind	[7]
moneo	monere, monui, monitus	*verb 2nd*	warn, advise	[2]
mons	montis	*noun m 3*	mountain	[5]
morior	mori, mortuus sum	*verb 3rd* dep*	die	[9]
mors	mortis	*noun f 3*	death	[5]
mortuus sum		(*perfect of* morior)		
motus	mota, motum	(*perfect passive participle of* moveo)		
moveo	movere, movi, motus	*verb 2nd*	move (something)	[7]
mox	*indecl*	*adv*	soon	[5]
multo	*indecl*	*adv*	much, by much	[7]
multus	multa, multum	*adj*	much, *pl* many	[3]
murus	muri	*noun m 2*	wall	[2]
nam	*indecl*	*conj*	for	[8]
narro	narrare, narravi, narratus	*verb 1st*	tell, relate	[7]
nauta	nautae	*noun m 1*	sailor	[3]
navigo	navigare, navigavi	*verb 1st*	sail	[1]
navis	navis	*noun f 3*	ship	[4]
-ne . . . ?	*indecl*	*adv*	(*makes open question, e.g.*) is it?	[4]
ne	*indecl*	*conj*	that . . . not, so that . . . not; (*after verb of fearing*) that, lest	[10]
nec/neque	*indecl*	*conj*	and not, nor, neither	[8]
nec . . . nec/neque . . . neque			neither . . . nor	[8]
neco	necare, necavi, necatus	*verb 1st*	kill	[1]
nemo	nullius	*irreg pron m/f*	no-one, nobody	[9]
nescio	nescire, nescivi	*verb 4th*	not know	[10]
nihil	*indecl*	*irreg pron n*	nothing	[7]
nisi	*indecl*	*conj*	if not, unless, except	[8]
nolo	nolle, nolui	*verb irreg*	not want, refuse	[8]
noli	*pl* nolite		don't! (+ *inf*)	[8]
nomen	nominis	*noun n 3*	name	[4]
non	*indecl*	*adv*	not	[1]
nonne . . . ?	*indecl*	*adv*	surely?	[4]
nonnulli	nonnullae, nonnulla	*adj*	some, several	[9]
nos	nostrum	*pron*	we, us	[5]
noster	nostra, nostrum	*adj*	our	[5]
novem	*indecl*	*num*	nine	[6]
novus	nova, novum	*adj*	new	[3]
nox	noctis	*noun f 3*	night	[4]
nullus	nulla, nullum	*adj*	not any, no . . .	[8]
num . . . ?	*indecl*	*adv*	surely . . . not?	[4]

num	*indecl*	*adv*	whether (*in indirect question*)	[10]
numquam	*indecl*	*adv*	never	[5]
nunc	*indecl*	*adv*	now	[1]
nuntio	nuntiare, nuntiavi, nuntiatus	*verb 1st*	announce, report	[6]
nuntius	nuntii	*noun m 2*	messenger, message, news	[1]
oblatus	oblata, oblatum	(*perfect passive participle of* offero)		
obtuli		(*perfect of* offero)		
occido	occidere, occidi, occisus	*verb 3rd*	kill	[10]
octo	*indecl*	*num*	eight	[6]
offero	offerre, obtuli, oblatus	*verb irreg*	offer	[8]
olim	*indecl*	*adv*	once, some time ago	[5]
omnis	omne	*adj*	all, every	[5]
opprimo	opprimere, oppressi, oppressus	*verb 3rd*	crush, overwhelm	[9]
oppugno	oppugnare, oppugnavi, oppugnatus	*verb 1st*	attack	[3]
optimus	optima, optimum	*adj*	best, excellent, very good	[7]
oro	orare, oravi, oratus	*verb 1st*	beg	[10]
ostendo	ostendere, ostendi, ostentus	*verb 3rd*	show	[8]
paene	*indecl*	*adv*	almost, nearly	[10]
paro	parare, paravi, paratus	*verb 1st*	prepare, provide	[1]
pars	partis	*noun f 3*	part	[7]
parvus	parva, parvum	*adj*	small	[3]
passus sum		(*perfect of* patior)		
pater	patris	*noun m 3*	father	[4]
patior	pati, passus sum	*verb 3rd* dep*	suffer, endure	[9]
patria	patriae	*noun f 1*	country, homeland	[3]
pauci	paucae, pauca	*adj pl*	few, a few	[7]
pax	pacis	*noun f 3*	peace	[5]
pecunia	pecuniae	*noun f 1*	money	[1]
peior	peius	*adj*	worse	[7]
pello	pellere, pepuli, pulsus	*verb 3rd*	drive	[10]
per	+ *acc*	*prep*	through, along	[1]
pereo	perire, perii	*verb irreg*	die, perish	[6]
periculum	periculi	*noun n 2*	danger	[2]
persuadeo	persuadere, persuasi	*verb 2nd*	persuade (+ *dat*)	[6]
perterritus	perterrita, perterritum	*adj*	terrified	[6]
pes	pedis	*noun m 3*	foot	[10]
pessimus	pessima, pessimum	*adj*	worst, very bad	[7]
peto	petere, petivi, petitus	*verb 3rd*	seek, beg/ask for, make for	[4]
plurimus	plurima, plurimum	*adj*	very much, *pl* very many, most	[7]

plus	*gen* pluris	*adj*	more of (+ *gen*); *pl* more	[7]
poena	poenae	*noun f 1*	punishment	[10]
poenas do			pay the penalty, be punished	[10]
pono	ponere, posui, positus	*verb 3rd*	place, put, set up	[5]
porta	portae	*noun f 1*	gate	[3]
porto	portare, portavi, portatus	*verb 1st*	carry, bear, take	[1]
positus	posita, positum	(*perfect passive participle of* pono)		
possum	posse, potui	*verb irreg*	can, be able	[3]
post	+ *acc*	*prep*	after, behind	[4]
postea	*indecl*	*adv*	afterwards	[8]
postquam	*indecl*	*conj*	after, when	[6]
postridie	*indecl*	*adv*	on the next day	[10]
posui		(*perfect of* pono)		
potui		(*perfect of* possum)		
praemium	praemii	*noun n 2*	prize, reward, profit	[8]
primo	*indecl*	*adv*	at first	[7]
primus	prima, primum	*adj*	first	[4]
princeps	principis	*noun m 3*	chief; emperor	[10]
pro	+ *abl*	*prep*	in front of, for, in return for	[9]
procedo	procedere, processi	*verb 3rd*	advance, proceed	[10]
proelium	proelii	*noun n 2*	battle	[8]
proficiscor	proficisci, profectus sum	*verb 3rd dep*	set out	[9]
progredior	progredi, progressus sum	*verb 3rd* dep*	advance	[9]
promitto	promittere, promisi, promissus	*verb 3rd*	promise	[8]
prope	+ *acc*	*prep*	near	[6]
propter	+ *acc*	*prep*	on account of, because of	[9]
proximus	proxima, proximum	*adj*	nearest, next to	[9]
puella	puellae	*noun f 1*	girl	[1]
puer	pueri	*noun m 2*	boy	[2]
pugno	pugnare, pugnavi	*verb 1st*	fight	[1]
pulcher	pulchra, pulchrum	*adj*	beautiful, handsome	[3]
punio	punire, punivi, punitus	*verb 4th*	punish	[2]
puto	putare, putavi, putatus	*verb 1st*	think	[9]
quaero	quaerere, quaesivi, quaesitus	*verb 3rd*	search for, look for, ask	[3]
qualis?	quale?	*adj*	what sort of?	[8]
quam	*indecl*	*adv*	than; how . . . ! how . . .?	[7]
quam celerrime (*or other sup adv*)			as (quickly) as possible	[7]
quamquam	*indecl*	*conj*	although	[6]
quando?	*indecl*	*adv*	when?	[4]
quantus?	quanta? quantum?	*adj*	how big? how much?	[8]
quattuor	*indecl*	*num*	four	[6]

-que	*indecl*	*conj*	and (*before word it is attached to*)	[3]
qui	quae, quod	*pron*	who, which	[6]
quidam	quaedam, quoddam	*pron*	a certain, a, one, some	[9]
quinque	*indecl*	*num*	five	[2]
quis?	quid?	*pron*	who? what?	[6]
quo?	*indecl*	*adv*	(*question*) where to? (*not question*) to where	[4] [10]
quod	*indecl*	*conj*	because	[6]
quomodo?	*indecl*	*adv*	how? in what way?	[8]
quoque	*indecl*	*conj*	also, too	[8]
quot?	*indecl*	*adj*	how many?	[8]
rapio	rapere, rapui, raptus	*verb 3rd**	seize, grab	[8]
re-	*indecl*	*prefix*	. . . back	[6]
reddo	reddere, reddidi, redditus	*verb 3rd*	give back, restore	[9]
redeo	redire, redii	*verb irreg*	go back, come back, return	[6]
refero	referre, rettuli, relatus	*verb irreg*	bring back, carry back; report, tell	[8]
regina	reginae	*noun f 1*	queen	[4]
regnum	regni	*noun n 2*	kingdom	[4]
rego	regere, rexi, rectus	*verb 3rd*	rule, reign	[5]
regredior	regredi, regressus sum	*verb 3rd* dep*	go back, return	[9]
relinquo	relinquere, reliqui, relictus	*verb 3rd*	leave, leave behind	[4]
res	rei	*noun f 5*	thing, matter, event	[10]
resisto	resistere, restiti	*verb 3rd*	resist (+ *dat*)	[7]
respondeo	respondere, respondi, responsus	*verb 2nd*	reply	[6]
rex	regis	*noun 3 m*	king	[4]
rideo	ridere, risi	*verb 2nd*	laugh, smile	[4]
risi		(*perfect of* rideo)		
rogo	rogare, rogavi, rogatus	*verb 1st*	ask, ask for	[5]
Roma	Romae (Romae = at/in Rome)	*noun f 1*	Rome	[1]
Romanus	Romana, Romanum	*adj*	Roman	[3]
sacer	sacra, sacrum	*adj*	sacred	[8]
saepe	*indecl*	*adv*	often	[5]
saevus	saeva, saevum	*adj*	savage, cruel	[5]
saluto	salutare, salutavi, salutatus	*verb 1st*	greet	[1]
sanguis	sanguinis	*noun m 3*	blood	[7]
scelestus	scelesta, scelestum	*adj*	wicked	[8]
scelus	sceleris	*noun n 3*	crime	[8]
scio	scire, scivi, scitus	*verb 4th*	know	[9]
scribo	scribere, scripsi, scriptus	*verb 3rd*	write	[2]
scripsi		(*perfect of* scribo)		

se	sui	*refl pron*	himself, herself, itself, themselves	[5]
secutus sum		*(perfect of* sequor)		
sed	*indecl*	*conj*	but	[1]
sedeo	sedere, sedi	*verb 2nd*	sit	[2]
semper	*indecl*	*adv*	always	[1]
senator	senatoris	*noun m 3*	senator	[6]
senex	senis	*noun m 3*	old man	[4]
sentio	sentire, sensi, sensus	*verb 4th*	feel, notice	[9]
septem	*indecl*	*num*	seven	[6]
sequor	sequi, secutus sum	*verb 3rd dep*	follow	[9]
servo	servare, servavi, servatus	*verb 1st*	save, protect, keep	[6]
servus	servi	*noun m 2*	slave	[1]
sex	*indecl*	*num*	six	[6]
si	*indecl*	*conj*	if	[8]
sic	*indecl*	*adv*	thus, in this way	[7]
silva	silvae	*noun f 1*	wood, forest	[5]
simul	*indecl*	*adv*	at the same time	[10]
simulac/ simulatque	*indecl*	*conj*	as soon as	[10]
sine	+ *abl*	*prep*	without	[7]
soleo	solere, solitus sum	*verb 2nd s-dep*	be accustomed	[9]
solus	sola, solum	*adj*	alone, on one's own, lonely, only	[7]
specto	spectare, spectavi, spectatus	*verb 1st*	look at, watch	[4]
spero	sperare, speravi, speratus	*verb 1st*	hope, expect	[9]
spes	spei	*noun f 5*	hope	[10]
statim	*indecl*	*adv*	at once, immediately	[3]
steti		*(perfect of* sto)		
sto	stare, steti	*verb 1st*	stand	[7]
stultus	stulta, stultum	*adj*	stupid, foolish	[3]
sub	+ *acc/abl*	*prep*	under, beneath	[8]
subito	*indecl*	*adv*	suddenly	[3]
sum	esse, fui	*verb irreg*	be	[1]
summus	summa, summum	*adj*	highest, greatest, top (of)	[8]
supero	superare, superavi, superatus	*verb 1st*	overcome, overpower	[5]
surgo	surgere, surrexi	*verb 3rd*	get up, stand up, rise	[8]
surrexi		*(perfect of* surgo)		
sustuli		*(perfect of* tollo)		
suus	sua, suum	*adj*	his, her, its, their (own) *(refl)*	[5]
taberna	tabernae	*noun f 1*	shop, inn	[2]
taceo	tacere, tacui, tacitus	*verb 2nd*	be silent, be quiet	[5]
talis	tale	*adj*	such, of such a kind	[10]
tam	*indecl*	*adv*	so	[10]
tamen	*indecl*	*adv*	however	[5]

tandem	*indecl*	*adv*	at last, finally	[3]
tantus	tanta, tantum	*adj*	so great, such a great	[10]
tempestas	tempestatis	*noun f 3*	storm	[9]
templum	templi	*noun n 2*	temple	[2]
tempus	temporis	*noun n 3*	time	[10]
teneo	tenere, tenui, tentus	*verb 2nd*	hold	[5]
terra	terrae	*noun f 1*	earth, ground, land, country	[3]
terreo	terrere, terrui, territus	*verb 2nd*	frighten	[2]
timeo	timere, timui	*verb 2nd*	fear, be afraid	[2]
tollo	tollere, sustuli, sublatus	*verb 3rd*	raise, lift up, hold up	[8]
tot	*indecl*	*adj*	so many	[10]
totus	tota, totum	*adj*	whole	[8]
trado	tradere, tradidi, traditus	*verb 3rd*	hand over, hand down	[5]
traho	trahere, traxi, tractus	*verb 3rd*	drag	[2]
trans	+ *acc, or as prefix*	*prep*	across	[6]
traxi		(*perfect of* traho)		
tres	tria	*num*	three	[6]
tristis	triste	*adj*	sad	[5]
tu	tui	*pron*	you (*sg*)	[4]
tuli		(*perfect of* fero)		
tum	*indecl*	*adv*	then, at that time	[5]
turba	turbae	*noun f 1*	crowd	[4]
tuus	tua, tuum	*adj*	your (of you *sg*), yours	[4]
ubi	*indecl*	*adv*	(*question*) where?	[4]
			(*not question*) when, where	[6]
umquam	*indecl*	*adv*	ever	[10]
unde	*indecl*	*adv*	(*question*) where from?	[4]
			(*not question*) from where	[10]
unus	una, unum	*num*	one	[6]
urbs	urbis	*noun f 3*	city, town	[4]
ut	*indecl*	*conj*	(+ *subjunctive*) that, so that, in order to; (+ *indicative, or no verb*) as, when	[10]
uxor	uxoris	*noun f 3*	wife	[6]
validus	valida, validum	*adj*	strong	[10]
vehementer	*indecl*	*adv*	violently, loudly	[10]
vendo	vendere, vendidi, venditus	*verb 3rd*	sell	[6]
venio	venire, veni	*verb 4th*	come	[2]
verbum	verbi	*noun n 2*	word	[2]
verto	vertere, verti, versus	*verb 3rd*	turn	[10]
vester	vestra, vestrum	*adj*	your (of you *pl*), yours	[5]
via	viae	*noun f 1*	road, street, way	[3]
vici		(*perfect of* vinco)		

victoria	victoriae	*noun f 1*	victory	[9]
victus	victa, victum	*(perfect passive participle of* vinco)		
video	videre, vidi, visus	*verb 2nd*	see	[2]
videor	videri, visus sum	*verb 2nd dep*	seem, appear	[8]
villa	villae	*noun f 1*	house, country villa	[1]
vinco	vincere, vici, victus	*verb 3rd*	conquer, win, be victorious	[5]
vinum	vini	*noun n 2*	wine	[2]
vir	viri	*noun m 2*	man, male	[2]
virtus	virtutis	*noun f 3*	courage, virtue	[7]
visus	visa, visum	*(perfect passive participle of* video)		
vita	vitae	*noun f 1*	life	[9]
vivo	vivere, vixi	*verb 3rd*	live, be alive	[9]
vixi		*(perfect of* vivo)		
voco	vocare, vocavi, vocatus	*verb 1st*	call	[1]
volo	velle, volui	*verb irreg*	want, wish, be willing	[8]
vos	vestrum	*pron*	you *(pl)*	[5]
vox	vocis	*noun f 3*	voice, shout	[8]
vulnero	vulnerare, vulneravi, vulneratus	*verb 1st*	wound, injure	[9]
vulnus	vulneris	*noun n 3*	wound	[9]

INDEX TO PART 2